*I dedicate this book to
God's Ambassadors throughout the world who,
like the one who sent them,
have laid down their lives
that Muslims may experience,
deliverance, forgiveness, and love
through the Messiah.*

99697

Contents

Tables

Preface

This book reflects a long pilgrimage. It emerged from my D. Min. studies and also includes numerous insights from my Ph.D. studies. But this book is not about academics. It's about people deeply loved by God and greatly in need of a Savior. It's about a people I love and a people I have served for over twenty years.

I have gained much insight into Muslims through my studies and in my ministry. But I have learned even more from my co-workers among Muslims – men and women of whom the world is not worthy (Heb 11:38). Their profound insights, sacrificial lifestyles and thrilling stories of the outbreaking of God's love among Muslims make me proud to be within their ranks.

Throughout this book I have made liberal use of Arabic pseudonyms to avoid unnecessary problems for my friends and co-workers and to reinforce that the principles I'm emphasizing have application throughout the world of folk Islam. For example, I am referring to the people group I served as the "Baahithiin." which means "the searching ones." When such a pseudonym is first used, it is accompanied by an asterisk and explicitly identified as a pseudonym.

Muslims, Magic and the Kingdom of God is a community project. Many people have made their mark on my thinking and deserve a special recognition. Many thanks to Darrell Dorr, Bob Blincoe, Meg Crossman, Greg Livingstone, Bill Jackson, Jim Reapsome, Phil Parshall, Don McCurry, and Clinton Arnold for reading and editing this work. Special thanks belongs to Chuck Kraft, who originally encouraged me to publish my studies on folk Islam.

I am also grateful for the hard work of Jeleta Eckheart. She more than anyone helped turn my scholarly work into a readable book. If there is even one ounce of literary gold in this book, it's because she quarried it out of me.

Muslims, Magic and the Kingdom of God

The felt need for power is so great among folk Muslims that their entire worldview is seen through the spectacles of power.

— J. Dudley Woodberry

Showman or Shaman?

The word "magic" conjures up different images for different people. To most Westerners, magic entertains. The magician is a showman—a specialist at illusion. Trickery and sleight-of-hand hold crowds spellbound.

Another kind of magic captures instead of captivates. This kind of magic holds crowds spirit-bound, not spellbound. It is based on delusion, not illusion, and centers on a shaman, not a showman.

The shaman is a "spirit practitioner" or the proverbial "witch doctor." Whether he's called a *marabout* (as in North Africa) or a *dukun* (as in Indonesia), through his relationship with demons he taps into supernatural power from the Evil One. The shaman knows the right rituals and precise prayers to manipulate spirits to lend help or bring harm.[1]

Superstition obviously plays its part in this magical worldview. There is a psychological aspect to magic, but there is also a Satanic component. Those who fear demons may be excessively affected by their magical worldview, but Scripture makes clear that real demons do seek to control people. The powers of darkness stand behind magical practice.

Hans Betz, a specialist in magic in New Testament times, explains the role of the magician:

> He knew the code words needed to communicate with the gods, the demons, and the dead. He could tap, regulate, and manipulate the invisible energies. ... [T]he magician served as a power and communications expert, crisis manager, miracle healer and inflicter of damages and all-purpose therapist and agent of worried, troubled, and troublesome souls (Betz 1992:xlvii).

Two points in Betz's definition show the contrast between magic and the Christian faith. Whereas Christianity emphasizes a *relationship* with God and *submission* to His will, magic focuses on the importance of *ritual* and *manipulation*. While Christians pray to God, magicians command the gods (demons). Magicians are not too concerned about having a personal relationship with God, loving others or understanding truth. Their major focus is pragmatic, utilitarian and self-centered. They want to manipulate the powers for their own interests.

Muslims, Modernity and Magic

More than a billion people daily confess, "There is no God but Allah and Muhammad is His apostle." These words summarize the essence of a Muslim's faith. Our effort here is to describe practically how to reach these people who know so little of the love and power of Christ, concentrating on approaches to that large segment of the Muslim world known as folk Muslims–those who are doctrinally Muslim but practically animist. Folk Muslims confess Allah but worship spirits and are more concerned with magic than with Muhammad. *Of the world's one billion Muslims, more than three-fourths are folk Muslims.*[2]

Because folk Islam blends animism with Islam, it is considered idolatrous by orthodox Muslims. Just as Western evangelical Christians grieve over the materialism and hedonism negatively impacting Christianity, so do orthodox Muslims grieve over magic practices infiltrating Islam. Evangelical Christians and orthodox

Muslims share a common belief that the one true, almighty God deserves our complete devotion and submission. Anything less is idolatrous, unworthy of His transcendent majesty.

In our focus on reaching folk Muslims, we must consider both animistic concerns and Islamic beliefs in order to develop an effective outreach among them. It is vital to understand and deal with the spirit realm issues of animism,[3] but reaching folk Muslims demands different strategies than reaching other animists since they see themselves as Muslims who, when challenged about their faith, respond like fervent fundamentalists, zealously confessing their creed and defending their faith. Though animistic in practice, folk Muslims maintain a strong emotional attachment to Islamic beliefs.

A friend describes working with folk Muslims in Southeast Asia.

> Early in our experience with [this people group], my wife sought to share Jesus with our next-door neighbor lady who had become a good friend. Knowing that [this people] are interested in the lives of the prophets, my wife read stories from the Gospels of Jesus calming the storm, healing the sick and revealing the secrets of men's thoughts. Our neighbor's response was, "That was interesting, but my own father does those things all the time!"
>
> After further questioning the lady, my wife discovered that her father, the village *imam* [the leader of the mosque], was known for his ability to access "Allah's power" in order to heal the sick, find lost people and possessions, and demonstrate other supernatural skills.
>
> Our friend therefore was not impressed to hear about the miracles of Christ performed 2,000 years ago! It was then we realized that our Western Bible college education had not prepared us to demonstrate the power of Christ.[4]

Some might object that we live in an urban world with half the world's population in cities, making folk Islam a relic of the past. "Modernity is in. Magic is out."

Clearly, urbanization is impacting Muslims. The United Prayer Track of the AD 2000 and Beyond Movement has given priority attention to the 100 least evangelized cities in the world, known as the "100 gateway cities." Massive Muslim cities like Cairo (population of 15 million), Istanbul (10 million), Tehran (7.5 million), Karachi (9.5 million), Dhaka (9 million), and Jakarta (11.5 million) claim strategic economic, political, and spiritual prominence in their respective nations. In fact, 51 of the 100 "gateway cities" are Muslim. Thus, Muslim mission is predominately urban mission. Commitment to Muslims means commitment to cities. Commitment to cities means commitment to Muslims.

However, the urban world does not exclude the magical world. Folk Islam is not just found among uneducated rural peasants or nomadic Bedouins; it is also part of city life. The urban realities of rock-and-roll music, high-tech lifestyles, college education, traffic jams, pollution and swelling populations do not preclude the magical practices of Muslims. Witch doctors thrive in the asphalt jungle.

Most research acknowledges that magic is more pervasive in the village than in the city. Villagers practice magic more frequently and more publicly than their wealthier urban counterparts. As one missionary shared with me, "magic among the rich and educated is practiced more privately, so it's harder to evaluate how pervasive it is." Since educated urbanites are more Westernized, they are not as apt to admit publicly their real beliefs and practices about the spirit realm – not wanting to sound superstitious or unsophisticated to interviewers from the West.

Yet the vast majority of Muslim cities still reflect a strong rural orientation to life. Many people live in the city but still think like villagers. In fact, this is one of the distinctives of cities in "developing nations." As the urban sociologist John Palen points out,

> Cities in the developing world are among the largest and fastest growing in the world. Nevertheless, it must be kept in mind that the growth of cities and a high level of urbanization are not the same thing. In the Western world the two things happened at the same time, but it is quite possible to find extremely large cities in overwhelmingly rural countries. ... A number of extremely large cities does not necessarily indicate an urban nation (Palen 1987:9).

J. Clyde Mitchell indicates that magic and animism is typical of cities in developing nations. Describing urban Africa, he writes:

It is difficult to secure accurate information on the degree to which African work-seekers make use of charms in their search for employment. Of 35 men who visited a doctor in Harare, 15 of them sought treatment primarily for a straightforward medical complaint such as a headache, constipation, or something similar. Of the remaining 20, no less than 10 sought charms to help them to secure employment or stay in it. The remaining 10 were seeking advice about sexual virility, love potions, gambling charms, or straightforward anti-witchcraft medicine (Friedl and Chrisman 1975:380).

I once discussed place spirits with a Baahithiin Muslim, an educated, young married man who would be considered "modern" or "urban" in his thinking. When I asked him if there are spirits in objects like trees, he replied, "I believe there are all kinds of spirits. But we are not supposed to focus our attention on them. We should not spend all our time worrying about them." Then in the next breath he began telling a story about a tree that couldn't be cut down because the spirits were too powerful.

This man is typical of urban folk Muslims who cling to their animistic beliefs–Muslim but fearful of spirits. According to numerous studies, magic is an integral and pervasive reality in Third World cities.[5] A modern, urban veneer should not blind us to the unseen realities affecting Muslim beliefs and values. Though more prevalent in rural settings, folk Islam is also alive and well in the city.

Cities can become cauldrons of animistic knowledge when the need for strong supernatural safety nets pushes Muslim urbanites toward animism and magic. For example, anthropologist Robert Wessing studied Sundanese culture in Indonesia and learned that "the best place to get an amulet to ward off children's diseases was the main mosque in Bandung [the capital of West Java with over two million people]" (Wessing 1978:14-15). Furthermore, the urban phenomenon of blood sacrifice is practiced at the highest levels of Indonesia's government. A reporter for *New Yorker* magazine, Raymond Bonner, makes these observations about this practice.

In 1983, before construction of a modern international airport for Jakarta could begin, Indonesian Muslims and French Christians (the French had the construction contract) offered up prayers during a ceremony in which the heads of five water buffalo were buried. In earlier times, a young girl or boy was sacrificed before land was disturbed – a gift to the spirits living on the land (Bonner 1988:3).

My own experience among the Baahithiin reveals a similar pattern. I found that the Baahithiin have a ceremony in which they offer a blood sacrifice to appease an evil god when they move or construct a new building. Originally, they slaughtered a large animal and buried its head at the spot where the person wanted to move. To this day most Baahithiin continue this ritual, but with the sacrifice of a smaller animal instead.

While it may be debated how many Baahithiin admit belief in this evil god, their widespread behavior confirms the belief. When asked if many people still believed in this god, a Baahithiin friend told me, "I think sacrifices were offered up for all of the major buildings in our regional capital. I'm sure [one of the newest and nicest shopping centers in this regional capital] had one. ... The brand new television station in the regional capital televised its sacrificial ceremony."

Since most Western missionaries come from a materialistic-oriented culture which relegates the supernatural to other-worldly concerns, when faced with the realities of the spirit realm they often either ignore the issues or offer naturalistic solutions to what are perceived by folk Muslims as supernaturally-caused problems – so opportunities for ministry are lost.

In addition, we Westerners fail to learn about spirit-realm issues because it is hard for us to take the stance of humble, hungry learners. I found the more I questioned my informants with neutral questions, the more they opened up to me and shared freely. But I had to dig to understand them, questioning numerous informants from various angles and framing my questions so as not to prejudice them in their answers. I asked with genuine interest, "What do Baahithiin believe about charms?" This approach elicited a truer response than, "Do the Baahithiin *still* believe in charms?" Or worse, "Baahithiin don't believe in magic, do they?" When I told my informants stories about spirits and magic that I had encountered, demonstrating that I believed in the supernatural, they were even more apt to share openly with me.

Phil Parshall, one of Evangelicalism's most prominent practical Islamicists, confessed regarding folk Islamic issues in 1983:

> In some senses, I have learned more in this short time [his last few years of ministry] about grassroots Islam than I did in my first 18 years. ... Amazingly, one can be surrounded by certain dynamic situations and still be quite unaware of what is happening. This is particularly true if one seeks to understand Islam from a Western perspective – which is what I sought to do during my early years as a missionary (Parshall 1983:13).

I recently heard of a similar situation. In an enormous Middle Eastern city, a church planter with a Pentecostal background – who believes in these kind of things – assured his mentor that the people he was working with did not practice magic. When his mentor asked a national coworker about folk Islam, he replied, "It's everywhere!"

Questions for Reflection and Discussion

1. What are the distinctives of folk Islam in your area? How does Islam clash with animism in your area, and how does Islam readily accommodate animism in your area? To what extent do Muslim leaders in your community bemoan or accept the influence of animism?

2. To what extent has your cultural background, education and training, and personal experience prepared you to address the felt needs of folk Muslims? Where do you think you need the most "remedial" education or equipping?

3. How can you take the stance of a "humble, hungry learner" regarding the spirit realm? What are 2-3 neutral, open-ended questions you could ask cultural informants to help you learn more about the spiritual worldview of the people you serve?

It will help you to better digest what you're reading if you take the time to reflect on and discuss such questions after each chapter. Also, I would value a glimpse of what you're thinking! I invite you (either now or later) to share with me (r_d_love@hotmail.com) some of your answers to these questions. You may have some good things to teach me.

Notes

[1] Clinton Arnold, who has written three scholarly works on magic in the New Testament, defines magic as follows: "Magic was based on the belief in the supernatural powers which could be harnessed and used by appropriating the correct technique. Magic can therefore be defined as a method of manipulating supernatural powers to accomplish certain tasks with guaranteed results. Magicians would not seek the will of the deity in a matter, but would invoke the deity to do precisely as they stated" (1993:580).

[2] It is important to admit that there are also millions of folk Christians in the world – those who confess Christ with their lips but who worship other gods or spirits.

[3] See Burnett 1988; Van Rheenen 1991 and Steyne 1989 for excellent summaries of animism.

[4] Excerpted from an unpublished critique of this manuscript in August 1996.

[5] See Gmelch and Zenner 1988:78; du Toit 1980; Moody 1977, Ortiz 1988 and Hard 1989 for further documentation.

Chapter 1

A Contextualized Approach to Church Planting among Folk Muslims

It is possible to establish Muslim-convert churches ... through a team, even where missionary visas are not available. ... Establishing viable congregations with their own national leadership among Muslims ... is a do-able task.

—Greg Livingstone

The Baahithiin. One of the largest unreached people groups in my land of missionary service. I sat and prayed about the daunting task of reaching this massive people group. Then it dawned on me. There was no single approach or emphasis that would make us successful. There was no silver bullet. We would need every missiological insight and approach available to be fruitful in our church-planting efforts. This book describes that quest.

Our team developed a three-dimensional approach to reaching folk Muslims. This model involves church planting, contextualization and kingdom theology.

Personally I find **church planting** to be the most biblical and strategic way to fulfill the Great Commission, while **contextualization** is God's approach to cross-cultural communication and **kingdom theology** is crucial to all ministry—and is especially relevant to folk Muslims. The planting of contextualized churches rooted in kingdom theology is the most effective way to reach folk Muslims.[1]

Our team had the privilege of testing this thesis by planting a church among the Muslim Baahithiin. A commitment to kingdom theology and biblical contextualization doesn't make the work of church planting easy; however, it will make it possible. Kingdom

9

theology and biblical contextualization offer no panacea. In fact, a true understanding of both is a call to spiritual warfare and sacrifice. If the parables of the kingdom teach us anything, they teach us that we are in a war against the world, the flesh and the devil. In addition, learning a language, adapting to a new customs and seeking to incarnate truth in a new culture demand blood, sweat and tears. Well, at least sweat and tears!

Contextualization: A Modern Missiological Theory or an Ancient Biblical Model?

What is contextualization, really? Several definitions vie for our attention. Fundamentally, contextualization concerns itself with how the *text* (of Scripture) relates to the *context* of a people group.

Since contextualization is a modern missiological buzzword, many people assume it is a modern theory. Not so. Although the term is modern, the concept and principles are as old as the Bible. A brief look at two doctrines, the inspiration of Scripture and the incarnation, will make this clear.

Evangelicals believe that the Bible is the word of God in the words of humankind. Because Scripture is divine, it is authoritative. We have a message from heaven that must be obeyed. Because Scripture is also human, written in words understood by humankind, we can examine how God has "contextualized" his transcultural truth in the languages and cultures of humankind.

Scripture is what Charles Kraft calls "receptor-oriented." In crossing the gap between God and God's creatures, God does not merely build a bridge halfway across, requiring humans to span the gulf from the other side. Rather, God employs our culture's principles of communication in language we can understand. God is revealed in a receptor-oriented fashion (1988:169).

To illustrate how God communicates to different contexts, we note that God used the Near Eastern literary forms of law, covenant and poetry in the Old Testament. These were the common literary forms of the day. In the New Testament God employed the genres of history, epistle and apocalypse – all having clear parallels with first-century literature. In each case, God adopted and transformed common literary forms to reveal God's truth to God's people.

In contrast to refined, classical literary Greek, the New Testament authors (under the guidance of the Holy Spirit) wrote in *koine*, or common Greek, the language of the street. God's primary concern was to communicate, to make plain the meaning of the good news. Accordingly, God adopted the heart language of the people to reveal God's purposes.

Perhaps the most striking example is the fact that God employed the Hebrew word *elohim* and the Greek word *theos* to describe himself. Originally, *elohim* (an Old Testament term for God) was the name of the high god in the Canaanite pantheon. The New Testament word for God, *theos*, originally referred to the high god in the Greek pantheon. God used these imperfect terms and transformed them to fit his purposes and reveal his truth (Kittle 1968; see also Gilliland 1989:36ff).

What lesson do we learn from God's contextualization of his message? In the words of pastor-theologian John Stott:

> The overriding reason why we should take other people's cultures seriously is that God has taken ours seriously. God is the supreme communicator. And his Word has come to us in an extremely particularized form. Whether spoken or written, it was addressed to particular people in particular cultures using the particular thought-forms, syntax, and vocabulary with which they were familiar (Coote and Stott 1980: vii-viii).

The ultimate argument for the necessity and priority of contextualization, however, is the incarnation. The incarnation is not just theologically *descriptive* of what God has done in Christ. It is theologically *prescriptive* of what we must do to imitate Christ. As the *Willowbank Report on the Gospel and Culture* affirms, the incarnation is the "most spectacular instance of cultural identification in the history of mankind, since by his incarnation the Son became a first-century Galilean Jew" (Stott 1980:323).

The incarnation demonstrates God's unabashed and sacrificial commitment to contextualization. In the Old Testament, God revealed himself historically through his deeds and propositionally through his words. This revelation was sufficient for a saving, personal knowledge of God (which a cursory reading of the Psalms makes clear). But this propositional revelation was foundational and preparatory. Ultimately, the infinite, almighty, sovereign God chose to reveal himself personally. He became flesh in order to show how God relates to a fallen, hurting world of sinners (Jn 1:18; 14:8-9). The incarnation demonstrates how a supra-cultural God relates to a culture-bound humanity.

Jesus' commission, "As the Father has sent me, even so I send you" (Jn 20:21), indicates we are to model our ministry after that of Christ. Moreover, Paul makes a clear connection between our lives and ministries and the incarnation: "Have this attitude in yourselves which was also in Christ Jesus, who although He existed in the form of God, did not regard equality with God a thing to be grasped, but emptied Himself, taking the form of a bond-servant" (Phil 2:5-7). While this has many implications, it clearly mandates that we are to be contextualizers of the gospel. We are to be incarnational in our approach to ministry: culturally sensitive communicators with a culturally relevant message.

The Bible not only proclaims God's *message* of salvation but also portrays God's *method* of communicating. The Bible is God's method book on contextualization.

Why Church Planting?

Nowhere in the New Testament do we find the command to plant churches. However, a cursory reading of the book of Acts indicates that the early church, and especially Paul the apostle, understood the command to "make disciples of all nations" in terms of church planting. In the New Testament, there were no disciples apart from believing communities; there was no evangelism without church growth (1 Jn 1:3).

Evangelism is not enough. To rescue the perishing or to reach Muslims is only the first step toward an even greater goal. We want to build committed, growing communities–communities of the King. To make disciples of all nations (in Greek, *panta ta ethne*–all the ethnic groups of the world), we must establish churches within each of these *ethne*. Jesus' implication in Matthew 28:19 is clear, and the rest of the New Testament provides us with a model.

The most concise summary of church planting in the New Testament is found in Acts 14:21-23:

> And after they had preached the gospel to that city and had made many disciples they returned to Lystra and to Iconium and to Antioch, strengthening the souls of the disciples, encouraging them to continue in the faith, and saying, "Through many tribulations we must enter the kingdom of God." And when they had appointed elders for them in every church, having prayed with fasting, they commended them to the Lord in whom they had believed.

This passage highlights a number of important points regarding the process of church planting. Luke summarizes Paul's church-planting efforts in three cities–Lystra, Iconium and Antioch. (All of these cities are in the region of Galatia and were the recipients of Paul's letter to the Galatians). The various steps that Luke mentions in each city draw a composite picture of the process of church planting: first evangelize, next build up the body, then appoint elders to lead that body, and finally, move on.

Paul preached the gospel and "made many disciples." The verb "make disciples" (*matheteo*) occurs only in Matthew 28:19 and Acts 14:21, which clearly links the Great Commission with this passage. The first step in church planting is evangelism. This is how the church is birthed.

Second, Paul gathered the new believers to nurture them by "strengthening" and "encouraging." The nurture of these young communities was central to Paul's church-planting strategy. On his second missionary journey, Paul and his team could be found "strengthening the churches" (Ac 15:41). Again on his third missionary journey, he "strengthened all the disciples" (Ac 18:23). After evangelization came edification. Thus the church is built.

Third, before he moved on to new territory, Paul trained elders who would lead the church. Thus, after evangelization and edification came organization. Paul evangelized the lost, built up the body and trained up leaders.

These verses raise two important issues. Paul appointed a plurality of leaders – a group of elders, not simply a single pastor. In addition, the passage describes these fledgling fellowships as "churches." Although immature and incomplete (lacking clearly-appointed leadership), these small groups of new believers were nevertheless described as "church" prior to the appointing of elders. (Titus 1:5 describes a similar situation years later in Crete). Obviously Paul's definition of the church was more flexible and fluid than most modern definitions.

It is worth noting that Paul prepares the church to suffer. In each city this passage mentions, Paul had met intense persecution. He had almost been stoned to death in Lystra. Is it any wonder that he exclaimed, "Through many tribulations we must enter the kingdom of God!" Paul promised no health-and-wealth gospel here! Suffering is normative both in the New Testament and in Muslim ministry (Phil 1:29; Col 1:24; Ac 9:15-16).

This simple outline of church planting in Acts 14 – evangelization, edification, organization – is much more complicated in practice. That's because church planting is comprehensive, both a science and an art.

Church planting is comprehensive. Church planting is comprehensive because it encompasses every aspect of ministry and all of life. At the very least, church planting involves evangelizing, discipling, small group leading, worship and music directing, counseling, teaching and developing leaders. Church planters are generalists rather than specialists. We may not be evangelists, but we must evangelize. We may not be counselors, but we must counsel. Church planting forces us to deal with a whole spectrum of issues. We must cover everything from the devotional life to the sex life. Truly, church planting is a comprehensive endeavor.

Church planting is a science. Science is experimental. Science is pragmatic. Science is inductive. Through many trials and errors, every church plant involves similar activities. Evangelism, discipling and leadership training are integral to any church plant. These steps in the process of church planting will follow a certain sequence.

Church planting is an art. Every person and every people group is unique. Complex problems do not fit neatly into a highly regimented, step-by-step approach to evangelism and discipling. Church planters develop the art of sharing the gospel in relevant ways with different people. Discipling men and women with radically different backgrounds, personalities and gifts requires a certain artistry. These relational and spiritual dimensions of church planting comprise the "art" dimension of the task.

While the scientific aspect of church planting is based on knowledge, the artistic dimension is based on wisdom. This is why Paul talks about wisdom when he speaks of church planting. In Colossians 1:28, Paul describes the role of the pioneer church planter as proclaiming Christ, admonishing and teaching everyone "with all wisdom." After planting a number of churches in a variety of settings, Paul describes himself as a "wise" master builder (1 Cor 3:10). He had learned the "art" of founding churches.

Books on church planting tend to focus on the "science" part of the task because the "art" part of the task is learned primarily through experience–in the trenches. Church planting with an experienced church planter is the best way to learn how to plant a church. But the "science" part of church planting, also quite valuable, can be learned through a book. At least Paul thought so; that's why he wrote Titus and 1 and 2 Timothy.

At the end of this book I offer two approaches to church planting that I have found especially helpful. Appendix 1 features a "master builder's blueprint" that I first developed for my own church-planting team among the Baahithiin. Appendix 2 features the "Church Planting Phase and Activity List" developed by leaders in Frontiers to help a wide variety of teams to monitor their progress, overcome obstacles, and anticipate next steps.

Why Kingdom Theology?

Most Evangelical theology skips over the kingdom of God. Evangelicals talk a lot about "a personal Savior," being "saved" or being "born again." Rather than the rule of God, our emphasis tends to be on reconciliation with God–which is biblical and in most cases relevant to a Western audience, but it doesn't do justice to the whole Bible. Nor is it particularly relevant to folk Muslims.

The kingdom of God is the dominant theological theme in the Gospels. Jesus' preaching, prayers, and person all center on the kingdom of God (Mk 1:14, 15; Mt 6:9-13; Lk 17:21). The kingdom is the subject of his sermons, the point of his parables, and the meaning of his miracles (Mt 5-7; 11:1-5; 12:28,29; 13:1-52; Mk 4). In fact, we can only understand the message and mission of Jesus if we understand the kingdom of God. The two are inseparable.

Many Evangelicals, however, misunderstand the nature of the kingdom. We give preeminence to the relational (or Godward) dimension of the kingdom, stressing our personal relationship with God, forgiveness, and fellowship. This emphasis is sound; it is biblical, yet it is incomplete.

There is a rescue (or Satanward) dimension to Scripture as well.[2] Jesus not only came to save us from our sins but also to destroy the works of the devil (1 Jn 3:8). Through Jesus' life, death and resurrection, we have been rescued from the kingdom of darkness. Jesus has defeated Satan and ushered in the kingdom of God on earth (Mt 12:28; Ac 10:38; Eph 1:20-21; Col 1:12-14; 2:15; Heb 2:14; 1 Pt 3:21-22).

Kingdom theology sees all of life in light of this clash of the kingdoms of light and darkness. It takes the devil seriously. It offers a message of deliverance. Kingdom theology provides us with biblical foundations and practical tools to minister among folk Muslims. Magic, healings and exorcisms are far more easily understood and practiced when they are understood in kingdom terms.[3] Scripture reveals four aspects of kingdom theology relevant to contextualized church planting among folk Muslims: 1) truth encounter; 2) power encounter; 3) moral encounter; and 4) cultural encounter.

The church-planting team and the emerging church must preach the good news that Jesus came to destroy the works of the devil (truth encounter), confront the powers of darkness through exorcism and healing (power encounter), model the values of the kingdom (moral encounter), and express the reality of the kingdom through culturally relevant rituals (cultural encounter). Each of these encounters will be elaborated in later chapters.

Richard R. DeRidder's experience among animists parallels ministry to folk Muslims and illustrates my point. As a conservative, Reformed missiologist, DeRidder, who served from 1956-1960 as a missionary in Ceylon, hardly sees demons behind every bush. But he does affirm the relevance of a Satanward gospel.

> ... One thing deeply impressed me: how irrelevant so much of traditional Reformed Theology was to these people and their situation, and how seldom this theology spoke to their real needs. ... [T]he questions that concern Satan, the demons, angels, charms, etc. are not of great concern, nor do they receive much attention in the West. These are living issues to the Christians of these areas, surrounded as they were by animism and the continual fear of the spiritual realm. Among the greatest joys that we experienced was to proclaim to men the victory of Christ over the powers and see the shackles of slavery to elemental spirits broken by Christ. This is a chapter of Reformed Theology that has still not been written, and perhaps which cannot be written by the West. When the "Five Points of Calvinism" were preached to these people, they often responded with the question, "What's the issue?" Missionaries and pastors were scratching where it didn't itch! (1971:222).

It is my hope that this book will enable its readers to scratch where folk Muslims itch.

=====

Questions for Reflection and Discussion

1. "The planting of contextualized churches rooted in kingdom theology is the most effective way to reach folk Muslims." Do you agree? Why or why not? (Tell me if your answers change after you've read the whole book. :))

2. This chapter introduces four aspects of kingdom theology especially relevant to folk Muslims: truth encounter, power encounter, moral encounter, and cultural encounter. Later chapters will describe these in more detail, but what are your initial impressions? Which of the four do you find most appealing, which do you find most daunting, and why?

3. Jesus came to destroy the works of the devil (1 John 3:8). Which of the devil's works are most prominent among the people you serve? Do expatriate Christians and national Christians (if any) answer this question differently, and (if so) how and why?

It will help you to better digest what you're reading if you take the time to reflect on and discuss such questions after each chapter. Also, I would value a glimpse of what you're thinking! I invite you (either now or later) to share with me (r_d_love@hotmail.com) some of your answers to these questions. You may have some good things to teach me.

Notes

[1] While this book focuses on folk Muslims, much of what I have to say relates to church planting in general. A contextualized kingdom approach to ministry is effective anywhere. Dean Gilliland, for example, says that "power encounter [one important aspect of kingdom ministry] is a legitimate, positive concept for evangelization among Muslims. This is true in the generic Muslim context, not just in folk Islam" (Wagner and Pennoyer 1990:332-333). Many of the principles and practices outlined in this book could be effective among animists, Buddhists and Hindus as well.

[2] See *Jesus and the Power of Satan* (1968) and *The Significance of the Synoptic Miracles* (1961) by James Kallas for the most thorough and cogent expositions of the Satanward dimension of Scripture.

[3] See *Signs, Wonders and the Kingdom of God* by Don Williams (1989); *Christianity with Power* (1989) by Charles Kraft and *Power Healing* (1987) by John Wimber for excellent summaries of how the theology of the kingdom of God can be translated into a ministry of signs and wonders.

Chapter 2

Folk Islam

In folk Islam ... [p]eople in everyday life are believed to be at the mercy of evil powers: spirits, ghosts, demons, evil eyes, curses and sorcery. Their only protection is to seek the aid of Allah, angels, saints, charms, good magic and other powers.

–Paul Hiebert

"Uthman*, why do you have to give offerings to the ancestor spirits? Why don't you just cast them out?" I asked.

"Oh no!" he replied. "You don't cast them out. They are your ancestors. You have to respect them!"

Welcome to the world of folk Islam!

The response of Uthman, a Baahithiin Muslim, illustrates the beliefs of folk Muslims. Specific expressions of folk Islam will vary from culture to culture and country to country, but the underlying animistic belief system and orientation to life pervades the Muslim world.

A good example of this underlying animistic belief system is described in Clifford Geertz' *Islam Observed*. Geertz contrasts Islam in Morocco, at the western tip of the Muslim world, with Islam in Indonesia, at the eastern tip of the Muslim world. The Arabs of Morocco and the Asians of Indonesia are radically different culturally. So, too, is their expression of Islam.

According to Geertz, the Islam in Morocco reflects an uncompromising rigor. It is "basically the Islam of saint worship and moral severity, magical power and aggressive piety" (1971:9). By contrast, the Islam in Indonesia is adaptive, patient, and all-embracing. Indonesians absorb "Islamic concepts and practices ... into the same general Southeast Asian folk religion into which it had previously

19

absorbed Indian ones, locking ghosts, gods, jinns, and prophets together into a strikingly contemplative, even philosophical, animism" (1971:13). Yet despite radically different expressions and values, animism holds Muslims captive in both Morocco and Indonesia.

I have interviewed missionaries serving Muslims in North Africa, the Middle East, Central Asia, South Asia and Southeast Asia. I have visited many of these workers on-site as well. They all confirm the practice of folk Islam in their countries.

For example, most folk Muslims fear curses. Those in one North African country worry that someone will use their fingernail trimmings to curse them. Those in one Middle Eastern country prefer using a person's hair to proclaim a curse. (Both cases illustrate what is known as "contagious magic," which will be discussed later.) In another Middle Eastern country, a missionary notes that Muslims in his city frequently practice "blood blessings." If a man buys a car, he will sacrifice a lamb and place the blood on the bumper of the car to protect himself from the forces of darkness. When these Muslims build a new house, they sacrifice a lamb and apply its blood to the door frames.[1]

One North African country has occult fairs that draw as many as 20,000 people! During these "Satanic signs and wonders conferences," people gather in small groups all over the countryside to witness supernatural feats, offer blood sacrifices, and receive blessing (*baraka*). Possessed by spirits, some participants slash themselves with knives yet do not bleed. Others dance in trances. Still others take bites of bread and then throw the bread out so the crowd can receive the blessing. Two veteran workers have described certain people possessed by animal spirits (like the spirit of a lion) who use their bare hands to kill and devour a cow or other animal.

Yet folk Islam also has its lighter side. A love potion in North Africa supposedly keeps men faithful to their wives. Women serve this magic potion to their husbands in a cup of tea that is "spiced" with the wife's urine. With a hearty laugh, an Arab worker reported that "every man in [our country] has drunk his wife's urine – from the king down to the poorest peasant!"

After I interviewed one worker from the Middle East about various types of magic practices among folk Muslims, including weekly all-night exorcism ceremonies, he exclaimed, "Dallas Theological Seminary didn't prepare me for this!" Most seminaries don't.

J. Dudley Woodberry's experience in Pakistan provides a good summary of the type of issues church planters struggle with in the Muslim world.

> I sat down to reflect. Here we were in the outskirts of Islamabad or the place of Islam, the capital of Pakistan or the pure land, in a nation created so Muslims could live according to the Law of God as they understand it. Yet the felt need of at least those who had gathered for religious purposes was power – the capacity to produce results. They had come at a time of power, a birthday or holy day of one or more saints. They wore objects of power, their amulets. The people came to visit a place of power, a shrine, and a person of power – a holy man. They wanted to offer a prayer for power, or receive a power incantation to ward off the power of the spirits (Wagner and Pennoyer 1990:314).

Scholars of comparative religions like to distinguish between two manifestations of religion. They contrast the higher or ideal forms of the religion (in our case, formal Islam) with the lower or more popular forms (folk Islam).

Formal Islam is a comprehensive and legalistic code of ritual and laws. The institutional religion preoccupies itself with truth, founded on revelation. Formal Islam approaches God with an attitude of submission ("Thy will be done") and supplication ("Give us this day our daily bread"). The issues of origin, ultimate destiny and the meaning of life loom large in formal Islam. "The call to abandon and repudiate all idolatry, to acknowledge the sole sovereignty of God ... 'to have no other gods,' either in creed or in trust, is the impervious demand of Islamic religion" (McCurry 1979:197).

Folk Islam, by contrast, takes a more spiritualistic orientation to life. Spirits and demons, blessing and curses, healing and sorcery are its domain. Folk Islam confronts the spirit world with an attitude of manipulation ("*My* will be done!"). Moreover, its concerns are primarily heart-felt, not cognitive, and focused on the here-and-now. The issues of well-being, success and health consume its time. Folk Islam is the power of a shaman to deliver blessings and prevent bad fortune in this world (see Table 1).

Formal Islam	Folk Islam
Cognitive, Truth-oriented	Heart-felt, Emotional
Legalistic	Mystical
Ultimate Issues of Life:	Everyday Concerns:
Origins, heaven,	health, guidance,
hell, purpose	success, prosperity
The Quran	Supernatural Power
Sacred Traditions	Spiritual Revelation
Institutional	Inspirational
Supplicative	Manipulative

Table 1: A Comparison of Formal Islam and Folk Islam

To Westerners, the practices of folk Islam contradict formal Islam. However, those who practice folk Islam rarely see themselves as syncretists. They view themselves as genuine Muslims. From their perspective, no conflict exists between their popular religion and its more orthodox variety. What Samuel Zwemer, the famous missionary to Muslims, experienced years ago is still true today, "Islam and Animism live, in very neighborly fashion, on the same street and in the same mind."[2]

According to Phil Parshall, "perhaps 70 percent of all Muslims in the world are influenced by a system we could properly term folk Islam" (1983:16). J. Dudley Woodberry agrees with this figure, but Don McCurry's estimates are even higher, suggesting as much as 85 percent of the Muslim world is animistic (1980). Conservatively we can conclude that over three-quarters of the Islamic world are folk Muslims.[3] According to one Arab evangelist who has worked for more than 30 years in six Arab countries, folk Islam is the most pressing issue we face in reaching Muslims.

Even more Muslim women practice an animistic form of Islam – perhaps as many as 95%. Because women in Muslim societies often feel helpless, they frequently turn to magic and holy men for help. Elizabeth Fernea's description of women in Morocco is true of the broader Muslim world: "The need to fill up whatever was lacking in their lives dominated the women and was met through regular visits to the tombs, or *marabouts* where they sought *baraka* [blessing]" (1980:257). It is not just the down-trodden and uneducated who pursue supernatural help, however. In North Africa even highly educated, miniskirt-wearing Muslim women practice magic.

One Baahithiin shaman told me that he received his supernatural powers while on the ritual pilgrimage in Mecca. His experience shows that folk Islam touches even Saudi Arabia, which takes pride in being the heartland of formal Islam. But even though this large percentage of the Muslim world are folk Muslims, this doesn't mean that their folk practices are the same, or even that they are similarly pervasive. There is a spectrum of practice – from frequent use of overt magical practices, to infrequent and covert use of magic during times of crisis. Table 2 illustrates the possibilities.

The practice of folk Islam breaks into six components, as illustrated in Table 3. These six components describe folk Islam in simple yet comprehensive terms.[4] Church planters can use this model as a diagnostic tool to study folk Islam among the people group they seek to reach.

My experience and research among the Baahithiin illustrate the components of folk Islam. Their animistic perspective and practices provide a good introduction to the problems facing missionaries among folk Muslims. (Power rituals will not be treated separately since they are linked with every one of the other five components.)

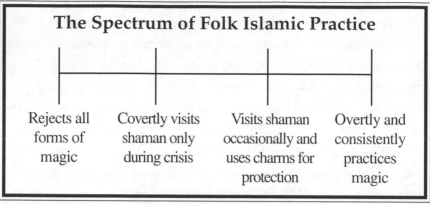

The Spectrum of Folk Islamic Practice

Rejects all forms of magic	Covertly visits shaman only during crisis	Visits shaman occasionally and uses charms for protection	Overtly and consistently practices magic

Table 2: The Spectrum of Folk Islamic Practice

Six Components of Folk Islam

	Examples from Folk Islam
Power(s)	demons, angels, mana
Power persons	imans, shamans
Power objects	charms, amulets
Power places	Mecca, saints' tombs
Power times	Muhammad's birthday, the pilgrimage
Power rituals	prayers and incantations using the Quran

Table 3: Six Components of Folk Islam

Power(s)

Baahithiin beliefs regarding spirit beings pervade the culture. These spirit powers can be evil or good, but evil spirits must be exorcised. One Baahithiin friend explained how the spiritual leader of my old neighborhood casts out demons: "He heals people possessed by spirits by talking nicely to the spirits either in his own language or spirit to spirit. ... He also quotes verses from the Quran. Sometimes he prays over water and then has the possessed person drink it. The minute they drink the water they are healed."

Good spirits help the Baahithiin during times of crisis. Another friend says this about ancestor spirits: "Occasionally, we need to call on our ancestor spirits to visit us when we need help. We ask for guidance from them because they know more than we do. They understand the spirit realm. For example, if I lose something, I will invite my ancestor spirits to come and then they will speak to me. I don't see them, but I hear their voices."

Besides Allah, the Baahithiin recognize five categories of spirit beings: 1) angels; 2) Islamic spirit beings; 3) evil spirits; 4) ancestor spirits; and 5) gods and goddesses. These varied categories of spirit beings and an abundance of specific names for evil spirits reflect the concerns and fears of the Baahithiin.[5]

The Baahithiin also believe in an impersonal power linked primarily with power objects, such as charms and amulets. R.H. Codrington, a missionary to Melanesia in the late 1800s, coined the term *mana* for this type of power. "He discovered that the inhabitants of the islands conceived of an impersonal supernatural force called *mana* that could reside in people and unusual objects. ... [M]ana worked more like ... electric power" (Spradley and McCurdy 1980:258).

Missiologist David Burnett's fourfold description of *mana* also accurately describes the Baahithiin belief:

First, *mana* is a power distinct from the ordinary powers of mankind. Secondly, ... *mana* may generally be understood as being an impersonal force very much like high voltage electricity. ... A third characteristic of *mana* is that it may be conceived of as being intrinsically amoral. A healer may use his *mana* to cure the sick, while a sorcerer may use his to cast a curse upon a person. ... Fourthly, *mana*, like any power, is valued by people. *Mana* can increase a person's prosperity, preserve a man from danger and enable a barren woman to bear children (Burnett 1988:26-27).

The Baahithiin understand powers as both personal and impersonal. But they also describe supernatural power in terms of white or black magic. If the supernatural power is for good or has its source in Allah, then it is considered white magic. White magic or power is usually linked with special prayer and verses from the Quran. Conversely, they use black magic, which has its source in Satan, to harm people.

Though most Baahithiin differentiate white magic from black magic on the basis of its source (the Quran) and its fruit (good or evil), some are more discerning. One of my informants said that intent differentiates white magic from black magic: Does he want to do good or evil with his power? Like others, he affirmed the fact that white magic has its source in the Quran. However, he admitted that people could even use verses from the Quran in an evil way, thus indicating that the Islamic holy book could be misused. Even an evil person could protect himself with an amulet filled with verses from the Quran.

Another informant mentions yet another difference between white and black magic. People with black magic will use their supernatural powers for demonstrations. They will eat glass, cut or slash their bodies and drive spikes into their stomachs to prove their invincibility. White magic, on the other hand, may not be used for demonstrations or to impress people. In addition, since white magic comes from God, it is more powerful than black magic.

A story from my experience may illustrate the reality of the magic practiced among the Baahithiin. It is not to be dismissed as merely a matter of superstition or sleight of hand (although every culture has its share of both). The power is real and supernatural.

One afternoon soon after arriving in this country, I was talking with a group of Baahithiin who told me of one of their friends with supernatural power enabling him to eat glass without harm. Being more than a little interested, I asked if I could meet the man. When I did meet him, he immediately offered to demonstrate his power. He asked for a rice meal and then had his friend break a light bulb and sprinkle its pieces among the rice. He then scooped the rice, put it in his mouth and crunched his "glass-rice" meal loudly and nonchalantly. He did not pray beforehand, nor was there any sign of blood.[6]

White magic and black magic are the most common categories of power for the Baahithiin. However, a functional analysis reveals four types of magic practiced among a wide array of folk Muslims: 1) productive magic; 2) protective magic; 3) destructive magic; and 4) divination.[7]

Productive Magic. Like peoples around the world, the Baahithiin hunger for blessing. The pursuit of prosperity, fertility and success is the major preoccupation of their lives. At the most practical level, they seek blessing in order to pass exams at school, find a mate, bear children, have a plentiful harvest or succeed in business. In these pursuits, they often turn toward what could be described as productive magic for success.

Productive magic is used to facilitate success in school. Uthman describes his experience of going to a shaman in order to pass an exam: "The shaman burned incense and prayed. Then I had to take a bath at midnight with seven types of flowers in the water. At the same time, I had to repeatedly mention the name of the principal of the school where I was going to take the exam. Praise God! I passed the exam."

The ability to bear children is another important aspect of blessing in every society. The Baahithiin use a certain kind of amulet to enhance fertility. A shaman prays over the amulet, then implants it under the woman's skin. Uthman exclaims, "My mother was not able to get pregnant, so she went to a shaman. The shaman implanted an amulet and then she had eight children!"

Although the Baahithiin are urbanizing, a large percentage of them still grow rice and are preoccupied by the need for a plentiful harvest. One informant used another kind of amulet as a means to ensure a good harvest. To keep mice from harming the crop and to enhance plant fertility, he buried a piece of paper with verses from the Quran in a path around the rice field.

Protective magic. Protective magic is possibly the most developed or comprehensive type of magic among the Baahithiin. They admit that fear is a major problem, so they seek supernatural measures in order to overcome these fears. They emphasize a supernatural approach to martial arts. For example, through incantations, rituals and prescribed conditions (fasting, keeping of certain taboos) the martial artist can knock a person backwards without touching him (using a push-like shove from a distance). Some are even able to withstand a forceful blow of a machete, without any trace of blood. Still others may bleed from a knife wound but are healed almost immediately. In addition, a flourishing use of charms and amulets gives further evidence of protective magic among the Baahithiin.

Destructive Magic. Destructive magic (black magic), common among the Baahithiin, uses various formulas, spells and incantations to control or harm people. For example, people use one type of black magic, *hejaab**, to get someone of the opposite sex to fall in love with him or her. One of my cultural informants describes this type as follows: "The practitioner of *hejaab* reads his incantations in Baahithiin, the national language and sometimes in Arabic. Along with this, fasting, fragrant oils and pictures are often part of the magical spell. When *hejaab* is used, a person that previously didn't like the person suddenly likes them."

In a more powerful form of black magic, conditions are stricter. In addition to fasting, prayer and various incantations, some shamans include scorpions and snakes as a part of the incantation. Practitioners most frequently use this form of black magic to make someone sick. Once the person becomes ill, he cannot be helped by a doctor. Only a shaman can heal someone who has been afflicted by this form of black magic.

Divination. In the most general sense, divination "means learning about the future or about things that may be hidden" (Lehman and Myers 1985:193). Two broad categories of divination among the Baahithiin are the inspirational/supernatural and the non-inspirational/ natural. The inspirational/supernatural approach seeks guidance from spirit beings, whereas the non-inspirational/natural approach seeks meaning in natural phenomena such as black cats, hairpins, astrology and numerology.

Folk Muslims use divination primarily in three practical areas: to discover the causes and cures of sickness or problems, to discover the future, or to help people make decisions about their future. One of my friends working among Muslims in Southeast Asia told me about an *imam* who was extremely accurate in divining lost or stolen possessions. He said that the local police would even come to this man to get help in solving their crimes!

Power People

Among Baahithiin two primary categories of power people (practitioners of magic) seem to exist: the occultic practitioner (shaman) and the Islamic practitioner (imam). While both types are believed to have some special type of supernatural power, power people also perform very natural functions. For example, power people might be midwives, circumcision experts, or masseurs. Some know the esoteric secrets to mysticism, while others foretell the future. Healing and sorcery are also a part of the power person's trade. An elder of a community is sometimes considered another type of power person.

Because definitions of religious specialists vary and often overlap, it isn't easy to define the power person. He or she may be a medicine man, a medium or a mystic. He or she may be a sorcerer, seeking to harm someone with black magic.[8] However, the power person could probably best be described as a shaman, "a ceremonial practitioner whose powers come from direct contact with the supernatural."[9]

The shaman receives his power either by inheriting it from his parents or by learning from another power person. In our community, Muhammah Lemiin* inherited his power from his father. When he was young, he memorized the prayers his father used when he would officiate at religious ceremonies. Later, his father gave him a book that had many prayers and mystical insights into the spirit realm. Muhammah Lemiin didn't really function as a power person, however, until his father died.

The occultic practitioner need not be a Muslim leader. He confesses Islam, often using verses from the Quran to heal and bless. Yet he is not perceived by the Islamic community as one of their leaders and does not function in the role of teacher. He is a Muslim who has supernatural powers. In some cases, his power is clearly evil. By contrast, Islamic practitioners (imams) function more like priests than shamans. As priests, they lead congregational prayer. They also preserve and explain the great traditions.

Other important differences distinguish the shaman and the imam. Whereas the occultic practitioner serves individuals on an occasional basis, Islamic leaders work with congregations as a part of a routine. Imams are institutional (backed up by an organization), while shamans are inspirational (dependent upon the inspiration of spirit beings for their practices). Imams approach the supernatural with an attitude of supplication, whereas shamans approach the supernatural with a view to manipulation.

However, in other societies the functions of the shaman and imam overlap. Many imams also operate in supernatural power. Like shamans, they have power to heal, bless and guide. However, their powers, unlike the shamans', are always linked with the Quran. Fasting, memorizing Quranic verses and special prayers are typical ways imams impart their blessings.

I have asked numerous informants to contrast shamans and imams, especially in the area of supernatural power. Daani's* response seems the most accurate. He said,

> Islamic leaders need to learn three things. They need to learn Arabic so they can understand the Quran, and [the national language] so they can teach it to us. They also need to learn the use of the Quran for supernatural purposes. In other words, there are many verses from the Quran that can be used to bless, guide and heal in a supernatural way. However, there are some Islamic leaders who only know Arabic and [the national language]. They haven't learned the supernatural use of the Quran. Maybe it's because they live in the city. Islamic leaders in the villages have more time to fast and pray, whereas those in the city are often too busy trying to make a living.

Power Objects

A charm (also known to Westerners as an amulet, fetish or talisman) is an object containing supernatural power to protect or bless people. Through power rituals, shamans empower (literally "fill") a normal object to turn it into a charm.

The charm generally has no efficacy until the recipient fulfills certain conditions or power rituals. While these power rituals vary according to the shaman and the charm, the most common include fasting, reading certain prayers or verses from the Quran, and not wearing the charm while going to the bathroom! Some Baahithiin argue that a real spirit being inhabits or attaches itself to the charm. Others contend that the "filling" of the charm refers to the entrance of that impersonal force or power described above as *mana*. One non-Western mission leader speaks of three kinds: personal charms, family charms, and royal charms (from the ancient kingdoms). Another informant classifies them this way: charms that are worn (rings or belts), charms that are stored or displayed (rocks or verses from the Quran), and charms that are implanted in the body.

The analysis of one of my informants is most thorough. He enumerates seven distinct categories of charms: 1) Weapons; 2) Verses written on paper or animal skin; 3) Pin-like objects implanted into the body; 4) Rings; 5) Family heirlooms; 6) Objects taken from a holy place, e.g., a splinter of wood from a tomb; and 7) Any object that has been filled by someone with supernatural power.

Probably the most famous Baahithiin charm is an ornamental sword or dagger called a *khanjar**. It protects one from natural calamities such as a storm. Or, functioning like a shield, it protects its wearer from personal harm, especially from an attack by someone evil.

One shaman described the function of his *khanjar* as follows: "Suppose someone wants to hurt you. If you hold onto this *khanjar*, praise God, nothing will happen to you. The person who wants to do you harm will immediately feel compassion for you and won't want to hurt you." *Khanjars* are usually handed down from ancestors, or they may be obtained from a shaman. They must be or empowered by a spirit or *mana*.

Many Baahithiin men like to wear rings with large stones for cosmetic purposes. However, some of these rings have more than natural beauty; they have been empowered by *mana*. The most popular of these rings are made from turquoise and can be purchased on the main streets in one of our major cities, where they are usually displayed along with other "normal" rings.

Another type of charm is a small pin implanted under the skin in order to make a person well-liked, stronger, more beautiful, or fertile. It can be inserted (usually by a power person) anywhere on one's body, but most people put it near their eyes, lips or chin, depending on where they want to draw attention. Baahithiin prefer pins made of gold or silver to make others like or love them. Silver ones are said to increase bodily strength or make a person stay young.

The pin charm's power depends on the keeping of certain taboos. For example, the wearer may be forbidden to eat certain foods like frogs or golden bananas. Sometimes the Baahithiin want to be released from the power of this charm. In particular, when a person is dying he or she usually wants to have the pin removed. They believe they will suffer a great deal more in death if they keep their charm. Also, people who are converted to a purer form of Islam will want to get rid of this charm.

A cultural informant told me of three ways a person can get rid of this charm's power. "First, the shaman who put it in can get it out. Secondly, you can break the taboos associated with the charm. And thirdly, an Islamic leader who has white magic can do it. He will pray over some water and then when the person drinks it, the charm will come out."

Another important amulet for the Baahithiin is a belt. Attached to this normal belt are verses from the Quran or Hadith (Islamic traditions, many of which are considered authoritative for Muslims). Sometimes the belt is constructed of brass with the verses carved into it. It derives its power not from a spirit, but from the inherent power or mana in the verses themselves. This belt is believed to provide protection from evil people.

Another type of amulet uses designs and verses from the Quran or the Hadith written on a piece of paper, metal or an animal skin. When I asked my informant about this kind of amulet, he handed me one from his wallet, while assuring me that he didn't believe in them. He said the designs and graphics originally come from Saudi Arabia, reflecting Arabs' pre-Islamic polytheistic beliefs. Baahithiin put these paper amulets over the doorways of their houses, keep them in wallets or store them in cupboards. Like the belt charm, they are thought to protect and bring good luck.

My informant's observations reflect his in-depth understanding of formal and folk Islam. According to Musk, some of the major sources of syncretistic folk Islam are the animistic practices that were prevalent throughout Arabia when Muhammad emerged as the founder of Islam (1989:229).

Power Places

The city of Al-Bait* is a center of spiritual power for the Baahithiin. From all over the country, people come to Al-Bait to seek blessing and power. It is not an exaggeration to say that for many, Al-Bait is a holy city. In fact, there is a ceremony in Al-Bait that is considered to be the spiritual equivalent of a Muslim going on a pilgrimage to Mecca.

In our region the tombs of three Muslim saints are reputedly centers of great blessing and esoteric power. Of these three, the one in Al-Bait is considered the most important. In fact, one spiritual guide said that a person is supposed to ask for permission at Al-Bait before he goes to the other tombs. According to another guide in Al-Bait, this is true because out of all the holy men who came to our region, Shaikh Al-Mutasawwif* was the closest relative of Muhammad.

Islam first came to the Baahithiin through Al-Bait. According to tradition, nine famous Muslim holy men came to spread the message of Islam throughout our region. Shaikh Al-Mutasawwif made Al-Bait his headquarters.

The tomb of Shaikh Al-Mutasawwif is now a center of spiritual blessing for the Baahithiin. It is a power place. Although people visit the grave throughout the year, most people want to visit this holy place during *Al-Mawlid Al-Nabawiyy**, Muhammad's birthday. During a three-hour visit to this grave during the month of *Al-Mawlid Al-Nabawiyy*, I noticed busloads of pilgrims from cities throughout the region.

The grave site of Shaikh Al-Mutasawwif consists of four sections. The first section is the entrance, where the spiritual guides and their fellow "soldiers" meet the visitors. The spiritual guides wear white coats with a traditional Baahithiin scarf around their heads and the Baahithiin dress, while the soldiers are shirtless, wearing only a scarf around their heads and the Baahithiin dress. They sell numerous amulets in this area. The most sought after in this area are oil, soil (taken from the saint's grave), dried rice, water, flowers and incense. The price for the amulet is left up to the visitor.

To the left of the entrance is the tomb. While there are hundreds of cement graves in the building (all relatives of Shaikh Al-Mutasawwif), the actual grave of Shaikh Al-Mutasawwif cannot be seen. Visitors are only allowed to pray in front of the two large wooden doors that enclose the grave.

This main area of the tomb is divided into three sections. In typical Muslim fashion, women are separated from the men, off to the right. Women who prayed in this section were usually there for a long period of time–for an entire day or even a whole week. However, women are allowed to pray with the men in the main (and central) section for up to three hours. To the left is a section especially for the bereaved and brokenhearted; I noted that these people had a pained, glazed look in their eyes and were subdued compared to the rest. The central section was buzzing with activity. The smell and smoke of incense filled the room. More than a hundred people were chanting the Quran and praying. Some people threw money at the door to the grave while shouting out their requests to God and Shaikh Al-Mutasawwif. People also caressed the doors in order to receive blessing.

Muslims make a pilgrimage, known as a *ziarah*, to a holy place with a variety of needs. Some seek financial success for their business, others want to pass important exams, while others come to pray to find a wife or to have children. Many come for blessing and physical healing.

Along with the normal Islamic practices of chanting the Quran and of prayer, *ziarah* at the tomb of Shaikh Al-Mutasawwif must include a number of unique rituals. Fasting and meditation are important as well. Petitioners must mention the name of Shaikh Al-Mutasawwif in their prayers. They must get containers of water from within the building and place them in front of the doors to the grave. They also buy flower petals to throw at the doors. The water and the flower petals are placed in front of these doors in order to absorb some of the blessing from the saint's grave. Supplicants then take the water and the flower petals home with them. If they are sick, they drink the water in order to be healed. They drop the flower petals into bath water so that they can take a holy bath of blessing to cleanse the soul.

Incense burns continually. Contrary to what most scholars assert, one spiritual guide assured us that incense had nothing to do with animistic or Hindu practices. Rather, they burn incense because the angels like it!

Musk's description of saint veneration in the Arab Muslim world is similar to my experience among the Baahithiin:

> The whole place was alive with the saint's baraka [blessing]. Many were there praying, crying, prostrating themselves and making requests of the saint. ... [T]here was holy water to drink, special relics to kiss, and a crowd of needy brothers and sisters to join with in prayer ... they touched the wooden screen separating them from the actual sarcophagus and wiped their faces and clothes with their hands. They wanted to carry home some of the baraka of the holy place (1989:48).

Power Times

Muslims all over the world celebrate Muhammad's birthday. The Baahithiin call this power time *Al-Mawlid Al-Nabawiyy*. Most Baahithiin celebrate *Al-Mawlid Al-Nabawiyy* in their own community. The day's events at the mosque include a sermon in commemoration of their prophet and a rice meal. (Meals are never eaten at the mosque for any other celebration.) Because of the occasion, the rice meal contains a special blessing.

Others celebrate Muhammad's birthday by intentionally seeking supernatural power. While the exact rituals and details of this *Al-Mawlid Al-Nabawiyy* celebration vary from community to community, a number of practices appear common to all. Central to the power ritual are the burning of incense and prayer. Washing a *khanjar* (the sword mentioned above as a power object) is another vital aspect of this ceremony. Through prayer, incense burning and washing the *khanjar*, they believe the *khanjar's* supernatural power will increase.

Some Baahithiin visit graves near their community to seek blessing, receive visions, and increase their power. *Al-Mawlid Al-Nabawiyy* is also a time to take a "holy bath." This ritual involves bathing under seven different waterfalls in order to be cleansed spiritually and increase one's spiritual power. To be effective, one has to bathe during the night before Muhammad's birthday. Since it is usually difficult for most people to find seven waterfalls within walking distance, only the most devout perform this ritual.

In one way or another, the *Al-Mawlid Al-Nabawiyy* holy day seems to be a time for Baahithiin Muslims to seek power. According to many, "during this night of *Al-Mawlid Al-Nabawiyy*, when cosmic power and influences abound, great amounts of power may be diverted from the cosmos to specific purposes."

Folk Muslims confess the greatness of Allah, but live in fear of the spirits. Because of this, their lives center around the manipulation of power. They are preoccupied with powers, power persons, power objects, power places, power times, and power rituals. Understanding this orientation to life helps prepare us to minister more effectively among them.

Questions for Reflection and Discussion

1. If you were to show Table 1 (comparing formal Islam to folk Islam) to a Muslim leader in your community, would he agree with the contrasts stated? Why or why not?

2. Use Table 2 (the spectrum of folk Islamic practice) and estimate what percent of your Muslim community would be aligned with what points on the spectrum. Discuss your estimates with 2-3 others, and see how and why your estimates vary.

3. Use Table 3 (six components of folk Islam) and identify examples of each of the six components in your Muslim community. Which components seem to be of greatest significance to your community? Which are more subtle, subdued, or complex? Which are most troubling or fascinating to you, and why?

4. How do the functions of the shaman and imam contrast or overlap in your society? How could you best relate to both types of leaders?

It will help you to better digest what you're reading if you take the time to reflect on and discuss such questions after each chapter. Also, I would value a glimpse of what you're thinking! I invite you (either now or later) to share with me (r_d_love@hotmail.com) some of your answers to these questions. You may have some good things to teach me.

Notes

[1] See Zwemer 1920 for further confirmation.

[2] Zwemer 1920:207. Musk describes it as follows: "The result should be a clash ... the surprising truth is that there is relatively little dissonance between the two domains. Official and popular expressions of Islam tend to live easily with one another. Indeed, both views may operate in veiled partnership within any one single Muslim. ... The lack of such obvious dissonance is, perhaps, the main reason why Western investigators, including Christian missionaries, have often failed to recognize the existence of the folk Islamic world (1989:224).

[3] I base my conclusion on eight years of missionary service, numerous informal interviews with various missionaries to Muslims, and extensive reading on the subject.

[4] These six components are described by J. Dudley Woodberry (in Wagner and Pennoyer 1990:314), although in this article Woodberry does not use these components as a model for analysis.

[5] A number of more orthodox Baahithiin Muslims no longer believe in ancestor spirits, gods and goddesses (believing only in angels, jinn and evil spirits) but they are in the minority. When questioned, many Baahithiin would deny belief in ancestor spirits, gods and goddesses because they know that these beliefs are not truly Islamic. Nevertheless, the task of the culturally sensitive cross-cultural worker is not just to document what a people say they believe, but to analyze what they do at the level of practice. One must infer beliefs from practices (Spradley 1979:8) and differentiate between the "ideal" and the "real" in culture. "Participant observation also avoids certain mistakes in understanding cultures. He or she learns to distinguish between real versus ideal culture. What people say is right and proper is ideal culture. Yet people do not often follow their own ideals. Observing actual behavior points to the realities rather than the ideals of cultural life" (Conn 1985:8; see also Kuper 1975:38, 49).

[6] See also Burnett 1988:207 for an example of this.

[7] See Koentjaraningrat 1990b:413-426 and Aune 1980.

[8] See Lehman and Myers 1985:81-87; Steyne 1989:165-174; and Burnett 1988:121-209 for a summary of the various definitions.

[9] Lessa and Vogt 1972:381. Spradley's definition of shamans is more comprehensive: They often possess a personal relationship with supernatural beings or know the secret medicines and spells necessary to use supernatural force. They do not head congregations, conducting their rites only when there is need for them. They are frequently associated with curing and are often represented in the popular literature as medicine men and witch doctors (1980:268).

* a pseudonym

Chapter 3

The Theology of the Kingdom of God

Redemption for Jesus was a broader concept than something merely internal, something infinitely greater than a theological dogma limited to the forgiveness of sins. ... For Jesus, redemption meant the arrival of the kingdom of God ... this means the destruction of Satan's rule both in the hearts of men and in their bodies and in their physical environment.
— **James Kallas**

The Theology of the Kingdom and the Whole Counsel of God

When I was a young associate pastor, my senior pastor asked me to teach a class on evangelism. As I studied a few key books and prayerfully reflected on the things I needed to teach, I became frustrated. How could I possibly combine the practicality of the "Four Spiritual Laws" with the theological depth of the gospel of the kingdom? My experience showed me that people need simple tools. I also knew that an in-depth understanding of the gospel of the kingdom was foundational for evangelism. If the "Four Spiritual Law" approach to evangelism was too simplistic, kingdom theology was too complicated. How could I ever explain the profundities and intricacies of the theology of the kingdom in a user-friendly way? No Bible scholar, to my knowledge, had ever integrated kingdom theology with hands-on ministry.

Thus began my long pilgrimage to make theology practical. I wanted to communicate the theology of the kingdom to thousands of Christians. This book is a snapshot of my pilgrimage. I share it with the hope that my struggles and summaries will be of help to others.[1]

The phrase "kingdom of God" is found primarily in the synoptic gospels (Matthew, Mark and Luke).[2] However, "the concept of the kingdom of God involves, in a real sense, the total message of the

Bible" (Bright 1963:7). It is a comprehensive construct – one of the few themes that summarizes the whole of Scripture.

The Old Testament describes God as an eternal king: "The Lord is a king forever" (Ps 10:16). His sovereign rule and kingship is a major theme in the Psalms: "The Lord has established his throne in the heavens; and his sovereignty rules over all" (Ps 103:19; see also Ps 93:1,2; 95:3; 145:10-13).

In one sense, God's sovereign rule as eternal king distinguishes the concept of the kingdom of God from other macro-theological models. For example, three major motifs of Scripture–the covenant, the promise and the salvation history approach[3]–are all linked solely with the acts of God in redemptive history. Prior to creation, however, there was no covenant, promise or salvation history. Yet even before creation, there was the kingdom of God–God ruled.

Moreover, the concepts of covenant, promise and salvation history focus on God and humankind. These themes generally do not relate to the universe and to the spirit realm. By contrast, the kingdom of God focuses on the totality of God's creation–the entire cosmos, as well as the spirit realm. Moreover, the kingdom of God provides us with a comprehensive framework for mission. It describes what missiologists call the *missio Dei* (God's mission), which is the restoration of God's rule over all creation. The kingdom of God is a macro-theological model, summarizing the whole counsel of God.

From one perspective, we can define the kingdom of God as *the sovereign reign of God*. He sovereignly controls the events and peoples of this world in such a way that his ultimate will is accomplished (Eph 1:11; Rm 8:28). This is how the term is often used, for example, in the Psalms.

Although the "sovereign" reign of God is an important aspect of the kingdom of God, our primary focus will be on *the saving reign of God*. The kingdom of God in this sense is inseparably linked with salvation, much the same way that Jesus uses it in the parables of the kingdom (Mt 13, Mk 4). It refers to God ruling practically in our lives. While God is king in the objective sense of his sovereign rule over all things, he is not king in my life personally (and subjectively) until I repent and believe in Christ. To preach the kingdom of God is to preach that Jesus is at once Savior and Lord.

The Theology of the Kingdom Made Plain

How can we summarize the multitude of verses and numerous themes related to the kingdom of God? While no single passage tells the whole story, one passage contains a full-orbed theology of the kingdom. Matthew 12:28-29 embodies what George Ladd describes as "the essential theology of the kingdom of God" (1974:66).

> But if I cast out demons by the Spirit of God, then the kingdom of God has come upon you. Or how can anyone enter the strong man's house and carry off his property, unless he first binds the strong man? And then he will plunder his house (Mt 12:28-29).

This passage describes six dimensions of kingdom theology. There are the dimensions of God as ruler and God as rescuer. There is a present dimension, a future dimension, a physical dimension and a spiritual dimension. These six themes are best understood in terms of three contrasting pairs.

The Dimensions of God as Ruler and God as Rescuer. The ultimate goal of redemptive history is the reign of God. All history is moving to this great climax when God rules over all, when all acknowledge God's kingship. This is the Godward aspect of the gospel.

But this rule of God is not simply a matter of having Jesus rule in our hearts and lives. Before God can reign, Satan must be deposed. Humankind must be rescued. God must conquer Satan. This is the Satanward aspect of the gospel.

First of all, Jesus casts out demons. The expulsion of demons describes kingdom ministry as deliverance. Second, the strong man (Satan) is bound. The binding of Satan was a common theme in Jewish thought and as such was linked to the future coming of the kingdom. Jesus uses this futuristic terminology, however, to describe his present mission.

While the concept of binding in this verse is metaphorical, it nevertheless depicts in some real sense a victory over Satan and a present curbing of his power. This binding or curbing of Satan's power is both a concrete manifestation of the kingdom of God in Jesus' earthly ministry and a foretaste of the future, when Satan is *defeated* at the cross (Col 2:15) and forever *destroyed* at the second coming of Christ (Rv 19:11-20:10).

Thus, the kingdom of God involves conflict and conquest. The kingdom of darkness must be overthrown. This is the ruler/rescuer dimension of the kingdom implicit in our Matthew passage.

The Present and Future Dimensions. Most kingdom of God passages in the New Testament focus on its future dimension (Mt 24; Rv). However, according to this passage, the kingdom of God is more than a future hope. It can also be experienced in the present. If demons are cast out, then the kingdom of God has come! Where Satan is driven back, the rule of God begins. This illustrates the present and future dimensions of the kingdom.

New Testament scholars generally understand the present and future dimensions of the kingdom as a two-stage invasion. In the person and mission of Jesus there is present fulfillment without consummation; the kingdom of God is both "already" and "not yet."

This two-stage invasion of the kingdom of God is described as a "mystery" in the New Testament (Rom 16:25-26). The Old Testament often presents the kingdom of God as an event in the future–a cataclysmic in-breaking of the reign of God:

> And in the days of those kings the God of heaven will set up a kingdom which will never be destroyed, and that kingdom will not be left for another people; it will crush and put an end to all these kingdoms, but it will itself endure forever (Dn 2:44).

The mystery of the kingdom, however, is the coming of the kingdom into present history. (See Jesus' parables in Mark 4 and Matthew 13.) This present manifestation of the kingdom is in hidden form, working secretly within and among men prior to its future manifestation in crushing power and unmitigated glory.

This understanding of the present and future dimensions of the kingdom of God sets forth what theologians refer to as the eschatological structure of the whole Bible. Since the fall of man, when Satan gained dominion, this age has been characterized by evil, bondage and suffering. After the Fall, God promised a new age, an age free from the burdens and blight of the rule of Satan. Scripture points toward a perfect future, when sin, Satan, sickness and death are banished, when all of creation will once again be restored to its original perfection and people will enjoy glorious eternal communion with God (Gn 3:15; Nm 14:21; Is 11:2-9, 65:17-25; 2 Pt 3:13-31; Rv 21:1-7).

However, since there is fulfillment without consummation, there remains a "not yet" aspect to the kingdom. Many people are not saved, a large number are not healed and multitudes remain demonized. Suffering characterizes this present age, and we find ourselves in an intense spiritual battle (Mt 5:10-12, Ac 14:22, Phil 1:29, 2 Tm 3:12).

The Physical and Spiritual Dimensions. In what ways, then, is the kingdom present? First of all it is manifested in the presence of the King. Jesus points to himself as the King:

> Now having been questioned by the Pharisees as to when the kingdom of God was coming, he answered them and said, 'The kingdom of God is not coming with signs to be observed, nor will they say 'Look, here it is!' or, 'There it is!' For behold, the kingdom of God is in your midst (Lk 17:20- 21).

The key to interpreting this passage is the phrase "in your midst." Some interpreters understand this to mean "within you," so that the kingdom of God here refers to God's rule in the individual soul. However, it is highly unlikely that Jesus would say the kingdom of God was "within" the Pharisees. The context of this passage, along with the rest of Jesus' teaching on the kingdom, clearly indicates that "in your midst" is the best interpretation. Wherever Christ reigns, the kingdom has come (Guthrie 1981:413; Ladd 1974:68).

The presence of the kingdom is manifested, second, in the preaching of the gospel. This is clearest in the parable of the sower (Mt 13:1-23), which Jesus describes as "the mystery of the kingdom" (v. 11). As noted above, according to the Old Testament, the kingdom of God would come in crushing power (Dn 2:44). Yet in this parable the sower works quietly and secretly. This is the mystery that the Old

Testament did not reveal! The kingdom is present, but it can be rejected.

> [The parable of the sower] emphasizes two things, *viz.*, its fruitlessness and the fruits of the sower's work. ... It points to the wonderful germinal force of the seed together with the failures. In the parable Jesus certainly does not want to draw our attention exclusively to the hidden manifestation of the kingdom threatened and handicapped by all kinds of powers; he also points out its miraculous operations and fruits. ... It consists in the revelation that the eschatological all-conquering coming of God into the world goes the way of the seed (Ridderbos 1962:131-132).

Third, according to Matthew 12:28, signs and wonders are proof of the presence of the kingdom. Jesus said, "If I cast out demons ... then the kingdom has come!" It is important to note that Matthew 12:28 is a commentary on Jesus' healing in verse 22: "Then there was brought to him a demon-possessed man who was blind and dumb, and he healed him, so that the dumb man spoke and saw."

Thus the exorcism was actually a healing in this case. Satan is portrayed in Scripture as a source of sickness. On numerous occasions in the Gospels, Jesus links sickness to a demonic source: "A woman was there who had been crippled by a spirit for 18 years" (Lk 13:11). "Then they brought him a demon-possessed man who was blind and mute and Jesus healed him so that he could both talk and see" (Mt 12:22; see also Mt 9:32-33, 17:14-19; Mk 9:17-18; Lk 11:14). The relationship between Satan and sickness is perhaps most explicit in Acts 10:38: "You know ... God anointed Jesus of Nazareth with the Holy Spirit and power and how he went around doing good and healing all who were under the power of the devil because God was with him." When Jesus drove out demons or healed the sick, he advanced the kingdom of God by pushing back the kingdom of Satan.

This is further illustrated in Luke 10:17-18: "And the 70 returned with joy, saying 'Lord, even the demons are subject to us in your name.' And he said to them 'I was watching Satan fall from heaven like lightning'." This text has been interpreted in various ways, but in light of the immediate context and the theology of the kingdom of

God we can clearly infer that through the ministry of evangelism, healing and exorcism, the 70 toppled the kingdom of Satan.

The kingdom of God is a spiritual realm, but it has physical implications. Because of the present inauguration of the kingdom of God, we can experience the blessings of the future age: we experience it now! Salvation, healing and power over demons are part of the "already" of the kingdom.

In summary, Matthew 12:28, 29 makes three significant points:

The dimensions of God as ruler and rescuer– The kingdom is advancing on the battlefield. Jesus has bound the strong man and he is plundering his kingdom. For God to rule in our lives, Satan must be overthrown.

The present and future dimensions– The kingdom is not just a future hope, it is also a present reality.

The physical and spiritual dimensions– The coming of the kingdom is linked to the presence of the king, evangelism and to signs and wonders.

The Kingdom of God and Church Planting

How does kingdom theology relate to church planting? Theologians rightly remind us that the kingdom of God should not be confused with the church itself. No simple, one-to-one correspondence links the kingdom of God and the church. The kingdom of God is a much more comprehensive concept. The church is created by the kingdom and the church proclaims the kingdom. (We never proclaim the church.) The kingdom refers to the rule of God (his dynamic reign), whereas the church refers to the people of God (the subjects of the kingdom).

Yet the distinction between the church and the kingdom can be overemphasized. While the kingdom and the church are not the same, neither can they be separated. Jesus Christ is at once king of the kingdom and head of the church. Moreover, Jesus' first words about the church, "I will build my church" are immediately followed by the promise, "I will give you the keys of the kingdom" (Mt 16:18-19). A clear relationship connects the church and the kingdom.

As noted earlier, the kingdom has both present and future dimensions. There is the "already" and the "not yet." The same is true of the church. While the church is not the kingdom which is to come, it is already under the rule of God which has begun.

The church is a partial manifestation of the kingdom. The church has begun to experience the reality of the kingdom, is commissioned to proclaim the kingdom, and is commanded to model the values of the kingdom. Although imperfect, the locus of God's reign on earth is in the church. In the words of Charles Van Engen, "local congregations are branch offices of the kingdom" (1991:101).

Matthew 24:14 makes a fascinating connection between the kingdom of God and the climax of history. "And this gospel of the kingdom shall be preached in the whole world for a witness to all the nations, and then the end shall come." This prophecy of the extension of the gospel before Christ's return implies that the church is the primary means through which the kingdom of God is extended on earth. In other words, the church proclaims the gospel of the kingdom with the goal of planting new churches in every ethnic group (nation) on earth. This witness goes forth, from nation to nation, climaxing in Christ's second coming. This means practically that the history of the kingdom of God on earth is the history of Christian missions (Fuller 1992:426).

Questions for Reflection and Discussion

1. From what or whom do members of your community long to be rescued? Do they evidence any hope of rescue?

2. How would you simply and practically explain the "kingdom of God" to a sincere seeker in your Muslim community? How would your summary vary from what you'd say to a comparable seeker in your own culture?

3. Which of the six dimensions of kingdom theology is most especially "good news" to your Muslim community? Why? Do your co-workers agree with your answer?

It will help you to better digest what you're reading if you take the time to reflect on and discuss such questions after each chapter. Also, I would value a glimpse of what you're thinking! I invite you (either now or later) to share with me (r_d_love@hotmail.com) some of your answers to these questions. You may have some good things to teach me.

Notes

[1] Many excellent books have been written about the kingdom of God. I have found James Kallas' *Jesus and the Power of Satan* and George Ladd's *The Theology of the New Testament* two of the best introductions to kingdom theology available. *Signs, Wonders and the Kingdom of God* by Don Williams and *Power Healing* by John Wimber have helped me translate the theology of the kingdom into a ministry of signs and wonders.

[2] Matthew, writing to Jews, prefers the term "kingdom of heaven," since many Jews would not pronounce the name "God." This is one way Matthew contextualized his message.

[3] See Robertson 1980; Kaiser 1978 and Cullmann 1967 for examples of each of these views.

Chapter 4

Contextualization

Christian contextualizations that are both authentic and effective are based on careful attention to both the biblical text and the respondent culture.
— David Hesselgrave and Edward Rommen

How Does the Text Relate to the Context?

As we talked about evangelism and a message for India, I asked him: "When you preach in India, what do you emphasize? Do you preach to them the love of God?"

"No," he said, "not particularly. The Indian mind is so polluted that if you talk to them about love they think mainly of sex life. You do not talk to them much about the love of God."

"Well," I said, "do you talk to them about the wrath of God and the judgment of God?" "No, this is not my emphasis," he remarked. "They are used to that. All the gods are mad anyway. It makes no difference to them if there is one more who is angry!"

"What do you talk to them about? Do you preach Christ and him crucified?" I guessed.

"No," he replied. "They would think of him as a poor martyr who helplessly died."

"What then is your emphasis? Do you talk to them about eternal life?"

"Not so," he said. "if you talk about eternal life, the Indian thinks of transmigration. He wants to get away from it. Don't emphasize eternal life."

"What then is your message?"

"I have never yet failed to get a hearing if I talk to them about forgiveness of sins and peace and rest in your heart. That's the product that sells well. Soon they ask me how they can get it. Having won their hearing I lead them on to the Savior who alone can meet their deepest needs" (Hesselgrave 1978:169).

This conversation between George Peters and an Indian evangelist named Bakht Singh illustrates some of the central issues of contextualization.

How can we model and proclaim the gospel so as to plant churches deeply rooted in Scripture and closely related to their culture? How can we proclaim God's *supracultural truth*, stripped of its Western cultural baggage and clothed in indigenous cultural forms and patterns of thought? How can we be true to Scripture and relevant to culture, avoiding the extremes of either cultural imposition or syncretism? These are the major concerns and priorities of contextualization[1] – modeled and articulated most clearly by the apostle Paul.

Paul: The Model Contextualizer

When it came to the content of the gospel message, Paul was both adamant and dogmatic. "If any man is preaching to you a gospel contrary to that which you have received, let him be accursed!" (Gal 1:9). The message was eternal and unchanging.

Yet in different contexts, the message had to be communicated differently. Thus, while Paul was dogmatic in his theology, he was flexible in his methodology. He communicated a passion for truth and a commitment to relevance. Paul was a model contextualizer.

1 Corinthians 9:19-23 can be described as the "Magna Carta" of contextualization, summarizing Paul's principles, defining clearly what the Bible teaches about contextualization:

> Though I am free and belong to no man, I make myself a slave to everyone to win as many as possible. To the Jew I became like a Jew, to win the Jews. To those under the law I became like one under the law (though I myself am not under the law), so as to win those under the law. To those not having the law I became like one not having the law (though I am not free from God's law but am under Christ's law), so as to win those not having the law. To the weak I became weak, to win the weak. I have become all things to all men so that by all possible means I might save some. I do all things for the sake of the gospel, that I may share in its blessings.

The *Purpose* of Contextualization

A structural analysis of this passage reveals three important points. Paul describes the purpose, the principles and the parameters of contextualization. First he shows the purpose of contextualization: evangelization:

- that I might win the as many as possible
- that I might win Jews
- that I might win those who are under the law
- that I might win those who are without law
- that I might win the weak
- that I may by all means save some

Paul's purposes are simple and straightforward: to win people to Christ.

Contextualization is an eternal, life-and-death issue. Paul would lovingly live as a Jew to the Jews or a Greek to the Greeks for the sake of the lost. Beyond and behind the cultural relativity of contextualization lies the ultimate reality of eternity.

Paul's strategy was shaped dramatically by this eternal orientation and these evangelistic purposes. In other words, the major mission in Paul's life was the planting of churches. He was first and foremost an apostle – single-mindedly focusing on the frontiers, zealously rescuing the perishing (Rm 15:16-21, 1 Cor 1:17-18; 2 Cor 2:15-16, 4:3).

The *Principle* of Contextualization

Next, Paul describes the principle of contextualization: identification. He was determined to "become like" the people he was trying to reach.[2] Five times, Paul reiterates his commitment to identify with a people. He mentions four specific groups and then concludes with a summary statement.

- I became like a Jew
- I became like one under the law
- I became like one not having the law
- I became weak

- I have become all things to all men

In what ways did Paul, the apostle to the Gentiles (Rm 11:13), become like a Jew to the Jews? The most striking examples are found in Acts 16 and 21.

When it came to non-negotiable truths, Paul the apostle was a dynamic defender of the faith, a powerful apologist. With dogged determination, he fought to uphold the truth of the gospel against Judaizing influences (see Gal and Ac 15). He boldly stood before the Jerusalem Council to present his case; he publicly confronted Peter when the truth of the gospel was at stake.

Yet this same Paul, who would not let Titus be circumcised because of his adamant stand for the liberty of the gospel, had Timothy circumcised in order to relate to the Jews (Ac 16:1-3). Paul was opposed to circumcision as a *basis* for salvation, but he was committed to circumcision as a *bridge* for salvation. Since Timothy was born of a mixed marriage (Jew and Gentile), he would be more readily accepted by the Jews if he were circumcised.

Acts 21:26 describes Paul's participation in a Jewish Nazarite vow: "Then Paul took the men, and the next day, purifying himself along with them, went into the temple, giving notice of the completion of the days of purification, until the sacrifice was offered for each of them." The implications of this passage are unnerving for many Christians. How could Paul, who proclaimed liberty in Christ, who proclaimed that Christ was the fulfillment of the Old Testament, actually offer sacrifices? This passage illustrates Paul acting as a Jew to the Jews. [3]

How did Paul become like a Greek to the Greeks? Paul's sermon at Athens (Ac 17) is a brilliant example of his way of relating to Greek culture. Paul begins his address by noting the religious devotion of the Athenians. "I observe that you are very religious in all respects" (v 22). Although this word can mean either religious or superstitious, the context clearly favors "religious."

Their religious actions took the form of pagan idolatry, which doubtless incensed Paul's monotheistic heart. Nevertheless, he saw in the Athenian religiosity a sense of respect for the divine implanted by God (Fernando 1987:40), a *sensus divinitas*. He was able to see a people groping for God (Rm 1:18-25). In his own words, Paul says that God created mankind "that they should seek God" (Ac 17:24-27).

After winning their attention, Paul noticed an altar (not an idol) "to an unknown God." This altar was an admission on the part of the intellectual Athenians that their knowledge of the supernatural was incomplete. *Paul had found his point of contact.* With a note of apostolic authority he exclaimed, "What therefore you worship in ignorance, this I proclaim to you" (v 23).

This sermon reflects Paul's wise use of cultural elements from the people to whom he ministered. In Acts 17:27-28 Paul quotes from two Greek poets (Aratus and Epimenides) to support his belief in God's immanence and our sonship. "He is not far from each one of us; for in him we live, move and exist, as even some of your own poets have said, 'for we also are his offspring.'" Clearly, Paul was familiar with the literature of the culture.

This issue of Paul quoting from pagan sources to support Christian truth is noteworthy because, as N.B. Stonehouse explains, "The quotations in their proper pagan contexts express points of view which were undoubtedly quite repugnant to Paul" (1957:27).

However, Paul believed in general revelation. To him, it was not a doctrine to be debated, but a foundational missiological fact. Bavinck's words aptly summarize Paul's perspective. "When a missionary or some other person comes into contact with a non-Christian and speaks to him about the gospel, he can be sure that God has concerned himself with this person long before" (1981:126). In the picturesque words of Harvie Conn, these quotations are "the footprints of God which are found in every culture" (1989).

Howard Marshall interprets these quotes as a case of outright adoption:

> Not only are these quotations from pagan poets but they also refer unequivocally to Zeus, the chief god in the Greek pantheon. And yet Paul uses them to depict the character of the Christian God. Evidently he was prepared to allow their truth, but only if Zeus was

recognized as somehow depicting Yahweh; yet it is obvious that much of what pagans said about Zeus certainly could not be applied to Yahweh. Only where it was in agreement with the Old Testament and Christian revelation in Jesus was Paul prepared to take the steps.[4]

Bruce, on the other hand, sees this as a case of transformation. "It is not suggested that even the Paul of Acts ... envisaged God in terms of the Zeus of Stoic pantheism, but if men whom his hearers recognized as authorities had used language which could corroborate his argument, he would quote their words, giving them a biblical sense as he did so" (1977:242). Whether Paul's use of these Greek sources is a case of adoption or transformation is less important than that he used them with great theological and contextual sensitivity.

While culturally sensitive and judicious in his presentation of the gospel, Paul nevertheless firmly and forthrightly confronts error. He proclaims a divine message from heaven, a message that is not indigenous to any earthly culture. First of all, he describes their worship as in "ignorance" (v 23). He also affirms the unity of mankind, removing "all imagined justification for the belief that Greeks were innately superior to barbarians" (Bruce 1988:358). Finally, he confronts their idolatry, calling them to repent and warning them of coming judgment (vv 29-31).

In his Areopagus address, Paul constructively engages the world-view of his audience, personally challenging the Athenian intellectuals to a new allegiance. Paul, a Jew to the Jews, was a Greek to the Greeks. This was identification – the principle of contextualization.

Just how far can we go in our contextualization? The answer to this is found in 1 Corinthians 9.

The *Parameters* of Contextualization

A third aspect of Paul's approach is described in 1 Corinthians 9: confrontation. There are limits to contextualization. Here Paul says he is *"under the law of Christ."* Although he always attempted to adapt his message to his audience, he was not free to "do his own thing" (like many of the Corinthians did), but worked within the theological and ethical boundaries of Christ's law.[5]

Paul realized the dangers of contextualizing the gospel. It was always possible that people would pervert the meaning of the gospel. He knew full well that the basic elements of the gospel could be lost and replaced by religious elements from the receiving culture. Because of this, he was adamantly opposed to syncretism. Any dilution or distortion of the gospel was forcefully denounced. Any syncretistic attempt to fuse irreconcilable beliefs and practices with the gospel was firmly rejected.

One of the clear theological implications of "being under the law of Christ" for modern-day contextualizers, then, is the priority of Scriptural authority. Our contextualization must not only be relevant, but also prophetic. We must be as flexible as possible and always seek to be culturally sensitive. However, the text always judges the context. Certain aspects of culture must be confronted. Ultimately, we have the words of eternal life, an authoritative message from heaven which prophetically engages every earthly culture.

The Three Dimensions of Contextualization:
Evangelistic, Didactic and Prophetic

One way of understanding contextualization is through word pictures. Generally speaking, the following three word pictures of contextualization are sequential. They reflect the stages of contextualization as it unfolds in the life of the missionary.

Contextualization is like planting a seed without the flowerpot. Harvie Conn says contextualization as "the art of planting the gospel seed in culture's diverse soils without also planting the flowerpot" (1982:12). This is the evangelistic dimension of contextualization.

To contextualize is to be jealous for the purity of the gospel (the gospel seed), while at the same time to be iconoclastic about Western forms or emphases that are irrelevant (the flowerpot). In other words, contextualization is the opposite of replication. We are not interested in the replicating the flowerpot, but in propagating the gospel seed. This focuses on the *core of truth*.

This dimension of contextualization is the missionary's first priority. Culturally relevant proclamation of the gospel becomes the major focus of the missionary team's first stage of service. This involves a diligent study of language and culture with the expectation of finding redemptive analogies and cultural bridges that will help communicate Christ. Before missionaries are able to plant the gospel seed without the flowerpot, they must have a good grasp of both the gospel and the culture of those they serve.

Contextualization is like planting a great variety of seeds. While Conn's definition of contextualization is simple and picturesque, the process is much more complex. Contextualization is more than planting a gospel seed. It involves more than communicating core truth. Biblical contextualization is concerned about the whole counsel of God (Ac 20:27). We are commissioned to teach all nations "to obey all that Jesus commanded" (Mt 28:20).

The imagery shifts from the flowerpot to the nursery–where there is a great variety of seeds just as the Bible has a great variety of teachings. Certain teachings speak with special relevance to our people group and must take root if we are obedient to the Great Commission. This is the didactic or teaching dimension of contextualization, and its focus is on the *comprehensiveness of truth*.

This dimension becomes important after the team has been on the field a number of years. It demands a deeper understanding of the language and culture, as well as of Scripture. The longer missionaries live among a people, the more effectively they will discover those portions of Scripture that speak to their needs. For example, in the Baahithiin culture we spent much time teaching on marriage, love and forgiveness. We also worked hard at developing biblically based, culturally relevant life-cycle ceremonies.

Contextualization is like hoeing weeds and removing rocks. Turning from the seeds to the soil, this aspect of contextualization focuses on the recipient's culture. Every culture's soil is polluted by sinful patterns and demonic strongholds. These weeds and rocks must be removed for the gospel seed to flourish. At this point, the missionary team must confront the people group's wrong presuppositions, perspectives and practices. This is the prophetic dimension of contextualization. The focus of this dimension is on the *judging nature of truth*.

In most cases, missionaries should not embark on this dimension of contextualization until they reflect competence in the evangelistic and teaching dimensions. To be most effective, the missionary has to earn the right to engage in this level of contextualization through years of study, prayerful reflection and intimate relationships. The clearest illustration of this in my ministry was in the area of confronting magic.

Five Steps to Contextualization

These dimensions of contextualization describe the early and tentative stages of contextualization modeled by the missionary. They are *tentative* because true contextualization is ultimately carried out by the emerging church. This is not to minimize the early attempts of the missionary. Our tentative attempts are necessary. By virtue of our very presence in the culture, missionaries model the gospel. The better we know the language, culture and Scripture, the more accurately we will contextualize early on. Over the long run, however, we must hold lightly our limited attempts at contextualization and open our hands to encourage the emerging church to join in the process of translating the gospel into its culture.

The leaders of the emerging church, along with the missionary, go through a five-step process:[6]

- Gather information about old beliefs and customs, especially as it relates to the message, the messenger and the church.
- Study relevant portions of Scripture.
- Evaluate the old beliefs and practices, in a Spirit-dependent atmosphere of open discussion.

- Create new contextualized Christian beliefs and practices. Then, as a community, experiment with them and evaluate them.
- Formalize the new beliefs and practices after evaluating their impact.

Gather information about old beliefs and customs, especially as it relates to the message, the messenger and the church. Contextualization is a comprehensive process that involves all of Scripture as it relates to all of life. The process of gathering information about old beliefs and customs takes a long time. Through numerous sources, especially older men and women or any written sources, the missionary team needs to learn about the presuppositions and perspectives of the people served. They must discover both the meaning and the function of the people's rituals and customs. This is the *cultural step* of contextualization.

We need to gather information in three major areas: relating to the message, the messenger and the church. For the gospel to truly take root among a people, all three areas must be contextualized. In my previous country of service, for example, some ministries seek to contextualize the message. They use the Quran as a bridge in their witness and speak of *Nabi Isa* or *Isa al-Masih* (Islamic names for Jesus) as Savior. They may quote Baahithiin proverbs as a starting point for communication. However, they fail to contextualize in the areas of the messenger and the church. While the ministry team may use contextual themes and terminology, they remain generally "churchy" in their overall style of communication.

Moreover, many of these ministries have no intention of planting new contextualized churches. The few converts who are won to the Lord are incorporated in the existing church, which is culturally foreign to the Muslim majority. The problem is that Muslims who are open to the gospel are closed to the idea of joining the culturally foreign church. While the gospel message may appeal to them, the idea of forsaking their cultural heritage and social network repels them.

Hence, failure to contextualize in all three areas has greatly hampered the outreach of these ministries.

All three areas—the message, the messenger, and the church—are crucial to contextualization. Our mouths must communicate the gospel, our lives must incarnate the gospel, and ultimately our churches must reflect the gospel. This process begins by gathering information.

Study relevant portions of Scripture. Contextualization is more than just a cultural exercise. There is also a *biblical step*. All three areas of contextualization mentioned above (the message, the messenger and the church) force us to rigorously study the text in light of the context. Therefore, it is vitally important that we understand, model and teach our churches the process of dynamic theologizing. We will surely teach them the major doctrines of the faith—the theological *product*. In the long run, it is just as crucial that they learn the theological *process*. As Bruce Nicholls emphasizes, with reference to contextualization, "the central issue is hermeneutics."[7]

The hermeneutical task of contextualization is primarily a dialogue between the text and the context. This early stage of contextualization is fairly limited, dealing with the application of specific portions of Scripture to concrete issues. The process of contextualization should always begin at this level.

It doesn't end here. There is a later stage of contextualization as well. The hermeneutical task of the contextualizer also involves theologizing at a "macro" level. Eventually one must interact with the great creeds of Christendom as part of the interpretive task, for we need to do our theologizing in dialogue with the church universal.[8] We have a right to interpret the Bible for our particular context, but also a responsibility to listen to the church at large, to work towards what Paul Hiebert calls a "transcultural theology" (1985:217).

Evaluate the old beliefs and practices, in a Spirit-dependent atmosphere of open discussion. After gathering information and studying Scripture, we are ready to evaluate the old beliefs and practices. This *evaluative step* of contextualization should be done, ideally, in a Spirit-dependent community.

Contextualization is a communal process, carried out by the church. As we noted earlier, missionaries should develop tentative conclusions about contextualization on numerous issues. However, ultimately the church, especially its leaders, must determine what biblical Christianity will look like in their culture. This community approach to contextualization helps the church stay balanced in its approach.

Contextualization is also a spiritual process; therefore, it must be guided by the Holy Spirit. One of the Holy Spirit's unique tasks is to guide the church into all truth. Biblical contextualization is not just a matter of good hermeneutics and anthropological insight. It does not boil down to a few principles or methods. It is a spiritual dialogue with the "Spirit of truth" (Jn 15:26, 16:13).

The biblical evaluation of culture requires a discerning dialogue with the culture that "continually challenges, incorporates, and transforms elements of the cultural milieu" (Gilliland 1989:12). God brings culture under his kingship in three ways:[9] 1) adoption; 2) confrontation; and 3) transformation.

Adoption. Because God created culture, there are divine dimensions to culture. Certain aspects of culture have no moral or religious overtones; they can be adopted outright. This is especially true of material aspects of culture like types of architecture, clothing and musical instruments. For this reason, "Christianity is wholly neutral to the vast majority of cultural components" (McGavran 1974:39). We can freely adopt many aspects of culture.

Confrontation. Because of sin, there are demonic or carnal elements of culture. Certain components of culture must be confronted and rejected. Some cultural patterns are not able to be transformed because they are explicitly linked with sinful practices. They are "still very close to the kernel of paganism and they must be rejected completely" (Bavinck 1960:174-175).

Hiebert gives an example of this from a Hindu context. "The use of aqua blue in Indian dramas signifies the Hindu god Krishna. It would be almost impossible to use that color on the face of an actor in a Christian drama without drawing in Hindu mythology" (Gilliland 1989:117).

Burnett describes beliefs and practices that must be confronted as "crunch issues":

> In the Old Testament, the people of Israel were condemned for going to the high places and having sexual relations with the "sacred prostitutes." This was part of their idolatrous worship of Baal, and continually condemned by the prophets as such. The local people recognized such practices as indicative that the person was worshipping Baal and not Yahweh. When a person became a true follower of Yahweh this practice had to end. Likewise, in all cultures today there are such crunch issues (1990:232).

Transformation. Missionary teams rarely have trouble discerning whether they should adopt or confront certain beliefs and practices. (It may be hard to do, but it's not hard to understand!) By contrast, transformation is almost always the most complex aspect of contextualization.[10]

Transformation has to take place within a culture. While it affects many rituals and cultural practices, changes in worldview and motivation are fundamental. "All culture needs transformation in motivation if not in content," says Hesselgrave (1978:82).

According to Hiebert, old forms can be transformed in at least five ways:

- *addition* –adding to the traditional forms. For example, culturally relevant Christmas and Easter celebrations became part of Baahithiin outreach.
- *subtraction* – deleting aspects of the traditional practice which convey heretical or sinful connotations. For example, among the Baahithiin we eliminated the burning of incense from the life-cycle ceremonies because it was intimately linked with ancestor worship.

- *substitution*—developing a new practice or form that meets many of the same needs and functions in many of the same ways as the old form but in an acceptable Christian way. For example, the Tonga team in Africa, led by Phil Elkins, had tea parties in place of beer parties.

- *reinterpretation*—giving an old form new meaning through systematic teaching and clear communication. For example, I know of one church-planting team that reinterpreted and participated with Muslim-background believers in the Ramadan fast. Instead of agreeing with the Islamic explanation that fasting garner "points" with God, the team repeatedly explained the fast in light of Isaiah 58 and the teachings of Christ on the subject. The missionaries emphasized that their main focus of prayer during the fasting month was that more Muslims would come to know the Messiah.

- *creation of new forms*—developing altogether new forms which still fit the cultural patterns. For example, among the Baahithiin we developed culturally relevant group singing during the life-cycle ceremonies.

The meaning of a form is the central issue in contextualization because forms are relative. Different forms may convey similar meanings in different societies. The reverse is also true: similar forms convey different meanings in different societies. For example, the form of holding hands conveys different meanings in different cultures. When two men hold hands in Southeast Asia or the Middle East, it is a sign of friendship and healthy affection; in America, it suggests perversion.

Because of this, the twin concepts of "form" and "meaning" (as espoused by the science of anthropology) are crucial for understanding contextualization, especially the task of transformation.[11] The forms of a culture are the things you can observe—both material (houses, clothing, furniture) and conceptual (marriage customs, religious rituals, grammatical patterns). According to Kraft, "The meaning of a cultural form consists of the totality of subjective associations attached to the form" (1979:65). That is, every form conveys various impressions, values and attitudes. A particular form is used in a particular culture to convey a particular meaning or meanings.

On the other hand, a form is inseparably linked to meaning since all meanings are expressed through forms. Therefore, when we consider adopting, confronting or transforming a cultural form we must first understand its meaning. Then we can determine how we will handle the form. Islam puts a great emphasis on external forms.

Although the average Muslim has little real understanding of the numerous legalistic observances, he or she nevertheless performs these obligations in order to obtain merit. This "works" orientation is incompatible with the gospel of grace. But does the Muslim have to change his forms? Do we have to import a whole new set of foreign "forms" into a Muslim society? No! What the Muslim needs is a change in meaning, not in the forms.

In fact, according to J. Dudley Woodberry, "what have come to be known as the 'pillars' of Islam are all adaptations of previous Jewish and Christian forms!" (Gilliland 1989:282). Therefore, the majority of Muslim forms, although heavily laden with a works meaning, can and should be re-converted. The focus needs to be on meaning, since the goal is conversion or worldview change.

Phil Parshall's illustration aptly describes this process:

> An unconverted North American may be very faithful in church attendance, give to the poor, love his fellow man, and be moral and ethical in his business dealings. He too looks on these functions as building merit, leading to the assurance of eternal life. Such a man may then encounter the message of grace and experience the New Birth. Does he now cease attending church, stop giving to the poor, begin to hate his friends and commence unethical business dealings? No, such a thought is preposterous. He continues in the same forms, but his purpose and perspective relating to these practices are totally changed.
>
> Gratitude and love to Christ have replaced merit-seeking. There is a new and deep meaning behind those external practices. The same basic dynamic can take place in the life of a Muslim as he infuses new meanings into forms which he retains – assuming these

forms are in no way prohibited by command or principle in the word of God (1980:59).

This emphasis on meaning is at once the most profound and difficult aspect of contextualization. In fact, the battle for biblical contextualization against heretical syncretism is fought here. Two different Muslim-background churches could be basically identical in their forms. Yet one could be contextual while the other syncretistic. The difference is at the level of meaning. Change at the meaning level comes through the Spirit-led study of the Scriptures in community.

Create new contextualized Christian beliefs and practices. Then, as a community, experiment with them and evaluate them. After evaluation comes the *creative and experimental step* of contextualization. The community will create new contextualized Christian beliefs and practices, then experiment with and evaluate them in order to discern their communicative impact.

Contextualization, like communication, is dynamic and difficult. Thus, if our newly created forms communicate wrong meanings, they must be changed. The emerging Baahithiin church, for example, is still at this stage. Many of their life-cycle ceremonies are being developed, evaluated and refined.

Formalize the new beliefs and practices after evaluating their impact. The fifth and final step of contextualization is the *formalizing step.* After the long process outlined above, the emerging church puts its stamp of approval on these newly developed expressions of faith. The most fundamental aspects of contextualization have been established.

Yet the creative and evaluative aspects of contextualization must not stop. The community that is true to both Scripture and its context will continually move back and forth between steps four and five. As long as there are unreached homogeneous units and social classes, as long as there are villages and cities without churches, the creative and experimental task continues.[12]

In summary, there are five steps in contextualization:

- cultural
- biblical
- evaluative
- creative and experimental
- formalizing

These five steps enable the Spirit-led community of national believers and missionaries to develop contextualized beliefs and practices. Together, they can decide, in light of Scripture and their cultural perspective, which practices can be used without modification (adoption), which are not usable (confrontation), and which can be used with new meaning (transformation).

Table 4 summarizes the five steps to contextualization. It guides at least one team I know in the process of contextualization.

Questions for Reflection and Discussion

1. Which issues in contextualization are most problematic or controversial in your area of folk Islam? About which issues do you feel most passionate, troubled, or ambivalent? Which forms might be transformed (rather than adopted or confronted), and how?

2. In what way might you parallel the apostle Paul's experience in Acts 17 of quoting from "pagan sources" to support Christian truth? Could such quotes represent adoption, or would they require transformation (cf. Howard Marshall, F.F. Bruce)?

3. Which stage in contextualization (evangelistic, didactic, or prophetic) have you and your colleagues reached? What tools and resources are you utilizing?

The Steps to Biblical Contextualization in Church Planting

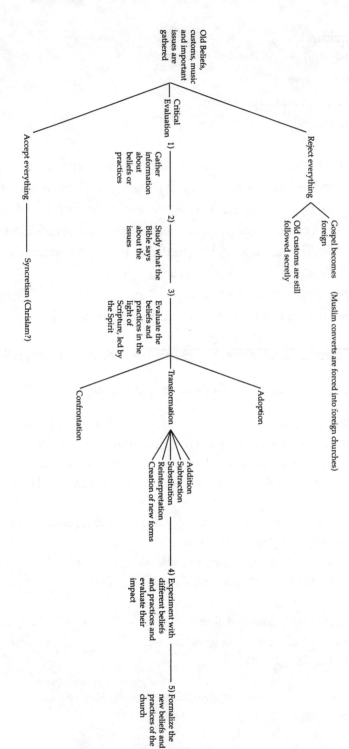

Table 4: The Steps to Biblical Contextualization in Church Planting (Adapted from Hiebert 1985a:188)

4. "Eventually, one must interact with the great creeds of Christendom as part of the interpretive task." Which of the great creeds are most useful to your context, and why?

It will help you to better digest what you're reading if you take the time to reflect on and discuss such questions after each chapter. Also, I would value a glimpse of what you're thinking! I invite you (either now or later) to share with me (r_d_love@hotmail.com) some of your answers to these questions. You may have some good things to teach me.

Notes

[1] The term "contextualization" has no commonly accepted definition among Evangelicals. However, a number of significant proposals and similar definitions have been put forth. Early in the debate, Charles R. Taber gave one of the clearest and most complete definitions: "Contextualization ... is the effort to understand and take seriously the specific context of each human group and person on its own terms and in all its dimensions–cultural, religious, social, political, economic–and discern what the gospel says to people in that context. ... It does not, for instance, ask how the gospel relates to 'the religions,' but how it relates to this religion as understood and practiced by this group or this person. What usable concepts and symbols does this religion provide for the approach of the gospel? ... What particular obstacles does it place in the way of a true understanding of the gospel?" (McCurry 1978:146).

In the early stages, the focus of contextualization was on relevance. But later in the debate, Harvie Conn reminded us that contextualization must be prophetic. We must emphasize the text (of Scripture) as well as the context. "There is also that inevitable confrontation between gospel and culture, the clash over the rock of ultimate offense. Contextualization ... must challenge the values and standards of the culture ... that mirror the demonic and dehumanizing forces of sin" (1984:257).

Thus, contextualization seeks to be both relevant and prophetic. It is a commitment to a culturally relevant communication and application of the gospel. Dean Gilliland's definition is one of the most balanced and comprehensive statements made to date, reflecting theological depth and missiological wisdom, born of experience. He highlights both the issues and the process of cross-cultural theologizing. "Contextualized theology ... is the dynamic reflection carried out by the particular church upon its own life in light of the Word of God and historic Christian truth. Guided by the Holy Spirit, the church continually challenges, incorporates, and transforms elements of the cultural milieu, bringing these under the Lordship of Christ" (1989:12).

[2] The phrase "become like" indicates that his identification was not total. He did not become a Jew to the Jews. He became *like* a Jew.

[3] See Longenecker 1980:245-252.

[4] Coote and Stott 1980:26; see also Stonehouse 1957:29.

[5] It is difficult to determine exactly what Paul meant by being under the law of Christ. However, Longenecker's discussion of the issues and interpretation are most satisfying. While giving due attention to the internal and spiritual dimensions of Paul's ethic, Longenecker rightly concludes that Paul possessed and proclaimed a tradition of Christ's person and teaching which he regarded as an external and authoritative norm and pattern for the outworking of Christian liberty: "The law of Christ stands as the standard of God for Paul. He views the teaching of Christ as the embodiment and one true interpretation of the Old Testament ... also he considers the person of Christ to be the tangible portrayal and example of the divine standard. ... Thus the Law of Christ must be understood in the thought of Paul as not only the teaching of Christ but also the example of the person of Christ" (1980:191).

[6] Paul Hiebert, Charles Kraft, Dean Gililland and Harvie Conn have been most formative in my thinking regarding contextualization. I owe much of what I say here to them.

[7] Bong Rin Ro, 1984:244. See also Larkin 1988; Hesselgrave & Rommen 1989:170-179.

[8] See Richard Muller 1991 for an excellent, comprehensive summary of these issues.

[9] H. Richard Neibuhr has developed a classic five-fold analysis of possible positions regarding Christ and culture (with some modification): (1) Christ against culture, (2) The Christ of culture, (3) Christ above culture, (4) Christ and culture in paradox, and (5) Christ the transformer of culture (Neibuhr 1951; Kraft 1979:103-115 and Hesselgrave 1978:79-82). Although there is some value to this grid theoretically (for it encompasses obscurantist and liberal views, etc.), it provides little practical help. The threefold model described here (adoption, confrontation and transformation) outlines concrete ways that God relates to culture.

[10] The Dutch missiologist J. H. Bavinck describes this transforming process as "possession": The Christian life does not accommodate or adapt itself to heathen forms of life, but it takes the latter in possession and thereby makes them new. ... Christ takes the life of a people in his hands, he renews and re-establishes the distorted and deteriorated; he fills each thing, each word, and each practice with a new meaning and gives it a new direction ... it is in essence the legitimate taking possession of something by him to whom all power is given in heaven and on earth (1960: 178-179). While I agree with Bavinck in principle, I prefer the concept of transformation to that of possession. Transformation conveys the idea of working from within culture, like the parables of the mustard seed and the leaven, whereas possession tends to connote the capture of a culture from without. The concept of transformation fits best with kingdom theology.

[11] Burnett 1990:133-136; Gilliland 1989:101-120.

[12] The creative and experimental aspects of contextualization continue in the church in America. The recent emphasis on the "seeker-sensitive church" is an example of this.

Chapter 5

Worldview and the Heavenly Places

The idea of a vitality of heaven in which angels and demonic powers are alive poses enormous problems to the modern view of the world in which cosmic life is understood as the outcome and manifestation of impersonal forces whose properties can be quantified by means of measurements, calculations, and the instruments available to the physicist.

– Ulrich Mauser

Supernatural Worldviews

More than 30 men, women and children gathered at the community leader's house to give thanks to God and honor us after the completion of the water project, our first major development project. This was a memorable occasion for us since only the poorest of the community were invited. It was the first time the people here have put on a communal feast especially for us.

In customary fashion, we sat in a circle on straw mats on the floor, with men and women separated. After formal greetings from various people, the spiritual leader (*shaikh**) of the community was asked to speak and pray.

The hosts placed four types of drinks in front of the *shaikh* (coffee, tea, a fruit drink and a punch drink). There were also a cigarette, a cigar and a rice mountain. I was told that these were food offerings for the ancestor spirits. They have a variety of foods because the different ancestor spirits have different tastes! They then put burning coals in front of the *shaikh*, and he began to invoke the ancestor spirits to come while he burned incense. All of a sudden, the *shaikh* started crying and asking for forgiveness. Next, he calmed down and continued the normal Islamic prayers. Then we all ate the rice meal together.

Afterward, the *shaikh* told me that when an ancestor spirit came upon him he started to cry. This was confirmed by two other participants afterwards. Both the *shaikh* and my friends said that this does happen infrequently, but that everyone knew that the *shaikh* had been possessed.

This experience, taken from my field notes during my early days in missionary service, illustrates the spiritual worldview of the Baahithiin. Even though these possession experiences are infrequent, the relaxed manner in which the people experienced this event and interpreted it to me highlights their supernatural approach to life.

Anthropologists call the topic of this chapter "supernatural causality." Understanding a people's supernatural worldview is fundamental for effective ministry among folk Muslims. Effective church planters must understand their perception of reality, especially because it differs so radically from the Western worldview. This understanding provides the starting point for communicating the gospel. However, the people group's perspective is not the only one a church planter needs to understand. The Bible's perspective of the supernatural, which also differs radically from the Western worldview, is of primary importance.

The Excluded Middle and the Expanded Middle

In 1982, Paul Hiebert published a watershed article on worldview entitled "The Flaw of the Excluded Middle." This "excluded middle zone" refers to the area where the spirit realm impinges upon this world. This middle zone encompasses the areas of ancestors, demons, witchcraft, sorcery and the like, and had not been adequately addressed by Evangelicals according to Hiebert. This was a blind spot in most Western missionaries' worldviews.

In his article Hiebert points out that missionaries have historically engaged in "truth encounter" – speaking to the cosmic issues of creation, redemption, heaven and hell. Missionaries have also been successful in what he describes as "empirical encounter," that is, addressing the sphere of nature through medicine and technology. Where the Western missionary movement has generally failed is in what he describes as the middle zone of the spirit realm. This must be addressed through "power encounter." (See Table 5.)

An avalanche of articles and books followed Hiebert's article. At the same time, God raised up John Wimber and the Vineyard Christian Fellowship to point out how the excluded middle negatively impacted Evangelical theology and practice in the area of power encounter. A new emphasis on signs and wonders and spiritual warfare was birthed.

But as often happens, the pendulum swung from one extreme to another. Whereas most Evangelicals used to be blind to the middle zone, over a decade later a number had become preoccupied with it. For some, the excluded middle has now become what Scott Moreau describes as the *expanded* middle (1995:25-36). Instead of becoming one important part of the believer's perspective on the Christian life, the middle zone or spirit realm has become dominant for some. The perceived root of every problem is demonic. The world and the flesh have not only taken a back seat to the demonic, they aren't even in the car![1] (See Table 6.)

Recently I was coaching a spiritually-minded, make-it-happen type of church planter who was having problems with one of his teammates, so he decided to have a half day of prayer and fasting for this person. I was impressed with his devotion to the Lord and to the spiritual welfare of his teammate. He then explained, "I want to have some warfare prayer over my troubled teammate so that she will be delivered from the forces of darkness causing the problem." This church planter got a sheepish grin on his face when I pointed out that his teammate's problem may not be demonic. Could she have problems with the "world" and the "flesh," I asked? "Whoops, good point," he replied.

Transcendent World Beyond Ours:
Includes:
- hells, heavens, other times, i.e. eternity
- high god (African); Vishnu, Siva (Hindu)
- cosmic forces; karma
- Jehovah, angels, demons

Religion
Truth
faith, miracles, other-worldly problems, sacred

Supernatural Forces on Earth:
Includes:
- spirits, ghosts ancestors, demons
- earthly gods and goddesses who live within trees, rivers, hills and villages
- supernatural forces: mana, planetary influences, evil eyes, power of magic, sorcery, witchcraft
- Holy Spirit, angels, demons, signs and wonders, gifts of the Spirit

Excluded Middle
by Westerners
Power

Empirical World of Our Senses:
Includes:
- folk sciences to explain how things occur
- explanations based on empirical observations (Person shoots an arrow into a deer; he attributes death to the arrow.)
- theories about the natural world (how to build a house, plant crops, etc.)
- theories about human relationships (how to raise children, treat spouses, etc.)

Science
Control
sight and experience, natural order, secular

Table 5: A Three-Level Analysis of Worldview and the Excluded Middle
(adapted from Hiebert 1982; Moreau 1995:34)

Upper Level
religious, spiritual
truth

Middle Level
religious/spiritual
physical/psychological
power

Lower Level
physical, psychosocial
control

Table 6: The Flaw of the Expanded Middle (Moreau 1995:34)

Supernatural Causality

What causes things? What power lies behind such causation? What forces are at work in the universe? In general, all cultures affirm natural, supernatural and human causality. Our main concern here, however, is supernatural causality, or the dynamic relationship between spiritual and human beings. Causality is well illustrated by David Burnett in his book, *Unearthly Powers*.

> *Tribesman:*   This man is sick because someone worked sorcery against him.
>
> *White Doctor:* This man is sick from malaria because he was bitten by an infected mosquito.
>
> *Tribesman:*   Yes, he was bitten by a mosquito, but who sent the mosquito? (1988:109).

This interplay between doctor and tribesman underscores a fundamental difference in worldviews. The doctor generally seeks to explain *how* things have occurred, whereas the tribesman focuses on *why*, in other words "causality." Another illustration, from urban Africa, might help clarify the point.

> They are likely to see in a motor accident not "bad luck" or an unfortunate misadventure, but rather the machinations of some witch who owes the victim a personal grudge, or the action of some aggrieved ancestor spirit who has chosen this way to express his displeasure to his descendants. This explanation is specific to the individual concerned: it explains why the accident should befall that particular person and not his workmate, who was perhaps traveling next to him. It explains ... the why of the event, rather than the how.[2]

The radical differences in perspective that these illustrations highlight may be described as the difference between two basic worldviews: the mechanistic/natural and the personal/spiritual. The mechanistic/natural worldview understands events only in terms of the empirical world, the natural cause and effect, without reference to the unseen world or the involvement of personal spiritual beings.

By contrast, the personal/spiritual worldview understands the empirical, natural world in terms of the unseen, spiritual world. This worldview sees reality in terms of personal and powerful spiritual beings as well as impersonal forces that are constantly interacting with human beings and with the natural world. Westerners usually adhere to the mechanistic/natural worldview, whereas folk Muslims, like most non-Western peoples of the world, take the perspective of the personal/spiritual worldview.

Understanding this personal/spiritual worldview is foundational to understanding the folk Muslim way of thinking. In *Unearthly Powers*, David Burnett details four major contrasts between these two types of worldviews. The following table summarizes his discussion with some modification.[3]

The Personal/Spiritual Worldview	The Mechanistic/Natural Worldview
1. The universe is not closed. The border between the natural and the supernatural is blurred. The natural and supernatural merge into each other.	1. The universe is a closed system. There is a sharp distinction between the natural and the supernatural (if one even believes in the supernatural).
2. The universe is greatly influenced by personal, powerful spirit beings and impersonal power. These invisible forces greatly affect our daily lives.	2. The universe is mechanistic. Everything can be explained rationally. Everything happens by cause and effect.
3. Humankind is essentially a part of the universe as a whole. Thus, man must live in harmony with his environment.	3. Humankind must dominate and control nature.
4. Humankind establishes harmony with the universe via spiritual techniques and rituals.	4. Humankind dominates and controls the universe via science and technology.

Table 7: Worldview Contrasts (adapted from Burnett 1988:14-21)

Worldview and Supernatural Causality in the Bible

The Bible contains numerous illustrations of the concepts of worldview and supernatural causality. Three incidents in the book of Acts are particularly helpful.

Paul at Lystra –Deified by a Polytheistic Worldview

And at Lystra there was sitting a certain man without strength in his feet, lame from his mother's womb, who had never walked. This man was listening to Paul as he spoke, who, when he had fixed his gaze upon him, and had seen that he had faith to be made well, said with a loud voice, "Stand upright on your feet." And he leaped up and began to walk. And when the multitudes saw what Paul had done, they raised their voice, saying in the Lycaonian language, "The gods have become like men and have come down to us. "And they began calling Barnabas, Zeus, and Paul, Hermes, because he was the chief speaker. And the priest of Zeus, whose temple was just outside the city, brought oxen and garlands to the gates, and wanted to offer sacrifice with the crowds. But when the apostles, Barnabas and Paul, heard it, they tore their robes and rushed out into the crowd, crying out and saying, "Men why are you doing these things? We are also men of the same nature as you, and preach the gospel to you in order that you should turn from these vain things to a living God, who made the heaven and the earth and the sea, and all that is in them" (Acts 14:8-15).

This story is a classic example of a confrontation between theistic and polytheistic worldviews. God manifested his power through Paul by healing a lame man at Lystra. However, the multitudes misinterpreted God's mighty act because of their Greek worldview. From their perspective, this was not a miracle of the one true God through his servant. Rather, this manifestation of power was proof that "the gods have become like men and have come down to us" (Ac 14:11). Barnabas was deified as Zeus, the chief god of the Greek pantheon. Paul, because of his speaking ability, was called Hermes, the god of eloquence and rhetoric. Apparently, "local legend told of earlier occasions when the gods had come down to them in the likeness of men, in particular, the two gods whom the Greeks knew as Zeus and Hermes" (Bruce 1988:291).

The multitudes at Lystra understood supernatural causality in polytheistic terms. In other words, their polytheistic presuppositions caused them to worship Paul and Barnabas–"the Priest of Zeus ... wanted to offer sacrifice" (14:13)–instead of worshipping the God they represented. Both Paul and Barnabas protested vehemently against this blasphemy by tearing their clothes. Paul then proceeded to preach a short sermon on the one true God, starting with the fact that they were mere men seeking to turn those at Lystra "from these vain things [idolatrous worship] to a living God, who made the heaven and the earth and the sea and all that is in them" (14:15).

Paul Before the Sanhedrin –Clash Between Theists and Secularists

> But perceiving that one part were Sadducees and the other Pharisees, Paul began crying out in the Council, "Brethren, I am a Pharisee, a son of Pharisees; I am on trial for the hope of the resurrection of the dead!" And as he said this, there arose a dissension between the Pharisees and Sadducees; and the assembly was divided. For the Sadducees say that there is no resurrection, nor an angel, nor a spirit, but the Pharisees acknowledge them all. And there arose a great uproar; and some of the scribes of the Pharisaic party stood up and began to argue heatedly, saying, "We find nothing wrong with this man; suppose a spirit or an angel has spoken to him?" (Acts 23:6-9).

This passage illustrates the clash between a secular and a theistic worldview. Paul was on trial for his faith before the Sanhedrin. However, he deftly turned the tables on the Sanhedrin by pitting the different belief systems of the Pharisees against the Sadducees. "For the Sadducees say that there is no resurrection, nor an angel, nor a spirit, but the Pharisees acknowledged them all" (23:8).

The Sadducees' belief system resembled a modern secular worldview. They denied the existence of a bodily resurrection and afterlife. They also rejected the Bible's teaching on the spirit realm. The Pharisees, by contrast, were committed to these beliefs, which (is worth noting) are fundamental to the gospel.

This clash of worldviews resulted in an uproar. Division and heated arguments erupted over these deeply held viewpoints. Due to their fundamental assumptions, the Pharisees could no longer pass judgment against Paul. Their conclusion? "We find nothing wrong with this man; suppose a spirit or an angel has spoken to him?" (23:9). Because the Pharisees believed in supernatural causality, they were open to Paul's message – at least compared to the Sadducees!

Paul among a Tribal People at Malta – Deification Revisited

But when Paul had gathered a bundle of sticks and laid them on the fire, a viper came out because of the heat, and fastened on this hand. And when the natives saw the creature hanging from his hand, they began saying to one another, "Undoubtedly this man is a murderer, and though he has been saved from the sea, justice has not allowed him to live." However, he shook the creature off into the fire and suffered no harm. But they were expecting that he was about to swell up or suddenly fall down dead. But after they had waited a long time and had seen nothing unusual happen to him, they changed their minds and began to say that he was a god (Acts 28:3-6).

Here is another illustration of supernatural causality within a polytheistic worldview. Shipwrecked on the island of Malta, Paul was gathering wood for a fire when a snake bit him. At first, the islanders interpreted this as the judgment of the gods on Paul. In their minds, tragic occurrences such as snake bites do not just happen randomly. According to their worldview, supernatural forces determine the events of history. Thus, this snake bite could not be just bad luck; it was divine judgment. When Paul was not harmed by the snake, the islanders were forced to reinterpret the situation. Since the snake did not kill Paul, they concluded that he was a god! From their perspective, only a god would be unharmed by a snake bite. Their worldview had no room for a sovereign God who could heal and protect his servants.

The Spirit Realm: "The Heavenly Places"

Confronting the supernatural worldview of folk Muslims forces church planters to rediscover what Bible says about the spirit realm, or the realm where personal spirits inhabit the cosmos. Ephesians is one of the most helpful letters in the New Testament regarding spirit realm issues because Ephesus was a center for magical practices. "Ephesians appears to have been written to a group of churches in western Asia Minor needing help in developing a Christian perspective on the 'powers' and encouragement in their ongoing struggles with these pernicious spirit-forces" (Arnold 1992a:167).

In the context of magic and miracles, Paul equipped the Ephesians to deal with the forces of darkness. In the course of his argument, he uses the phrase "heavenly places" five times (1:3, 1:20; 2:6; 3:10; 6:12). In four out of these five verses, evil spirits are either implicitly or explicitly mentioned. The powers of evil are found in the immediate context of every one of these references to "heavenly places" except Ephesians 1:3. More than any other phrase in the Bible, "heavenly places" most succinctly describes the spirit realm as folk Muslims understand it.

Spiritual blessings in the heavenly places. According to Paul, we have been "blessed with every spiritual blessing in heavenly places in Christ" (1:3). Through Christ, the heavenly realm has invaded the earthly realm. The kingdom has come in Christ, and we can enjoy a foretaste of heaven now.

Seated at the right hand of God. God has raised Christ from the dead and "seated him at his right hand in the heavenly places far above all rule and authority and power and dominion" (1:20-21). In the context of his prayer for the Ephesians, Paul reaches breathtaking heights in expounding Christ's resurrection and enthronement: "he raised him from the dead, and seated him at his right hand."

Next, he underscores the unrivaled authority of Christ's rule. "He has been raised and seated *far above* all rule and authority and power and dominion and every name. And he put all things in subjection under his feet."

The piling up of power terms—rule, authority, power, and dominion—gives us some insight into the occultic context in which Paul ministered. Every one of these terms is found in Jewish and the Greek magical texts of the first century (Arnold 1992a:52-56). The phrase "every name that is named" also alludes to an environment steeped in magic. Magic is based on the chanting of ritual incantations, calling on the names of various spirits and deities to carry out the wishes of the practitioner, such as the seven sons of Sceva attempted to do with the name of Jesus in Acts 19:13-16.

By his resurrection, Christ conquered all the powers of darkness. He reigns over all the cosmic forces of evil. For a people converted out of a background of magical practices, like those at Ephesus or folk Muslims today, this is a powerful, liberating message!

We are seated with him in heavenly places. By his grace, God has "raised us up with him [Christ] and seated us with him in the heavenly places" (2:6). This third use of "heavenly places" points to the believer's exaltation into the heavenly places.

Admittedly, this verse is difficult to understand. However, it is not just meaningless mysticism. Two things are clear: First, whatever else it may mean to be seated with Christ in the heavenly places, at least it means that we share in his authority over the powers of darkness. Second, we share in that authority over the powers of darkness through faith. Paul mentions the Ephesians' faith several times in this connection. He has heard of their faith (1:15). He speaks about Christ's power as something to be appropriated by those who believe (1:19). And he affirms that our salvation – including being raised up with Christ in the heavenlies – is by faith (2:8). Magicians manipulate spirits through *formulas*. Followers of Christ resist spirits through *faith*.

The manifold wisdom of God is made known in heavenly places. According to Paul, the manifold wisdom of God is "made known through the church to the rulers and authorities in the heavenly places" (3:10). The fourth use of the phrase highlights the centrality of the church in God's global plan. The church is an object lesson of God's wisdom for all creation – including spirit beings.[4] God manifests his wisdom through the power of the gospel to reconcile the estranged and unify the divided among all nations (2:11-3:9). As God's reconciling power in Christ becomes effective in his church, it produces a united, multiracial community of "peoples." Because spirit beings are not omniscient, they have not grasped God's purpose of the ages to reach all nations (3:5-6,11). John Stott describes it well.

> So then, as the gospel spreads throughout the world, this new and variegated Christian community develops. It is as if a great drama is being enacted. History is the theater, the world is the stage, and church members in every land are the actors. God himself has written the play, and he directs and produces it. ... But who are the audience? They are the cosmic intelligences, the principalities and powers in the heavenly places. We are to think of them as spectators in the drama of salvation. Thus, "the history of the Christian church becomes a graduate school for angels" (1979:123-4).

Spiritual warfare in the heavenly places. The last and most famous reference to heavenly places in Ephesians indicates that our struggle is "against the spiritual forces of wickedness in the heavenly places" (6:12). We are in a battle against the hosts of hell that takes place in the spirit realm. The phrase "heavenly places" is used almost like a technical term in Ephesians, since it is found nowhere else in the New Testament. It should not simply be equated with "heaven" as the dwelling place of God, distinct from earth. The word "heaven" or "heavens" is used in the sense of God's dwelling place several times elsewhere in Ephesians (1:10; 3:15; 4:10; 6:9).

Instead, "heavenly places" refers to a broader concept. "It is the spiritual world, the timeless, supra-material realm where those spiritual events referred to take place" (Bratcher and Nida 1982:10-11). Stott interprets this phrase as the "sphere of invisible reality," "the unseen world," or the "unseen world of spiritual reality" (1979:246,266,273).

In what way can the "heavenly places" – the spirit realm – be the dwelling place of God and at the same time the scene of Satanic struggle? The Jews in New Testament times believed in seven heavens. While Paul does speak of "the third heaven" (2 Cor 12:2) and the author of Hebrews says that Jesus passed through the heavens (plural, 4:14), there is no explicit mention of seven heavens or even a semi-complete description of heaven in the Bible. Yet it is probably valid to describe the heavenly places "as comprising a succession of levels, with the throne of God on the highest of these and the hostile forces occupying the lowest" (Bruce 1984:406).

The concept of "heavenly places" is a biblical term for the spirit realm.[5] This leads to at least two important conclusions. First of all, Christ's death and resurrection are specifically related to the spirit realm (1:19-20, 2:4-6). Second, the church's life and ministry are also directly linked with the spirit realm (3:10, 6:12). In other words, in the epistle to the Ephesians, the church's salvation, ministry and warfare can only be fully understood in light of the spirit realm.

The Western worldview is very different from the folk Muslim's worldview. However, the Bible equips us to deal with these differences. The worldviews encountered by the early church were similar to the animistic worldview of folk Islam. Church planters need to be true "people of the book," as the Quran describes Christians, and develop a truly biblical worldview of the spirit realm.

As Vern Poythress affirms, "The Bible's worldview should be the one that all theologians [I would say "all Christians"] adopt for themselves. All their study of the Bible should be in terms of the framework of assumptions about God and the world that the Bible itself supplies. This orientation is very important ... It is submitting to what God says" (1987:21).

What Does God Say About Spirits and Causality?

The biblical concept of "the heavenly places" in Ephesians offers important insights into understanding spirit realm issues. It will also be helpful to look at the issues of worldview and supernatural causality in a broader theological framework. In *The Universe Next Door*, James Sire examines various worldview options such as deism, pantheism and monism. He then describes theism, summarizing its eight essential elements. These eight propositions provide a good starting point for the theological aspect of our discussion (1988:25-43).

1. God is infinite and personal (triune), transcendent and immanent, omniscient, sovereign and good.
2. God created the cosmos 'ex nihilo' to operate with a uniformity of cause and effect in an open system.

3. Human beings are created in the image and likeness of God and thus possess personality, self-transcendence, intelligence, morality, gregariousness and creativity.
4. Human beings can know both the world around them and God himself because God has built into them the capacity to do so and because he takes an active role in communicating with them.
5. Human beings were created good, but through the Fall, the image of God became defaced, though not so ruined as not to be capable of restoration; through the work of Christ, God redeemed humanity and began the process of restoring man to goodness, though any given man may choose to reject that redemption.
6. For each person, death is either the gate to life with God and his people, or the gate to eternal separation from the only things that will ultimately fulfill human aspirations.
7. Ethics is transcendent and is based on the character of God as good (holy and loving).
8. History is linear, a meaningful sequence of events leading to the fulfillment of God's purposes for humanity.

Sire cogently outlines what he considers to be the main aspects of a theistic worldview; his outline of theism reflects some of the best insights of modern Evangelicalism. "It recognizes the reality of the unseen world, and of a supreme Creator who is distinct from and greater than his creation. It also recognizes clearly defined moral absolutes based on the fact that there is an ultimate Creator. Further, it recognizes the presence of evil as well as good within the created order" (Burnett 1988:246). Nevertheless, Sire's analysis also reflects the weakness of conservative Evangelical theology. He, too, has failed to adequately deal with the spirit realm. Maybe we should give him the benefit of the doubt and say that he is outlining only a "theistic" as opposed to a "biblical" worldview. Whichever way we interpret him, however, these eight propositions still fail to address a major component of a biblical worldview: angels and demons. Two more propositions are necessary to develop a proper theological foundation for a biblical worldview:

9. God also created spirit beings. A host of these spirit beings have rebelled against God and have set up a counter-kingdom. Satan is the leader of these demonic hordes and this counterfeit kingdom. However, a multitude of these spirit beings, called angels, have not rebelled against God and remain faithful to the administration of his

kingdom, a kingdom which is in continual warfare against the kingdom of Satan.

10. Through the person and work of Christ, Satan has been defeated, his kingdom overthrown. Moreover, through the Holy Spirit, the church has been given power to defeat Satan and the powers of darkness in its mandate to establish the kingdom of God among all the peoples of the world.

A fully biblical worldview must not only be theologically accurate, but also holistic. It must encompass both the natural and the supernatural, giving a comprehensive view of reality. A biblical worldview must also explain the dynamic relationship between the spirit realm, nature and humanity. The following table seeks to describe something of this dynamic in light of the ten theological affirmations above.[6]

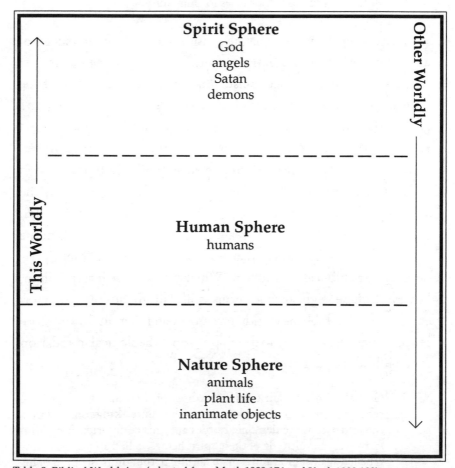

Table 8: Biblical Worldview (adapted from Musk 1989:176 and Kraft 1989:199)

This table illustrates the overlapping nature of the physical and spiritual realms and highlights the interaction between the spheres. The arrows between the spheres and the broken lines underscore the interplay between these three dimensions. Spirits affect us and we affect the spirit realm. Human beings can be demonized or filled with the Holy Spirit. Shamans can call upon evil spirits for help. Through prayer, preaching the gospel and healing the sick, Christians can extend the kingdom of God, which affects the spirit realm.

The arrow to the nature sphere, however, only goes one direction. While the spirit sphere impinges upon the nature sphere, the reverse is not true. Through various shamanistic rituals and prayers, spirits can empower rocks, rings, swords and belts to become amulets.

The Bible speaks about the spirit realm impacting the nature sphere. For example, God empowered Moses' staff to do miracles in Egypt (Ex 4). He also anointed Paul in such a way as to perform "extraordinary miracles ... so that handkerchiefs or aprons were even carried from his body to the sick, and the diseases left them and the evil spirits went out" (Ac 19:11-12). While these are not necessarily models to imitate, they do indicate that the spirit realm can affect the natural sphere.

In addition, the Bible indicates that the spirit realm can affect animals. God spoke through Balaam's donkey (Num 22) and rescued Daniel by closing the lions' mouths (Dan 6). Jesus also permitted a legion of demons to enter a herd of swine (Mk 5).

We can communicate more effectively and biblically if we understand folk Muslims' perceptions and motivations. Perceptions of the unseen world affected Paul's interactions with polytheists and secularists in the book of Acts. In the same way, today's church planters must be prepared to encounter the biblical reality of the heavenly places, dealing with magic and the forces of darkness as Paul describes in the letter to the Ephesians.

Supernatural causality is not just an anthropological concept. The Bible clearly teaches that the spirit realm impacts the physical realm. Folk Muslims rightly discern supernatural forces affecting their lives.

Their views may be excessive, even superstitious – what we described earlier as the "expanded middle" view of the spirit realm. But behind their spiritualistic perspectives are real demons.

Understanding this enhances our ability to communicate through word and deed to their needs. It enables us discern biblical bridges that speak relevantly to their fears (truth encounter). It also pushes us to address the power dimensions of their lives (power encounter) – the two major subjects of our next few chapters.

Questions for Reflection and Discussion

1. To what extent has your background and worldview been shaped by either the flaw of the excluded middle or the flaw of the expanded middle? How have such distortions handicapped your approach to the Muslim people you serve?

2. What is your community's phrase for the spirit realm or the "heavenly places"? Which of the apostle Paul's references to the "heavenly places" in the book of Ephesians could be of greatest usefulness in your witness to your community?

3. Do you believe it is valid to describe the heavenly places as comprising a succession of levels? Why or why not? Does it make any significant or practical difference?

4. In this chapter I add two propositions to James Sire's eight to round out a biblical worldview. Can you identify any other propositions that you believe must be added?

5. Behind the spiritualistic perspectives of folk Muslims lie real demons. Have you confronted such demons? What did you do, and how well did you fare?

It will help you to better digest what you're reading if you take the time to reflect on and discuss such questions after each chapter. Also, I would value a glimpse of what you're thinking! I invite you (either now or later) to share with me (r_d_love@hotmail.com) some of your answers to these questions. You may have some good things to teach me.

Notes

[1] See Arnold 1997 and Moreau 1997 for balanced, scholarly and practical studies on spiritual warfare that address the world, the flesh and the devil.

[2] Friedl and Chrisman 1975:377-378; see also Kuper 1975:100.

[3] The chart is adapted from Burnett 1988:15-21.

[4] In this passage, the phrase "rulers and authorities" probably refers to both angelic and demonic forces. See 1 Pet 1:12.

[5] It is worth noting that the Baahithiin translation of Ephesians 6:12 correctly chooses a phrase meaning "the spirit realm or the realm of the supernatural" to translate that which is rendered "heavenly places" (NASB) or "heavenly realm" (NIV).

[6] This chart is a modification of Musk (1989:176) and Kraft (1989:199).

* a pseudonym

Chapter 6

Truth Encounter: A Defeated Foe

Paul preached the gospel and planted churches among people who believed in the existence of evil spirits. This fact had an impact on how he preached the gospel and on what he taught those new Christians in his letters.
— Clinton Arnold

I get passionate about spiritual warfare. In fact, I get angry when I see the devil defeat God's people. We must know about our enemy if we are to defeat him. Some brothers and sisters act as if the Bible teaches, "Ignore the devil and he will flee from you!" Yet, Paul exclaims, "We are not ignorant of his [the devil's] schemes" (2 Cor 2:11). Too many Evangelicals are quite ignorant of his schemes. We ignore our enemy to our peril.

On the other hand, I know many other believers who go to the opposite extreme. The devil becomes an unbeatable, Goliath-like "Darth Vadar." Every circumstance in life is understood as warfare. They don't see demons behind every bush; these people see demons behind the demons behind every bush! What's so bad about this perspective is not that life is full of demons. I believe it is. What bothers me is that they are more impressed with the devil than they are in awe of Jesus. They focus more on the powers and principalities than they do on the one who has been raised far above every power and principality (Eph 1:21-22). They walk in fear instead of faith. They reflect anxiety instead of confidence.

There is no doubt about it. The devil is a powerful foe. But he is also a defeated foe. He is no match for Jesus:

- The one who created all things (Jn 1:3)
- The one who upholds all things by the word of his power (Heb 1:3)
- The one who works all things after the counsel of his will (Eph 1:11)
- The one who is head over all rule and authority (Col 2:10)
- The one who has been given the name above all names (Phil 2:9)
- The ruler of the kings of the earth (Rev 1:5)

In this book I am attempting to present an integrated, comprehensive approach to spiritual warfare. Spiritual warfare practices such as personal purity, prayer, fasting, exorcism, or resisting the devil by quoting Scripture are usually studied in isolation from the gospel. Most books on spiritual warfare rarely mention the vital relationship between the gospel and warfare. Yet *the gospel of the kingdom provides a massive biblical foundation for spiritual warfare.* According to the gospel of the kingdom, Jesus' words and work and his death and resurrection are all aspects of spiritual warfare. They are attacks on the kingdom of darkness. Spiritual warfare begins with the gospel.

This gospel of the kingdom breaks into a people in four ways: through truth encounter, power encounter, moral encounter and cultural encounter. The next few chapters will address each of these kinds of encounter. But the kingdom approach to ministry begins with truth encounter. Church planters need to preach the gospel in such a way as to confront folk Muslims with the truth of the good news of Christ.

This concept of *truth encounter is both personal and propositional.* First of all, truth encounter is personal. Jesus is the truth (Jn 14:6). The Gospel of John teaches that the good news centers around a relationship with him: "But as many as received him, to them he gave the right to become children of God" (Jn 1:12). "And this is eternal life, that they may know you the only true God, and Jesus Christ whom you have sent" (Jn 17:3). Thus, truth encounter involves an encounter with the living person, Jesus.

Second, truth encounter is propositional. Believers not only encounter the living Christ, but they must also believe certain truths (good news) about him. Jesus is a prophet of God as Muslims contend. But he is more than a prophet; he is the Savior of the world. The Gospel of John also affirms the propositional nature of the gospel: "These have been written that you may believe that Jesus is the Christ, the Son of the Living God; and that believing you may have life in his name" (Jn 20:31; see also 8:31-32).

Unmasking the Dark Powers

The truth that needs to be proclaimed first among folk Muslims should be the rescue dimension of the gospel – God's ability to bring them from the darkness into the light. This must be the church planter's starting point because it is a felt need for folk Muslims.[1]

Paul defined his pioneer church-planting ministry among the nations as a rescue operation. Jesus commissioned Paul to go to the nations "to open their eyes so that they may turn from darkness to light and from the dominion of Satan to God" (Ac 26:18). In other words, church planting among unreached peoples involves encountering the kingdom of darkness.

Folk Muslims use charms, practice magic and fear evil spirits for a good reason. Dark angels are diabolically plotting to destroy humanity. To understand the plight of folk Muslims and prepare for spiritual battle, church planters must understand what the New Testament teaches about the kingdom of light and the kingdom of darkness.[2] An objective reading of the New Testament highlights the importance of the rescue view of salvation. Spirit powers are mentioned in almost every book of the New Testament, and this clash of the kingdoms is a primary theme in the books of Mark, Ephesians and Colossians.

The early church viewed the good news from this angle, too. The first confessions of faith, summarizing the core of Christianity, frequently mentioned Christ's victory over the forces of darkness. Spirit powers are mentioned in the early church's ...

> ... sermon paradigms, formalized *kerygma*, primitive professions of faith, and hymns and Eucharistic prayers. ... [F]rom the earliest age, the Church's preaching and professions of faith contained references to what we call "principalities and powers" (Schlier 1961:7-8).

According to Oscar Cullmann, "the express mention of the victory of Christ over the demons, powers and authorities belongs to all the earliest confessions up to the year 150" (1949:24).

While the rescue view of the gospel is presently downplayed among Evangelicals, this hasn't always been the case. This theme has played an important role in church history and historical theology. Gustaf Aulen describes this rescue view of the gospel as the classical or dominant view of the atonement for the first thousand years of Christian history:

> Its central theme is the idea of the Atonement as a Divine conflict and victory; Christ–Christus Victor–fights against and triumphs over the evil powers of the world, the "tyrants" under which mankind is in bondage and suffering, and in Him God reconciles the world to Himself (1986:4).

Historical theologian Richard A. Muller points out that the early church focused on God's divine rescue operation because that view of the good news made most sense in their cultural context.

> W]riters ... throughout the patristic era selected ... the theme of Christ's victory over the powers ... not because these themes necessarily appeared to them to be the central themes of the New Testament in its own right, but because this particular New Testament way of understanding Christ's work spoke directly to their own cultural and historical context (1991:206).

Unmasking Dark Angels

Jesus described Satan as "the ruler of this world" (Jn 12:31, 14:30, 16:11). Paul uses similar terminology. Satan is "the god of this age" (2Cor 4:4) and "the prince of the power of the air" (Eph 2:2). The Apostle

John says that "the whole world lies in the power of the evil one" (1 Jn 5:19).

However, we shouldn't be overly impressed with our enemy. *Satan's authority is temporary and conditional.* It is temporary because the presence of the future – the age to come – has invaded the present evil age. Jesus has come to reclaim his creation and conquer this counter-kingdom. Satan's authority is conditional because even though Satan has immense power, he is still a created being (Col 1:16). He exists and has power in this age only because of, and as long as, God allows him to do so (*cf.* Lk 22:31-32).

The book of Ephesians strikes a perfect balance between God's absolute sovereignty and Satan's temporary rule. God is the one who chose us in Christ before the foundation of the world (Eph 1:4) and the one who works all things after the counsel of his will (Eph 1:11). Yet this same letter closes with one of the most pointed passages in the New Testament on spiritual warfare (Eph 6:10-18). The realization of God's sovereignty brings us great comfort. It greatly lessens the distress and struggle of spiritual battle with the powers of darkness. But it in no way minimizes or eliminates the pain. Thus, Paul calls us to "put on the full armor of God" that we "may be able to stand firm against the schemes of the devil" (Eph 6:11).

A host of terms depict the forces of darkness throughout the New Testament. In fact, the enormous number of terms used to describe the demonic realm highlight its significance and centrality in the New Testament. Moreover, "superhuman forces are mentioned in almost every place where Christ's complete lordship is being discussed" (Green 1981:81-82).

The most frequently used terms in the Gospels are "evil spirits," "unclean spirits" and "demons" (Mk 1:23,34; Ac 19:12). The first two terms underscore the blatantly evil nature of the counter-kingdom. The hosts of hell are described as "evil" and "unclean." While the word "demon" originally stood for a god or intermediary between God and humans, by the time the New Testament was written all demons were considered evil – agents of Satan. Satan's lieutenants are described occasionally as "angels." Jesus portrays hell as being "prepared for the devil and his angels" (Mt 25:41). The apostle John also describes these evil forces as angels (Rev 12:7).

Paul's demonology puts the emphasis in a different place. The Gospels focus on the possession of individuals. They speak of demons in relationship to people. Paul was familiar with both the theology and experience of casting demons out of people (Ac 16:16-18, 19:11-12). However, Paul's terminology indicates that he was more concerned with the relationship between demons, this age, and the cosmos.

Paul gives us the most thorough understanding of demonology in the New Testament. While he does use the terminology of the Gospels (e.g., bad angels, Satan, the devil and demons), he also describes the demonic realm in terms of "rulers," "authorities," "powers," "thrones," "dominions," and "world rulers of this darkness."

Folk Muslims may use some of these same terms to describe the hostile spirit world they face. They will most likely have their own terminology and their own categories as well. In some cases, they may even view these spirits in a positive light, like my friend Uthman, who welcomes ancestor spirits.

Ultimately, whatever the name and however the culture views these forces, the kingdom of darkness stands behind them. The purpose of truth encounter is to unmask and defeat these powers. Power encounter may liberate people, but only truth encounter can truly transform them. Folk Muslims must understand the evil nature of their animistic practices and how Christ conquered this kingdom of darkness.

Christ's Defeat of the Dark Angels

Christ's confrontation with the forces of darkness is displayed throughout his life and ministry. This is seen most dramatically in his ministry of exorcism. In the gospel of Mark, particularly, Jesus is portrayed as the great exorcist. His very presence terrifies demons; his word of command expels them. The ministry of Christ is an assault on the kingdom of darkness.

However, Christ's victory over Satan and the forces of darkness takes place preeminently in his death, resurrection and exaltation. At the cross Christ disarmed and triumphed over "the rulers and authorities" (Col 2:15; cf. Heb 2:14). In his resurrection and exaltation, he was raised far above all the spiritual forces of darkness (Eph 1:21-22; 1 Pet 3:22). In their various New Testament letters, Paul and Peter explicitly mention lists of these defeated spirit powers in numerous categories. The following table lists the varied terminology.

New Testament Categories of Defeated Spirit Powers			
Col. 1:16	Col. 2:15	Eph. 1:20-21	1 Pet. 3:21-22
thrones			
dominions		dominion	
rulers	rulers	rule	
authorities	authorities	authority	authorities
		power	powers
angels			

Table 9: New Testament Categories of Defeated Spirit Powers

Bruce's comments on the spiritual forces in Paul's letters (he mentions only five categories of spirit powers, excluding Peter's sixth category, "angels") are valid for the entire New Testament and provides a fitting summary for this subject.

> In all, five classes of angel-princes seem to be distinguished in the NT– thrones, principalities, authorities, powers and dominions. These probably represent the highest orders of the angelic realm, but the variety of ways in which the titles are combined in the NT

warns us against the attempt to reconstruct a fixed hierarchy from them. ... The point is that the highest angel-princes, like the rest of creation, are subject to Christ (1988:63-64).

With great vigor and clarity, the New Testament teaches that Christ is the conqueror of every type of spiritual power.

Christ's Destruction of the Dark Angels

The book of Revelation vividly portrays the final overthrow and ultimate defeat of Satan and the kingdom of darkness (Rev 19, 20). However, more relevant to our discussion is Paul's account in 1 Corinthians 15:24: "Then comes the end, when he [Christ] delivers up the kingdom to the God and Father, when he has abolished all rule and all authority and power."

This verse highlights the close relationship between eschatology (end times) and demonology. First of all, Paul speaks of the end of all things, the consummation of the kingdom. Then he shows that this eschatological fulfillment of the kingdom involves the ultimate destruction of the powers of darkness. Christ will abolish all rule, authority and power.

> These three words are probably not used to define various kinds of authority with precision. But the putting of them together gives emphasis to the thought that in that day there is no governing power of any kind that will not be completely subservient to him (Morris 1973:216).

Church planting involves turning a people from darkness to light, from the dominion of the devil to the kingdom of God. In other words, ministry among folk Muslims must be understood in terms of spiritual warfare with the powers of darkness. This spiritual warfare will be most successful if church planters encounter the darkness with the truth of the rescue view of the gospel. Christ defeated the powers of darkness at his first coming and will ultimately destroy the powers of darkness at his second coming.

Questions for Reflection and Discussion

1. Contrast the emphases in demonology in the Gospels and the ministry of the apostle Paul. How might these complementary emphases improve your witness to your community?

2. What terms and categories does your Muslim community use to describe the hostile spirit world they face? Do you understand these terms and categories well? Who or what can help you to understand them better?

3. What might it practically mean or "look like" for you and your colleagues to "unmask" the dark powers in your community? What might be your approach?

It will help you to better digest what you're reading if you take the time to reflect on and discuss such questions after each chapter. Also, I would value a glimpse of what you're thinking! I invite you (either now or later) to share with me (r_d_love@hotmail.com) some of your answers to these questions. You may have some good things to teach me.

Notes

[1] Ultimately, our folk Muslim friends must understand and cherish the relational dimension of the gospel. The relationship and rescue (or Godward and Satanward) views of the gospel are only differing emphases of the one gospel. Even in the key verses describing the rescue view of the gospel, the relational dimensions are mentioned as well. See chapter 3 on the kingdom of God.

[2] Charles Kraft likes to make a distinction between the personal and propositional nature of what I call truth encounter. He prefers to speak about truth encounter (the propositional dimension) and commitment (or allegiance) encounter (the personal dimension). But his very definition admits the strong overlap in the two concepts: "Commitment encounters, involving the exercise of the will in commitment and obedience to the Lord, are the most important of the encounters. For without commitment and obedience to Jesus, there is no spiritual life. ... Initial commitment and the relationship that proceeds from it are tightly linked to truth, both because they are developed within the truth encounter and because a relationship with God is the true reason for human

existence" (1992c:74-75). Therefore I prefer to use the term "truth encounter" to encompass both dimensions of truth.

Chapter 7

Truth Encounter: A Liberating Lord

Satan's power is in the lie, and when his lie is exposed by the truth, his plans are foiled. ... You just have to out-truth him. Believe, declare, and act upon the truth of God's Word, and you will thwart Satan's strategy.

– Neil Anderson

I got little response from my Muslim friends when I told them that "Jesus was sent by God to take away our sins" (1 Jn 3:5). This standard presentation, which focuses on forgiveness, didn't meet their felt need. However, when I said, "Jesus was sent by God to destroy the works of the devil" (1 Jn 3:8), I received their undivided attention.

How can we show our folk Muslim friends that the gospel is actually good news for them? How can we open up our Bible and actually preach a rescue gospel?

The Power Passages

Let's look at five passages which best summarize the rescue view of redemption and help us communicate the gospel to folk Muslims more effectively: Colossians 1:12-14 and 2:14-15; Hebrews 2:14, Ephesians 1:20-22, and 1 Peter 3:22. Church planters can use each of these passages to powerfully present the gospel from a kingdom perspective.

Colossians 1:12-14

... giving thanks to the Father, who has qualified us to share in the inheritance of the saints in light. For he delivered us from the domain of darkness, and transferred us to the kingdom of his beloved Son, in whom we have redemption, the forgiveness of sins.

This passage is full of explicit kingdom terminology: inheritance, domain of darkness, kingdom. Paul describes our salvation in terms of conflict between the kingdom of darkness and the kingdom of light.

First of all, Paul says that the Father has "qualified" us to share in the inheritance of the saints in light. The word "qualify" (*hikanosanti*) denotes an accomplished act, the gracious decree of a loving Father. This verb emphasizes the relational dimension of salvation: our relationship with God has been restored. Before we aligned ourselves with God's kingdom, we had stood before the eternal judge, condemned as guilty sinners. Now, by his grace, we have been adopted into the family, so that by faith and with confidence we can call the judge "our Father."

Next Paul describes the rescue view of salvation. We have been delivered and transferred. Again, in both cases the verb tense emphasizes "the already" of the kingdom of God.

We are delivered from the domain of darkness – a rebel kingdom characterized by opposition to the light. We have been transferred into the kingdom of his beloved Son (translated literally – the Son of his love). The phrase, "the kingdom of his beloved Son," highlights the Christ-centered nature of the kingdom. While Paul usually describes the kingdom as "the kingdom of God," he does, on occasion, use the terms interchangeably (Eph. 5:5; *cf.* Rev. 11:15).

Verse 14 links the concept of the kingdom with the cross. Entrance into the kingdom of Christ is based on redemption. The word "redemption" (*apolutrosis*) refers to purchase from the slave-market. "In verse 14 the metaphor changes from 'the victor who rescues by force of arms ... to the philanthropist who releases him by the payment of a ransom' " (Morris 1974:43).

Paul describes our entry into the kingdom of God as emancipation from slavery. We have been set free from the dominion of the devil. In Christ, we are no longer slaves of Satan. This redemption is further defined in terms of forgiveness. It is noteworthy that Paul describes his apostolic calling in words similar to those used in Colossians 1:12-14. He was sent to the nations "to open their eyes so that they may turn from darkness to light and from the dominion of Satan to God, in order that they may receive forgiveness of sins and an inheritance among those who have been sanctified by faith in [Jesus]" (Ac 26:18).

According to Paul, through Christ the kingdom has come. God had already qualified the Colossians to share in the inheritance; he had already delivered them from the kingdom of darkness and had already transferred them to his Son's kingdom.

Colossians 2:14-15

... having canceled out the certificate of debt consisting of decrees against us and which was hostile to us; and he has taken it out of the way, having nailed it to the cross. When he had disarmed the rulers and authorities, he made a public display of them, having triumphed over them through him.

These two verses explain both the relationship and rescue views of salvation. Verse 14 describes salvation in terms of forgiveness, while verse 15 highlights Christ's triumph over spiritual powers. As Wright says,

Paul notes the two barriers which stand between human beings and membership in God's family: The written code, with its regulations, that was against us and that stood opposed to us, on the one hand, and the powers and authorities on the other. God has apparently canceled the former and disarmed the latter (1986:110-111).

While there are exegetical difficulties in the passage, the general thrust is clear. Paul says that this certificate of debt has been "canceled out." "The Greek verb *exaleiphein* means to rub out, wipe away and so obliterate from sight, as writing on wax or a slate was removed" (Martin 1981:86). Clearly, this word pictures the divine action of God erasing our hostile debts.

However, God not only erases our debts, he also removes them from his presence: "He has taken it out of the way, having nailed it to the cross." The verbs "canceled" and "nailed" are in the aorist tense, denoting a once-for-all act. By contrast, the verb "has taken it away" is in the perfect tense, underscoring the abiding significance of this divine removal. Paul "illustrates the freeness and graciousness of God's forgiveness (*charizomai*) from the ancient custom of canceling debts" (Stott 1986:233).

The words "disarmed," "public display," and "triumphed" are the keys to interpreting verse 15.[1] The emphasis is on conquest. The military imagery of disarming must be understood in light of the words "public display" and "triumphed over"–allusions to the practice of Roman generals who paraded their captives of war in chains through the streets of the city to display their victory (Bruce 1988:111). Leivestad rightly explains:

> It is not of great significance whether we imagine a humiliating degradation of the powers, whereby their mantles and other insignia are taken from them, or a military conquest at which they are deprived of arms and weapons by the conqueror. The important thing is that the crucifixion of Jesus is, in one way or other, depicted as a divine triumph over the cosmic powers (1954:104).

How does the victory of Christ over the cosmic powers in verse 15 relate to the canceling of the decree mentioned in verse 14? Christ has blotted out the record of our indebtedness by his death. In doing so, the damning indictment, formerly used by the principalities and powers to control us, has been forever canceled. These demonic powers no longer have the right to rule over us. Their power over us is broken because the foothold they have had into our lives, due to sin, has been taken away.

Hebrews 2:14

Since then the children share in flesh and blood, he himself likewise also partook of the same, that through death he might render powerless him who had the power over death, that is, the devil.

The author of Hebrews begins with an affirmation about the incarnation: Jesus took on flesh and blood. This emphasizes the perfect humanity of Christ. However, the verses immediately preceding our passage (2:5-9) give further insight into the author's understanding of the incarnation. He describes Christ in terms of Psalm 8, implying that by his incarnation, Christ came to fulfill God's original purpose for humanity to rule the earth.

To regain humanity's lost dominion, Christ had to do more than just become a man. He came to die. The incarnation led to the crucifixion. This redemptive goal of the incarnation is made explicit in the final purpose clause: "in order that" through death he might *katargeo* him who had the power of death. The New American Standard Bible translates *katargeo* as "render powerless," whereas the New International Version translates it as "destroy." The context clearly favors "renders powerless." The devil has not yet been destroyed, but his power has been broken and his kingdom toppled.

At the cross, Christ defeated the devil and thus death itself. As Guthrie says,

> The death of Christ has brought deliverance to man and destruction to the devil. Both are potential rather than actual, for the devil is still active and most men still fear death. Nevertheless, the death and resurrection of Jesus have demonstrated once and for all that the devil is no longer master of death (1986:93).

Leon Morris' description of the rescue view of the gospel in Hebrews provides an apt conclusion.

> In common with the other New Testament writers, the author of this Epistle thinks of God as in continual conflict with the devil. Jesus came to earth expressly in order that He might enter into this conflict and destroy the devil (Heb. 2:14). His whole life might be understood as a struggle against Satan (*cf.* the witness of the Gospels to the temptations at the beginning of the ministry, and to the casting out of the demons, Satan's henchmen, throughout it). But preeminently it is the struggle seen in His death, which is the focal point of it all (1977:280).

Ephesians 1:20-22

He raised him from the dead, and seated him at his right hand in the heavenly places, far above all rule and authority and power and dominion, and every name that is named, not only in this age, but also in the one to come. And he put all things in subjection under his feet.

In the context of his prayer for the Ephesians, Paul reaches breathtaking heights expounding Christ's resurrection and rule: "he raised him from the dead, and seated him at his right hand." This was a central part of the early church's proclamation (Ac 2:32-35; Rom 8:34).

The resurrection and enthronement points to Christ's exalted status and unrivaled authority. He has not only been raised from the dead. He has been raised and seated *far above* all rule and authority and power and dominion and every name. And he put *all things* in subjection *under his feet.*"

This passage points out the fulfillment of the Old Testament messianic prophecy in Psalm 110: "The Lord says to my Lord, 'Sit at my right hand, until I make your enemies a footstool for your feet" (Ps 110:1). Cullmann comments, "Ps. 110, from which comes the statement about Christ's present sitting at the right hand of God and his victory over the powers, is the most frequent Old Testament citation to occur in the New Testament, and therefore the statement is to be found in almost all the old confessional formulas" (1967:171). This underscores the importance of the rescue view of the gospel in the early church.

The final clause, "he put all things in subjection under his feet," comes from Psalm 8:6. Originally this psalm, which functions as a commentary on Genesis 1:26-28, describes the majesty of humankind. We were created in God's image to rule the earth.

In this passage, however, Paul contextualizes this psalm in two ways. First he describes Christ as the last Adam. Although the first Adam lost his dominion to Satan, the second Adam regained it. Through his death and resurrection, the last Adam won back for us what the first Adam lost. "The full dominion which God intended man to enjoy is now exercised only in the man Christ Jesus" (Stott 1979:60). Through Christ and in Christ we are restored to our true dignity. Second, in the original passage, the objects of subjection were sheep, oxen, birds, and fish. Here, however, Paul indicates that spirit powers are now subject to Christ.

By his resurrection, Christ conquered all the powers of darkness. He reigns over all the cosmic forces of evil. For people converted out of a background of magical practices (like those at Ephesus or folk Muslims today), this is a powerful, liberating message.

1 Peter 3:21-22

… through the resurrection of Jesus Christ, who is at the right hand of God, having gone into heaven, after angels and authorities and powers had been subjected to him.

Peter, like Paul, also describes Christ's resurrection and en-thronement as a victory over evil spirit powers. The word "after" implies that the subjugation of angels, authorities and powers were necessary before Christ could reign.

Like the parallel passage in Ephesians 1:20-22, this passage alludes to Psalm 110. C. H. Dodd describes this messianic psalm (and by implication the rescue view of the gospel) as a fundamental element of the early church's *kerygma* : "Wherever we read of Christ being at the right hand of God, or of hostile powers being subjected to him, the ultimate reference is to this passage. In view of the place which Ps. CX. [110] holds in the New Testament, we may safely put it down as one of the fundamental texts of the primitive *kerygma*" (1980:15).

This verse underscores the "already/not yet" tension of the kingdom of God. Christ's rule is described in the present tense. Yet the people to whom Peter is writing are suffering. The devil is still prowling about like a roaring lion seeking someone to devour (1 Pet 5:8). Nevertheless, because of Christ's resurrection and enthronement, the ability of the powers of darkness to afflict the church is not the last word. The reign of Jesus is!

These five passages outline a concise presentation of kingdom theology as it relates to overcoming the powers of darkness. Ernest Best's comments on 1 Peter 3:21-22 provide a fitting summary:

The NT tradition associates the Christ event with a victory over these angelic powers. This victory may be depicted as future (1 Cor. 15:24), connected to the ascension as here (cf. Eph. 1:21), or related to the death of Jesus (Col. 2-15). ... In 1 Peter 3:22 it is to be assumed that their subjection took place as Christ went to heaven, for they were believed to inhabit the region between earth and the highest heaven (cf. Eph. 2:2, 6:12; Testament of Levi 3:1ff, 2 Enoch 7:1-5, 18:3-6) (1971:148-149).

Using Kingdom Theology in Evangelism

In order to be effective communicators of the kingdom, church planters must be able to proclaim the gospel simply. For example, my co-workers and I developed one such approach in a contextualized tract. The tract uses an attractive cover, intriguing title, and a story line taken from a well-known traditional epic showing the struggle between two kingdoms – one evil and one good. The tract explains that, just as the protagonist was saved from the kingdom of darkness, so also Jesus delivers us from the kingdom of Satan.

The tract utilizes an eight-step approach to sharing the gospel using kingdom theology:

1. God is the king of the universe (Gen. 1:1; Ps. 103:19).

2. Men and women were created and blessed to rule the earth as God's representatives (Gen. 1:26-28).

3. Adam and Eve disobeyed God and so were expelled from the kingdom of God (Gen. 3:22-24, Gal. 5:19-21).

4. Because of sin, Satan now rules the earth (1 John 5:19; 2 Cor. 4:4; John 12:31; 14:30; Eph. 2:2).

5. Consequently, men and women have become enslaved by Satan and are now under the wrath of God (1 John 5:19, Eph. 2:1-3, John 3:36).

6. Men and women seek to enter God's kingdom by means of good works but fail (Rom. 3:23; Isaiah 64:6).

7. God still loves men and women and sent Jesus Christ to defeat the devil, to deliver them from the kingdom of darkness, and to save

them from the wrath of God (1 John 3:8, Heb. 2:14, Col. 1:13-14, Col. 2:15, Eph. 1:20-21, 1 Pet. 3:22).

8. If men and women want to enter into the kingdom of God, they must repent and believe (Acts 2:38, 26:18; John 1:12).

Table 10: The Bridge to Life from a Kingdom Perspective

This approach can be summarized as in Table 10 in a diagram adapted from the Navigators' "Bridge to Life." In the tract we included a number of diagrams to show the step-by-step progression of points 1 through 8. Here, for the sake of brevity, I include only the final, complete diagram.

We are not just interested in evangelism among folk Muslims. We want to plant churches, or rather to establish kingdom communities that demonstrate who the King is and what he can do. Thus, kingdom theology must find expression in the church. The following confession of faith, written by a missionary and a national leader, is presently used in a folk Muslim convert church. This confession is not comprehensive. It reflects an early stage of contextualization. However, within it the gospel is clear, and the theology is relevant. This confession emphasizes the unity of God, describes the gospel in terms of kingdom theology, and adheres to biblical terminology throughout.

A Confession of Faith
from a kingdom perspective and for a folk Islamic context

I confess there is one God. There is no God but Allah.

I confess there is one God, and one mediator also between God and humankind, Isa al-Masih, himself human.

I believe that Isa al-Masih appeared for this purpose that he might destroy the works of the devil.

I believe that through Isa we have been delivered from the domain of darkness and transferred into the kingdom of God.

I believe that Isa gave himself as a ransom for all.

I believe that Isa al-Masih was raised from the dead and is at the right hand of God, having gone into heaven, after angels and authorities and powers had been subjected to him.

I believe that this is eternal life, that we know the only true God and Isa al-Masih whom he has sent.

Now to the King eternal, immortal, invisible, the only God, be honor and glory forever and ever.

Amen.[2]

The devil is defeated. Christ is exalted. The one true God must be praised and honored. Warfare ultimately leads to worship.

===

Questions for Reflection and Discussion

1. Which of the five biblical passages exposited in this chapter do you find most helpful to your ministry and community? Why?

2. Review the modified "Bridge to Life" illustration of proclaiming kingdom theology simply. Would this approach be useful in your context? What modifications might you want to make?

3. Review the confession of faith at the end of the chapter. Might this confession be useful in your context? What modifications might you want to make?

It will help you to better digest what you're reading if you take the time to reflect on and discuss such questions after each chapter. Also, I would value a glimpse of what you're thinking! I invite you (either now or later) to share with me (r_d_love@hotmail.com) some of your answers to these questions. You may have some good things to teach me.

Notes

[1] Some commentators have understood this disarming or stripping to refer to Christ either stripping off his demonic tormentors or stripping off his weak flesh. Morosco points out, "Neither of these views makes this stripping a real victory, however; rather it is more like an escape, which makes them both unsatisfactory in this context" (Morosco 1974:339).

[2] This confession of faith is taken from Mark 12:32, 1 Timothy 2:5, 1 John 3:8, Colossians 1:13, 1 Timothy 2:6, 1 Peter. 3:21-22, John 17:3, and 1 Timothy 1:17.

Chapter 8

Power Encounter: Offensive Attack

Satan's chief tactic is deception and ... this deception operates both in the realm of truth and in the realm of power. Christian ministry must therefore have a proper balance of ... proclamation of Christian truth and demonstration of Christ's power.

—**Timothy Warner**

The Need for Power Encounter

Greg Livingstone, the founder of Frontiers, likes to tell a story from the early days of this mission agency. Greg asked a Pentecostal team leader how he was planning to reach Muslims. The missionary replied, "We're going to raise the dead!"

Shaking his head, Greg queried, "Do you have a Plan B?"

People usually laugh at this story.[1] Still, the majority of missionaries to Muslims—whether or not they came from Pentecostal or charismatic churches—wrestle with the issues of signs and wonders. For example, one missionary with Frontiers in Central Asia (a Baptist by denomination and a Campus Crusade leader by training) led a Muslim shaman to Christ. Even though this Muslim convert wanted to serve Christ, he was still drawn to shamanistic practices. Truth encounter alone was not enough! When some non-charismatic Frontiers leaders came to encourage and coach this missionary, the missionary questioned them about the spirit realm and signs and wonders. Since they had not dealt with this before, they encouraged him to contact other Frontiers missionaries who had experience in these matters. He sent out an e-mail to a number of our missionaries and within 72 hours received counsel from five other team leaders. This missionary to Central Asia told me recently that every time their Muslim-convert church meets, they have a healing service! He now believes that power encounter must be part of the church-planting process.

A Presbyterian missionary in Central Asia describes his experiences of power encounter in one of his prayer letters:

> You may find it interesting to know that we have seen more cases of "demonization" here than anywhere we have ever been before. [He has served in two other Muslim countries.] We see cases weekly in cell meetings and on Sunday. The stories I could tell you would really shock some of you. But this is reality here. We are making inroads into a people group where the gospel has never existed before. ... Have you ever seen a demonized person scream and yell because the written Word of God was being read or spoken? We have![2]

Although once primarily the domain of Pentecostal and charismatic Christianity, the issue of power encounter is now a major concern of the broader Evangelical world. Respected professors have written on the subject: Timothy Warner (formerly) of Trinity Evangelical Divinity School (1991); Neil Anderson (formerly) of Talbot Theological Seminary (1976); Philip Steyne of Columbia International University (1989) and Charles Kraft of Fuller Theological Seminary (1989). An entire issue of the *International Journal of Frontier Missions* (1993) dealt with this theme as well. Power encounter is also a "hot" subject in Muslim ministry. Arthur Glasser (1979), Bill Musk (1989), Paul Hiebert (1989), J. Dudley Woodberry (1990), Phil Parshall (1983) and Vivienne Stacey (1989) all claim power encounter is very relevant for reaching Muslims.

"Power encounter" is a relatively new technical term in missiology that has its origin with Alan Tippett. For Tippett, power encounter is always connected with evangelism. Consequently, power encounter is a term used for those who are making a commitment to Christ or have just made one. It is "an encounter between their old and their new God. ... They have rejected the supernatural resources on which they once relied, and are challenging the old power to harm them" (1987:83).

Peter Wagner, on the other hand, does not link power encounter with evangelism and defines it more supernaturally.

> The kind of power encounter I am speaking of is a visible, practical demonstration that Jesus Christ is more powerful than the spirits, powers or false gods worshipped or feared by the members of a given people group. While every conversion is a power encounter in a sense, since an individual is delivered from the power of darkness to the power of light (see Col. 1:13), I refer here to the more public visible challenge that pits God against Satan (1988:150).

Definitions tend to fall into one of two camps. The narrower definition emphasizes signs and wonders, while the broader definition focuses more on spiritual warfare as including any conflict between a believer and the powers of darkness. I believe the Bible emphasizes a broader definition.

Power encounter is:
- the demonstration of God's power,
- through God's servants,
- over the work of Satan and demons,
- based on the work of Christ, the Great Commission and the ministry of the Holy Spirit,
- resulting in the salvation of the lost, the upbuilding of the Body and the glory of God.

The following story taken from a missionary's prayer letter vividly illustrates power encounter:[3]

> We arranged a meeting with Abdullah and his uncle regarding the cousin with the "jinn." It quickly became apparent that we must take a woman along. Anyway, it was decided that Cheryl and I should go. Our stated purpose was to gather more information direct from the source. It soon became clear, as we heard more firsthand descriptions, that this girl must be dealing with a demon. I suggested that we pray briefly and then schedule our next visit. I praised the Lord for many things related to our salvation and prayed briefly that the girl be freed from this oppression. Then, as I was

beginning to talk about our next visit, the mother pointed to her daughter and said, "Look, it's beginning!" The demon began manifesting with wailing and sobbing, then uncontrollable laughter. We were immediately struck with irrational terror. But the Lord was with us. Cheryl took hold of the girl and prayed fervently. Then I began praying in the local language. As the demon began to utter things in the local and trade languages, we commanded it to be silent in Jesus' name. It never uttered a word after that. We were embroiled in this for over an hour and the Lord revealed many things. There may be more than one demon. In the midst of it I had the complete freedom to share the gospel in the local language with the family members. The demon writhed at the quoting of Scripture, especially in the local language. I've never seen a look of intense hatred like this in my life. The family members had been in the habit of calling out the demon's name and engaging in casual conversation with it!! They tried to do it this time and the demon couldn't utter a sound. Even without the use of words the demon tried to mock me with smiles and nods of the head. I forbid it to do that also in the name of Jesus and it stopped. We spoke of the cross and of salvation as we prayed. We sensed that this demon had authority to be there–through the family heritage and the girl's own fantasies. I told Abdullah to go get the local-language translations from the car and before he could return the girl came back to normal. I told the family it was because the demon didn't want the rest of them to hear God's word in their own language. Abdullah's uncle read some anyway! We will be meeting them again Saturday in a different location. I plan to warn them from Luke 11:24-28 and I John 3:8b that if the Spirit of Jesus Christ does not replace the demon that leaves they could all be in for worse trouble! Then we will read from the Scriptures, discuss the good news, and see what happens.

The signs and wonders movement has done an excellent job of promoting kingdom theology as the basis for power ministry (Wimber 1986; 1987; Williams 1989). However, as I learned among the Baahithiin, there is a difference between doing power ministry in America and actually confronting magic in a folk Islamic (or power-oriented) society. Most Americans don't live in fear of demons or curses. They don't use charms or amulets. They are not dominated by a power-oriented worldview. However, folk Muslims are.

Missiologists have noted our ineffectiveness at dealing with syncretism in power-oriented societies. The chronic problem of dual allegiance is found throughout the world. Charles Kraft ably describes this problem and offers a balanced approach to these issues (1992).

However, most books and articles on "power issues" are not written for power-oriented societies. Even if they are, they rarely focus on the Scriptures that specifically address magic. I hope to rectify this in this chapter and the next. We will begin by examining what the Bible teaches about magic, beginning with Moses.

Moses and Magic

When you enter the land which the Lord your God gives you, you shall not learn to imitate the detestable things of those nations. There shall not be found among you anyone who makes his son or his daughter pass through the fire, one who uses divination, one who practices witchcraft, or one who interprets omens of a sorcerer, or one who casts a spell, or a medium, or a spiritist, or one who calls up the dead. For whoever does these things is detestable to the Lord, and because of these detestable things the Lord your God will drive them out before you. You shall be blameless before the Lord your God. For these nations, which you shall dispossess, listen to those who practice witchcraft and diviners, but as for you, the Lord your God has not allowed you to do so. The Lord your God will raise up for you a prophet like me from among you, from your countrymen, you shall listen to him (Dt 18:9-15).

This passage is not usually found in most discipleship study guides! In fact, for most American evangelicals this text is irrelevant. However, this is a classic text on the occult. Many of the occultic practices of the Canaanites forbidden in this passage parallel the occultic practices of folk Muslims.

Note the literary structure of this passage. It describes two ways people discern the divine will: through the prophetic word or through occultic practices. Moses contrasts those who seek revelation through God's appointed spokesperson, the prophet, with those seeking revelation illegitimately through magic practitioners.

Prohibitions against magic are scattered throughout the Old Testament (Ex 22:18; Lev 18:21; 19:26, 31; 20:2-6, 27). However, in this passage we find a comprehensive summary of teaching on magic in the Old Testament. Moses begins with a list of nine magical practices: making one's son or daughter pass through the fire, using divination, practicing witchcraft, interpreting omens, practicing sorcery, casting a spell, functioning as a medium, functioning as a spiritist and calling up the dead (vs 10-11).

Making one's son or daughter pass through the fire refers to human sacrifice to the false god, Molech (2 K 23:10; Jer 32:35). This might seem irrelevant to most of us. I was shocked to find that the Baahithiin have a type of magic in which someone makes a contract with a spirit being in order to get rich. This type of magic involves blood sacrifice, at times even human sacrifice.

The next three terms (divination, witchcraft and omens) refer to various types of divination or fortune-telling – supernatural methods of discerning the will of the gods. The next two terms (sorcerer and one who casts a spell) refer to magic, that is, the use of supernatural methods to control events or people. The last three terms (medium, spiritist or one who calls up the dead) refer to spiritism or communication with the spirit world.

Thus, Moses gives a blanket prohibition against the three major types of occultism: divination, magic and consultation with the spirit world.[4] God's perspective on these issues is clear. Three times he says these practices are "detestable" in his sight (vs 9,12). The people of God shall not imitate these practices (v 9), nor will the Lord allow his people to practice witchcraft or seek counsel from diviners (vs 14).

This passage not only prohibits these practices, it also gives us some insight into why people engage in them. Verse 14 says that these people "listen" to those who practice witchcraft and consult diviners. The Canaanites, as well as folk Muslims, are seeking guidance in life. They want to know the purpose of heaven and unlock the secrets of the future. They need help. They seek it from the spirit realm. Their motivation isn't necessarily bad, but their method is! They are seeking revelation from the wrong source.

There is an important contrast between verse 14 and 15. The people of God are forbidden to listen to spirit practitioners, but they are commanded to "listen" to the prophet that God will raise up in the future. Instead of going to a diviner, shaman, or magician, Moses calls the people of God to listen to the coming prophet–the prophet, Jesus (*Nabi Isa;* see Acts 3:20-22; John 6:14; 7:40).

The verses following Deuteronomy 18:9-15 address the issues of both the future prophet (vs 16-18) and the prophetic ministry in general (vs 19-22). The divinely appointed prophet, who declares God's word, provides God's people with guidance that is at variance with that of its neighbors. The same is true today. We have the written Word and Jesus, the Living Word, to guide us. No other sources can compare!

Moses' teaching on magic can be summarized in two words: prohibition and prediction. He links his great predictions of the coming prophet, Jesus, with prohibitions against magic and witchcraft. This reminds us that truth encounter and power encounter must go together. Folk Muslims need a power encounter to be delivered from their spirit practices, but ultimately they need truth encounter to be transformed. Moses says, "The Lord your God will raise up for you a prophet like me from among you, and from your countrymen, you shall listen to him" (v 15). True deliverance for folk Muslims depends on submission to the true prophet and true God, Jesus Christ.

Four Models of Power Encounter in Acts

The book of Acts addresses the issues of confronting magic in power-oriented societies. Luke has developed a "curriculum" for dealing with power-oriented societies–in story form. [5]

Signs and wonders (power encounters) were an important part of the early church's expansion. Philip led the way to Samaria and into a major clash with a magician and the powers of darkness (Ac 8:5-24). A power encounter with a magician also provided the first door-opener for Paul and Barnabas as the gospel moved to "the ends of the earth" (Ac 13:4-12). Paul's first church in Europe, at Philippi, included a power encounter, when a demonized fortune teller was set free (Ac 16:16-18). Another major invasion into enemy territory took place in Ephesus, where Paul confronted a society bound by Satan and black magic (Ac 19). He "performed extraordinary miracles ... so that handkerchiefs or aprons were even carried from his body to the sick, and diseases left them and the evil spirits went out" (Ac 19:11-12). The result? "The word of the Lord was growing mightily and prevailing" (Ac 19:20).

Luke writes to a context where magic flourished.[6] Magic was a very real temptation for the early church–just as it is for those who come to Christ from a folk Islamic context. Because of this, Luke has carefully crafted his narrative to equip the church to confront magic in power-oriented societies. Luke intentionally selects key stories and develops them in such a way as to: 1) clarify the difference between magic and miracle,[7] 2) equip the church for spiritual warfare against the forces of darkness most focally expressed in magic, and 3) make a clear connection between pioneer missions and power ministry.

Luke develops an anti-magic polemic in Acts. He records these encounters not only to demonstrate the supernatural confirmation of the gospel through signs and wonders, but also to contrast Satan-inspired magic with Holy Spirit-empowered miracle. One is based on formulas and manipulation, having its source in Satan; the other is based on faith and supplication, having its source in God. As Howard Kee notes, "There is clear evidence that the power of the Holy Spirit and that of magic are seen to be in competition, beginning with the launching of the mission of the church to the Gentiles" (1983:119).

Sir William Ramsay concurs:

> There is no class of opponents with whom the earliest Christian Apostles and missionaries are brought into collision so frequently, and whose opposition is described as being so obstinate and determined, as the magicians. *They play a very considerable part in the book of the Acts*" (1953:113 emphasis added).

Susan Garrett's outstanding book, *The Demise of the Devil: Magic and the Demonic in Luke's Writings,* also underscores the importance of magic in Acts. She notes that "Luke's particular treatment was extensive and consistent: he demonstrated that magicians have no chance of success in the new era inaugurated by Christ's resurrection.

... Luke's treatment of magic and magicians bears upon the interpretation of all of Luke-Acts" (1989:10 emphasis added).

Luke records four "showdowns" between missionaries and magicians in Acts. These power encounters function like windows into the world of the occult, which is so much like the world of folk Islam. These "duels" illustrate various aspects of magic and portray different approaches to defeat the devil.

Acts 8:5-24

And Philip went down to the city of Samaria and began proclaiming Christ to them. And the multitudes with one accord were giving attention to what was said by Philip, as they heard and saw the signs which he was performing. For in the case of many who had unclean spirits, they were coming out of them shouting with a loud voice and many who had been paralyzed and lame were healed. And there was much rejoicing in that city. Now there was a certain man named Simon who formerly was practicing magic in the city, and astonishing the people of Samaria, claiming to be someone great: and they all from the smallest to greatest, were giving attention to him, saying "This man is what is called the Great Power of God." And they were giving him attention because he had for a long time astonished them with his magic arts. But when they believed Philip preaching the good news about the kingdom of God and the name of Jesus Christ, they were being baptized, men and women alike. And even Simon himself believed; and after being baptized, he continued on with Philip; and as he observed signs and great miracles taking place, he was constantly amazed. Now when the apostles in Jerusalem heard that Samaria had received the word of God, they sent them Peter and John ... then they began laying their hands on them and they were receiving the Holy Spirit. Now when Simon saw the Spirit was bestowed through the laying on of the apostles hands, he offered them money, saying "Give this authority to me as well, so that everyone on whom I lay my hands may receive the Holy Spirit." But Peter said to him, "May your silver perish with you, because you thought you could obtain the gift of God with money! You have no part or portion in this matter, for your heart is not right before God. Therefore repent of this wickedness of yours and pray the Lord that if possible, the intention of your heart may be forgiven you. For I see that you are in the gall of bitterness and in the bondage of iniquity."

Luke purposely selects this account to remind us that missions is all about turning people from darkness to light, from the dominion of

Satan to the kingdom of God (26:18). The whole world does lie in the power of the evil one (1 Jn 5:19). Thus, when the gospel enters new territory, it is entering enemy territory. A clash between the kingdom of darkness and the kingdom of light undoubtedly will follow. It is no coincidence that Philip encounters magic in Samaria.

Philip was one of the original seven called to minister with the Apostles by serving tables (Ac 6:1-7) and the only person in the New Testament specifically described as having the gift of evangelism (Ac 21:8). His ministry in Samaria is the quintessential model of what John Wimber calls "power evangelism" (1986). Truth encounter was coupled with power encounter. This spirit-filled evangelist proclaimed the gospel with signs following. In other words, the *manifestations* of the kingdom pointed to and corroborated the *message* of the kingdom.

Philip's gospel centered around Jesus and the kingdom of God (8:5, 12). Two important themes are implicit in this gospel presentation. First, the close connection between the kingdom of God and the name of Jesus implies that Jesus is the way that the kingdom of God is experienced in our lives. The name of Jesus is the means by which God's kingly power is manifested among us.[8] Second, by proclaiming the kingdom of God Philip indicates that his preaching focused on the relationship and rescue (Godward/Satanward) dimensions of the gospel. This kingdom orientation means he not only spoke of *reconciliation* with God, but also *release* from Satan, emphasizing *forgiveness* through Christ as well as *freedom* from Satan.

Luke says that the Samaritans *heard and saw* the signs which Philip was performing. They saw God heal many who were paralyzed and lame. They also heard the signs because those with unclean spirits were shouting with a loud voice (v 7; see Mk 1:26, 5:5,7). This was a boisterous evangelistic meeting!

Philip was engaged in what Peter Wagner refers to as *ground-level spiritual warfare* – healing and casting demons out of ordinary people. But Luke indicates that Philip also engaged in *occult-level spiritual warfare*, which means confrontation with magicians, witches or shaman (1994:217). Philip met Simon (a power person), the first magician mentioned in Acts.[9]

Through the use of repetition, Luke underscores important facts about Simon. Twice he mentions that Simon practiced magic and says that Simon astonished the people of Samaria with his arts (vs 9, 11). Simon's self-acclaimed greatness (v 9) and the public affirmation of his greatness ("the great power of God," v 10) are recorded.

The description of Simon as the great power of God must be understood against the backdrop of a magical worldview. The word *dunamis* (variously translated as power or miracle) is described in Moulton and Milligan as "one of the most common and characteristic terms in the language of pagan devotion. 'Power' was what the devotees respected and worshipped" (1929:172). This is quite similar to the pursuit of power among folk Muslims today.

Some commentators believe that these affirmations of greatness imply that Simon was regarded as some kind of a god (Newman and Nida 1972:175). Even if he was not, these words smack of idolatry and self-deification. At the very least, these facts also suggest that Simon was no mere novice or underling in the realm of darkness. He was a powerful servant in Satan's kingdom.

Simon believed the gospel and was baptized (v 13). He then followed Philip around, "like a fan of a rock star" (Witherington 1998:285), watching him minister. Luke highlights important differences between Simon's power and Philip's power. The greatness of Philip's signs (vs 6, 13) are contrasted with Simon's magic (vs 9, 11), for Philip's power astonishes even Simon (v 13).[10] In addition, the very terms Luke uses underscore the difference. While Simon's power is described as magic, Philip's power is described as a "sign." It is a marker, if you will, pointing to the kingdom of God. The miracle points to the message.

Simon's astonishment changed to greed, however, when Peter and John joined Philip's outreach. Simon saw Peter and John lay hands on people to receive the Holy Spirit.[11] He mistakenly assumed that the laying on of hands was some kind of new power ritual.[12] Although there is no mention of tongues (as elsewhere in Acts), something visibly supernatural was clearly taking place that demonstrated the

Holy Spirit had come upon people. Simon tried to "bargain" with Peter for his power: "Give this authority to me as well, so that everyone on whom I lay my hands may receive the Holy Spirit" (v 19). Simon the magician, the power person, reverted to his old ways. He was thinking like a magician again, and magicians generally charged a fee for their services. The one who was accustomed to acclaim as "the great power of God" now wanted the same power demonstrated by the apostles. As a magician, he was looking for customers, not converts (Talbert 1997:85). He wanted power for the wrong reasons and sought it through the wrong methods. Susan Garrett sums up the situation:

> Simon's offer of money to Peter is for Luke not only blasphemous but absurd: the magician wanted to purchase divine authority while himself still trapped under diabolical authority. ... Christian authority is in no way like magical-Satanic authority, for the latter can be bought but the former is solely a gift of God. The Holy Spirit can be used and is used by God to confirm the word proclaimed by God's servants, but it cannot be used to bring glory to an individual.[13]

Peter's "meaning is 'To hell with you and your money!'" (Dunn 1996:112). This condemnation is stern but appropriate for a magician like Simon. Peter was not rebuking an overzealous new believer. He was confronting one who was experienced in the powers of darkness. Peter's scathing rebuke and pointed call to repentance exposes the deeper issues of Simon's heart (vs 21-22). He was not right before God; he was wicked, in the gall of bitterness and in the bondage of iniquity. Thus, "the story ends with Simon, the magician, depicted as one who is baptized but not changed and as one with whom God is not pleased" (Talbert 1997:87).

Luke includes this account in the history of the church's advance in order to equip us to evangelize people mesmerized by magic and steeped in the occult. He makes two practical points about dealing with magic.

A magical view of power is incompatible with the gospel. First, magical power exalts the magician rather than the Messiah. Second, magical power has no meaning beyond itself. It is not a sign confirming a message. Third, magical power has monetary motivations, whereas the message of the kingdom and the miracles of the kingdom are expressions of grace, freely given.

Power evangelism includes truth encounter. In one sense, Philip and Peter outdid the magicians at their own game. They did not shrink back from power encounter because it might not be understood.[14] They healed the sick, cast out demons and prayed for the fullness of the Holy Spirit. A power-oriented society must be confronted by power.

However, truth encounter is ultimately what distinguishes Satanic power from the Spirit's power.[15] Simon "was more interested in the great acts of power accompanying Philip's preaching than God's reign in his life" (Longenecker 1981:358). As a typical magician, Simon wanted possession of the power without submission to the source of the power. Philip preached the kingdom of God. This message demands submission to the king. It also includes repentance – turning from the kingdom of darkness. Truth encounter and power encounter go hand in hand to extend the kingdom.

> **Acts 13:8-12**
> But Elymas [also called Bar-Jesus] the magician ... was opposing them, seeking to turn the proconsul away from the faith. But Saul, who was also known as Paul, filled with the Holy Spirit, fixed his gaze upon him, and said, "You who are full of all deceit and fraud, you son of the devil, you enemy of all righteousness, will you not cease to make crooked the straight ways of the Lord? And now behold, the hand of the Lord is upon you, and you will be blind and not see the sun for a time." And immediately a mist and a darkness fell upon him, and he went about seeking those who would lead him by the hand. Then the proconsul believed when he saw what had happened, being amazed at the teaching of the Lord.

The first recorded event of Paul's first missionary journey is a power encounter on the island of Cyprus.[16] Luke's selection and placement of this as the frontispiece to Paul's missionary career indicates its significance. Moreover, "in narrating the apostles' confrontation with Bar-Jesus, Luke focuses more on the defeat of the magician than on the conversion of the proconsul. Bar-Jesus is introduced before Sergius Paulus and in greater detail. He is the more prominent actor in the narrative as the opponent of Christ's messengers" (Johnson 1997:172-173).

There are also significant contrasts between the magic of Simon and the magic of Bar-Jesus. Whereas Simon astonished the Samaritans with his powerful acts, Bar-Jesus guided the proconsul with his prophetic words. Simon's magic demonstrated supernatural power, while Bar-Jesus' magic stressed supernatural knowledge.

Luke includes a number of important details about this dramatic encounter. First, Bar-Jesus the magician worked closely with Sergius Paulus, a Roman proconsul. Apparently this magician served in the governor's court. Second, Bar-Jesus is specifically described as a magician (in Greek, *magos*). *Magos* is a "Persian loan word, which originally referred to one who was a member of a particular kind of priesthood ... [and] had come in New Testament times to mean 'sorcerer,' 'magician,' or even 'swindler' or 'charlatan' " (Newman and Nida 1972:247). Third, Bar-Jesus was also a Jewish false prophet (Ac 13:6), that is, he falsely claimed to be a medium of divine revelation. Fourth, this magician and false prophet tried "to turn the proconsul away from the faith" (Ac 13:8).

Because the magician sought to interfere with the preaching of the gospel, Paul confronted him. This was no mere rebuke. After being filled with the Spirit (v 9), Paul speaks forth a piercing string of condemnatory charges (v 10):

- "You are full of all deceit and fraud"
- "You son of the devil"
- "You enemy of all righteousness"
- "Will you not cease to make crooked the straight ways of the Lord?"

These Spirit-inspired words unmask the magician's diabolical motivations and intentions. Paul's description could not be stronger or more vivid. This magician is not just deceptive or fraudulent, he is *full* of *all* deceit and fraud. He does not just have enemies, but is himself the enemy of *all* righteousness. His crooked ways are contrasted with the straight ways of the Lord, and thus Paul calls him the "son of the devil." Next, Paul pronounces a judgment or curse upon the magician. Through Paul's prophetic word, God blinds the magician, so that he goes "about seeking those who would lead him by the hand" (v 11).

Luke concludes his account by focusing on the response of the proconsul to the encounter. "Then the proconsul believed when he saw what happened, being amazed at the teaching of the Lord" (v 12). The teaching of the Lord was confirmed by a sign from the Lord— again both a truth encounter and a power encounter. The proconsul believed when he saw the encounter and heard the word. Luke "brings before his readers a dramatic power encounter, in which the Holy Spirit overthrew the evil one, the apostle confounded the sorcerer, and the gospel triumphed over the occult" (Stott 1990:22).

What significance does this encounter with a first-century magician have for those of us working among folk Muslims? There are at least four principles of note in this account.

The kingdom of darkness stands behind magicians. While the primary orientation for the kingdom of darkness is ostensibly power, in reality its ultimate orientation is a moral one—or more precisely, immoral. An implacably evil spiritual kingdom seeks to hinder the spread of the gospel. Both the confrontation with Bar-Jesus and Luke's commentary underscore the nature of our warfare. This magician was seeking to do in the physical realm what the "god of this world" does in the spiritual realm: "blinding the minds of the unbelieving that they might not see the light of the gospel of the glory of Christ" (2 Cor 4:4). Though at times its servants appear as an angel of light (2 Cor 11:14), the kingdom of Satan is nevertheless a kingdom of darkness and wickedness (Eph 6:12).

The fullness of the Spirit is key to power encounter. Paul was "filled with the Holy Spirit" just before his supernatural encounter with the magician who was full of all deceit and fraud. The same was true of Philip. While not directly stated in the story of Philip and Simon,

Luke makes it clear that it was a Spirit-filled Philip who penetrated Samaria through signs and wonders (Ac 6:3,5).[17]

Evangelism should involve both truth encounter and power encounter. Paul's power encounter with Bar-Jesus took place while he was evangelizing Sergius Paulus. Again, kingdom proclamation and kingdom demonstration go hand-in-hand.

Curses or judgments may be used in power encounter.[18] This passage describes what Paul did, but it does not imply that this is normative for us. We may approach magicians in the same highly confrontational approach, by using a curse, but this is by no means normative. The text allows for it but does not demand it. However, if this apostolic practice is imitated, we had better be filled with the Spirit and led by the Spirit! Anyone experienced in power ministry knows that the Spirit's leading and anointing is crucial to the success of the encounter.

Comparisons between this encounter and other important power encounters in the Bible provide us with further context. For example, when Moses encounters the magicians of Egypt, he is not confrontational, as Paul was with Bar-Jesus. Nor does he resort to a direct curse upon the Egyptian magicians (Ex 7-14). Elijah's power encounter with the prophets of Baal is closer to Paul's encounter with Bar-Jesus (1 K 18). Elijah uses a highly confrontational approach. Still, he pronounces no direct curse upon the prophets of Baal – although afterward he slays them all!

The other encounters with magicians in Acts do not include a cursing model of power encounter. Simon the magician is not cursed (Ac 8).[19] The fortune-telling slave girl is not cursed (Ac 16), and there is no mention of cursing in Paul's encounters at Ephesus (Ac 19-20). Hence, while cursing has apostolic precedent, it is not a typical nor normative approach to confronting magic.

Acts 16:16-18

And it happened that as we were going to the place of prayer, a certain slave-girl having a spirit of divination met us, who was bringing her masters much profit by fortune telling. Following after

Paul and us, she kept crying out, saying, "These men are bond-servants of the Most High God, who are proclaiming to you the way of salvation." And she continued doing this for many days. But Paul was greatly annoyed, and turned and said to the spirit, "I command you in the name of Jesus Christ to come out of her!" And it came out at that very moment.

The third recorded power encounter in Acts takes place between Paul and a girl with a spirit of divination–literally, a python spirit (*pneuma pythona*). This slave girl was doubly bound–spiritually and economically. Her masters oppressed her physically and made great profit from her spiritually.

The comment that she brought profit to her masters seems to imply that she was controlled by a powerful spirit. C. Peter Wagner observes, "How was it that they could make so much money through this fortune-teller? The obvious answer is that this slave girl was good at fortune telling. She knew the future, and she had built a sound reputation for accuracy. ... The slave girl had not gained her stature in the occult community by making constant mistakes" (1995:69).

This python spirit originally referred to "a snake, and in particular the snake which guarded the celebrated oracle at Delphi and which was said to have been slain by Apollo" (Marshall 1983:268). According to this mythology, the pytheness was inspired by Apollo to predict the future.[20]

During their numerous encounters, the demonized fortune-teller carried out a promotional campaign for Paul's team. She followed them around for many days, crying out, "These men are bond-servants of the Most High God, who are proclaiming to you the way of salvation" (v 17). Finally, Paul confronted the slave girl. Why he waited so long to confront the demon is puzzling. We are not told why he waited. We can infer that he was waiting on God's timing for the encounter. Since our authority comes from God, we must wait on him for anointing and timing.

Paul commanded the python spirit to come out in the name of Jesus. When the slave owners saw their hope of profit gone, they seized Paul and Silas, beat them and threw them into prison. Spiritual encounter led to physical persecution. But the underlying reason for the persecution was economic. Johnson rightly notes, "The operative motive for the practitioners of divination is neither the quest for truth nor the pursuit of holiness. Rather, profit is their bottom line" (1997:177).

What are the practical implications of this encounter for us?

We have spiritual authority over the powers of darkness. There are significant differences between Jesus' and Paul's exorcisms. Jesus' authority is personal and direct; he commands the demons to come out and they obey. People were amazed at his authority to exorcise demons (Lk 4:36). Whereas Jesus' authority is personal and direct, Paul's authority is centered in Christ and derived from him. Jesus says merely "Come out," but Paul (and we) must say, "Come out *in Jesus' name!*" The authority of the believer is rooted in Christ. It flows out of relationship (in contrast to ritual) and is based on faith (in contrast to formulas). We have authority because Christ dwells in us, commissions us and accompanies us (Col 1:27; Jn 20:21; Mt 28:18-20; Eph 2:6). This principle provides a foundation for all spiritual warfare (Eph 6:10).

We command demons. Paul did not ask God to cast out the demon. He commanded the demon to leave. This method of exorcism – what some call the prayer of command – is an apostolic practice based on the biblical principle of Christ's authority. Jesus commanded sick bodies to be healed and demons to leave the demonized (Lk 4:35-36, 39). This authoritative approach to the demonic realm is unique to the signs and wonders dimension of Scripture and was the practice of the early church (Ac 3:6; 9:34, 40). This is a *power ritual.*

Acts 19:8-20

And God was performing extraordinary miracles by the hands of Paul, so that handkerchiefs or aprons were even carried from his body to the sick, and the diseases left them and the evil spirits went out. ... Many also of those who had believed kept coming, confessing and disclosing their practices. And many of those who practiced magic brought their books together and began burning them in the sight of all; and they counted the price of them and found it fifty thousand pieces of silver. So the word of the Lord was growing mightily and prevailing.

Paul labored in Ephesus for approximately three years – evangelizing, teaching, healing the sick, casting out demons, raising up leaders and sending out church planters (or church-planting teams) to the surrounding region. Power encounter was an important aspect of Paul's ministry in this city famous for its magic. We have a fairly detailed account of both the magic encountered and the method employed by Paul. In fact, Acts describes more accounts of the demonic in Paul's ministry at Ephesus than in any other location.

Luke says that "God was performing extraordinary miracles by the hands of Paul" (Ac 19:11). The Greek construction in verses 11-12 implies that Luke has in mind two types of extraordinary miracles (Longenecker 1981:496; Haenchen 1971:562). First, miracles were done by the hands of Paul, implying that these miracles took place through the laying on of hands. Laying on of hands is an important part of apostolic tradition, though there are other models of power ministry in the New Testament (Ac 5:12; 8:17; 9:34, 40; 14:3, 9,10; 16:18). Bruce says, "Not merely Paul's agency but the active use of his hands is implied" (1990a:410). While the laying on of hands is more than a mere ritual, it is also that. Paul uses a *power ritual* that was well known among Jews (Twelftree 1993:158) and Hellenistic Greeks (Edelstein 1945, 1:448, 456).

Second, in order to open up this new field, the message of the kingdom (Ac 19:8, 20:25) was accompanied by the manifestations of the kingdom: "extraordinary miracles" (Ac 19:11-13). The word "extraordinary" seems odd alongside the word "miracle," for a miracle is by nature "extraordinary." However, in this demon-infested environment, polluted with every kind of evil magical practice, the type of power encounters necessary to bring this city to Christ had to be dramatic. Hence, the miracles described by Luke at Ephesus were different in kind. Not only did signs and wonders take place *directly* through the laying on of Paul's hands, but also *indirectly:* "Handkerchiefs or aprons were even carried from his body to the sick, and the diseases left them and the evil spirits went out" (Ac 19:12). Here is a case where *power objects* were used to heal. Again, this is not the normal means of power encounter in the New Testament. I. Howard Marshall comments:

It is undeniably difficult to distinguish what is described here in verse 12 from primitive and crude beliefs in *mana*, i.e., in a quasi-physical power emanating from the healer and infecting his clothes so that these can be the vehicles of supernatural power. It is surprising that Luke, who is so critical of pagan magic, can allow that similar magical beliefs in a Christianized form were effective in the apostolic ministry. Perhaps we may suggest that God is capable of condescending to the level of men who still think in such crude ways (1980:310).

God is not only capable of condescending to communicate to us, he has done so. Alongside Paul's handkerchiefs at Ephesus, God empowered Moses' staff to do miracles in Egypt (Ex 4), Elisha's bones brought a man back to life (2 K 13:21), a woman was healed by touching the hem of Jesus garment (Mk 5:27-30), Jesus used saliva to heal the sick[21] (Mk 7:33, 8:23) and Peter's mere shadow brought healing (Ac 5:15). While these are not necessarily models to imitate, they indicate that God has indeed condescended in this fashion.[22]

Apparently the Ephesian magicians practiced what is known as contagious magic, in contrast to imitative magic. Imitative and contagious magic are terms originally coined by the anthropologist Sir James G. Frazer. Imitative magic refers to formulas that imitate the ends sought by the magician and is based on the law of similarity. Perhaps the most familiar example of this is when someone wants to injure or destroy an enemy by injuring or destroying an image of him (1963:14).

Contagious magic, on the other hand, assumes that materials or substances once in contact with the intended victim can be used against him. This is the law of contact. This is practiced, for example, when someone finds a victim's hair or nails and uses them to work his evil purposes on the victim from a distance (ibid:43).

Luke's account does not make it clear whether these encounters took place because of Paul's initiation or because of God's accommodation. If Paul took the initiative, then he used the methods of the magicians. Dean Gilliland exclaims, "What a risk he took! The orthodox would have accused him of syncretism ... Paul's method was that of contagious magic all right, but the consequence was healing, demonic confrontation and, 'the name of the Lord was extolled.' " (Wagner and Pennoyer 1990:337).

If in fact Paul did use the methods of contagious magic, he did not water down the gospel or compromise truth in adopting these forms. He was contextualizing. Three things kept these (questionable or at least interesting) methods from being syncretistic. First of all, Paul's ministry of signs and wonders was done in the context of a teaching ministry. For two years he was "reasoning daily in the school of Tyrannus" (Ac 19:9-10). He was actively teaching the "whole counsel of God" (Ac 19:8; 20:25, 27). Paul's ministry at Ephesus was both supernatural and rational. It was Spirit-empowered and biblically-based. It involved power encounter and truth encounter.

Second, Paul's teaching centered around the kingdom of God (Ac 19:18, 20:25), and this emphasis on the kingdom would have clarified the differences between the kingdom of God and the kingdom of Satan, thus highlighting the distinction between miracle and magic.

Third, Paul demanded true repentance and faith. In his farewell address to the Ephesian elders, he summarized his message as "repentance toward God and faith in our Lord Jesus Christ" (Ac 20:21). There was a moral and volitional dimension to his message. This emphasis brought the Ephesian believers to make a clean break with the occult by renouncing their demonic practices and destroying their charms, amulets and magical paraphernalia (Ac 19:18-19).

However, Paul may not have been using the methods of the magicians. These encounters could just as easily be understood as taking place outside of Paul's initiation. If this is true, then Luke's account still describes a case of contextualization, but rather than Paul, it was God who was contextualizing – choosing to manifest his healing power in ways that those from a magical background could fathom. He met them at their point of need, within their frame of reference.

Whether is was Paul's initiation or God's accommodation, teaching about the kingdom of God and repentance insured that these encounters would not be misunderstood. These *manifestations* of the kingdom pointed to and corroborated the *message* of the kingdom.

Paul's power encounters at Ephesus not only resulted in fruitful ministry, but also syncretistic response. True power ministry has Satanic counterfeits. The power demonstrated in Paul's ministry was obviously impressive. It was especially impressive to some Jewish exorcists, *power people*, who wanted to add some Christian tools to their Jewish occultic practices.[23]

The Jewish exorcists (the seven sons of Sceva) wanted to borrow the *power ritual* of Jesus' name to enhance their powers. In a magical worldview, to know the name of someone or something was to ensure one's control over it (cf. Oster 1974:48-53). The superficial resemblance between what they saw and heard Paul doing, and their specialty, led them to appropriate this new ritual. This attitude was typical of Jewish *power people* during the New Testament era.[24]

However, this mechanistic or ritualistic use of the name proved futile. The demon they sought to cast out responded both verbally and physically. First, he questioned the Jewish exorcists. "I recognize Jesus, and I know about Paul, but who are you?" (Ac 19:15).[25] Second, the demonized man attacked and severely wounded the would-be exorcists.[26]

The name of Jesus was like an unfamiliar weapon that exploded in their hands. Jesus would not let his name be reduced to a magical formula. He is nobody's lackey. Thus, Luke employs this dramatic encounter as an implicit polemic against magic. Without actually preaching directly to his audience about the folly of magic, he makes his point unmistakably clear (Kurz 1993:146-147).

This failed attempt at power encounter became well known with startling results. First of all, there was a general sense of awe: "Fear fell upon them all." There was the realization that the name of Jesus was not something to be toyed with. Second, the very name that was used as a mantra was now being magnified. Third, those who were involved in the occult began burning their magic books as a sign of repentance.

Luke says that many of those who "had believed" (*pepisteukoton*) were confessing and disclosing their practices (v 18). The use of *pepisteukoton,* a perfect participle, indicates that Luke has the Ephesian Christians in mind.[27] Paul's ministry, along with this incident, "stirred the saints to confess the hold that the occult had retained on them even after they became believers" (Harrison 1986:312).[28] They made a clean break from their dual allegiance and syncretistic understanding of truth.

Why this dramatic response? "The obvious answer is that in Luke's understanding the Ephesians perceived the defeat of the seven sons to be a defeat of magic in general: magic has become obsolete (Garrett 1989:95).

Luke's description of the event is enlightening. Since magic is based on secret ritual, the way to break its power over people is through public confession and disclosure of its practice (Ac 19:18). There was also the public destruction of the magical paraphernalia. "They brought their books together and began burning them in the sight of all" (Ac 19:19).

The books probably include magical paraphernalia similar to those found in the magical papyri–ancient magical formulas for healing, protection, blessing and cursing (Betz 1992 and Preisendanz 1973, 1974). These would most certainly include the famous "Ephesian Letters" (*Ephesia Grammata*). The Ephesian Letters were "the most noted magical formula of antiquity ... the magical formula *par excellence* in the Hellenistic world" (McCown 1923:128). These were *power objects* that were used in *power rituals.*

Perhaps Paul's persuasive call to repentance was based, at least in part, on Deuteronomy 7:25, "The graven images of their gods you are to burn with fire; you shall not covet the silver or the gold that is on them, nor take it for yourselves, lest you be snared by it, for it is an abomination to the Lord your God."

Luke says that 50,000 Greek drachmas worth of magical books were burned. Commentators differ as to a contemporary financial equivalent. Larkin posits $35,000 worth of books (1995:278), Newman and Nida feel $50,000 is a good estimate (1972:369), while Harrison believes "it is impossible to estimate the amount involved" (1986:313). According to Haenchen, a drachma was the equivalent of a day's wage (1971:567). Thus Wagner concludes, "If each piece of silver represents a day's wage, in today's terms at $10 an hour for eight-hour days, or $80 a day, it would total $4 million. Quite a book burning!" (1995b:169). Whatever the precise equivalent may be, Luke's emphasis is clear. The burning of the magical books was an expensive affair. True repentance can be costly.

Acts 19:20 functions as a climax and summary for the entire section: "So the word of the Lord was growing mightily and prevailing." Through Paul's ministry of teaching and power encounter, the gospel was advancing and the kingdom of God was being extended. In fact, Paul's ministry at Ephesus "has the characteristics of a people movement, especially considering the communal decision to burn magical books and other paraphernalia publicly" (Wagner 1996:215).[29]

Principles of Confronting Powers

What is Luke saying to the church about confronting power-oriented societies? Three principles stand out.

We may employ power objects in our healing ministries. Some Evangelicals will feel uneasy about this approach, but it is biblical. God used Paul's handkerchiefs and aprons to convey His healing power. God met the Ephesians within their frame of reference, at their point of need. He has and will continue to do so in power-oriented societies. Though it has biblical warrant, this approach is not normative– it is an approach we "may" employ.

Miracle is based on relationship, whereas magic is based on ritual. The name of Jesus is not a power ritual that can be used indiscriminately. Talbert explains:

> Since a magician has no personal relationship with the power involved but simply uses it for his own purposes, these exorcists who are not disciples of Jesus attempt to use the name of Jesus, with whom Paul has the relationship. The Lukan point is that the spiritual power manifest through Jesus' disciples like Paul is not appropriated or dispensed as a commodity (see 8:18-24) but is the result of a personal relationship with the risen Lord (1997:176).

Dual allegiance or syncretism is denounced. Renunciation of the occult and repentance from all ties with magic are demanded. Luke's polemic against magic climaxes with the burning of the magic paraphernalia. Luke records this act of public repentance to underscore the depth of repentance necessary for true conversion.

The chart that follows summarizes some of the main themes in each of Luke's four accounts of magic in Acts. These passages raises two other missiological issues related to power and spiritual warfare. 1) How does power ministry compare with magic? 2) Was Paul confronting a territorial spirit at Ephesus when he encountered Artemis (Acts 19:23-41)? We consider these questions below.

Magic versus Miracle

How does power ministry compare with magic? A superficial, "outsider's" perspective of healing and exorcism in the New Testament could lead many to believe that Christian miracle is no different than pagan magic. For example, Christians can appear to be manipulating God (or the gods) when they command demons. Prayers

Text	Acts 8:4-24	Acts 13:4-12	Acts 16:16-18	Acts 19:11-20
The Magician	Simon the magician	Elymas the magician	a slave girl with a python spirit	Jewish exorcists
The type of Magic	Power (productive, protective and destructive?)	divination	divination	power (productive, protective, and destructive?), contagious magic
Evangelistic Approach	power and truth encounter	power and truth encournter	power encounter	power and truth encounter
Role of the Magician(s)	a professing convert	an opponent	a bystander	bystanders and converts?
Weapons of our Warfare Emphasized	the fullness of the Holy Spirit	the fullness of the Holy Spirit	the name of Jesus (properly used)	the name of Jesus (improperly used)
Errors Exposed	economic motive, manipulation instead of submission, evil intents of the heart, syncretism	economic motive and evil intents of the heart	economic motive	manipulation instead of submission, syncretism

Table 11: Comparing and Contrasting Luke's Four Accounts of Magic in Acts

of healing and deliverance in the Bible are not usually prayers addressed to God but rather authoritative commands addressed to demons or sickness:

- "Be quiet!" Jesus said sternly. "Come out of him!" (Lk 4:35).
- So he [Jesus] bent over her and rebuked the fever and it left her (Lk 4:39).
- "In the name of Jesus Christ of Nazareth, stand up and walk" (Ac 3:6).
- Turning toward the dead woman, he said, "Tabitha, get up" (Ac 9:40).

- Paul looked directly at him ... and called out, "Stand up on your feet!" (Ac 14:10).
- Paul became so troubled that he turned around and said to the spirit, "In the name of Jesus Christ I command you to come out of her!" (Ac 16:18).
- "Brother Saul, receive your sight!" (Ac 22:13).

It would also be easy to interpret other Christian methods of healing as *power rituals*. For example, Jesus used spittle and mud to heal (Mk 7:33, 8:23, Jn 9:6), the early church used the name of Jesus (Ac 3:6, 16:18), and both Jesus and the early church used the laying on of hands (Lk 4:40, Ac 28:8). All these rituals, which could be easily imitated, appear to be central to the success of the miracle. As noted, Simon the magician (Ac 8:17-24) thought the laying on of hands was some sort of key to spiritual power. Outsiders like Simon would not necessarily realize that there is no inherent power in any of these rituals. Nor would they know that intimacy with Christ and the fullness of the Spirit are the vital factors in a healing ministry.

An analysis of the six components of folk religion (*powers, power people, power objects, power rituals, power places, power times*) indicate that some of the components are central to Christian power ministry, others may be evident, while still others should probably not be imitated. The Christian faith unequivocally affirms *power* (the Holy Spirit), *power people* (Christians anointed and gifted by the Holy Spirit) and *power rituals* (the use of the name of Jesus, the laying on of hands, baptism, the Lord's Supper).[30] *Power objects* are possible in unique contexts (Paul's handkerchiefs and aprons, Moses' staff) but are by no means normative.

I struggle more with the relevance of *power places* and *power times* because there is no New Testament precedent for them (like we see for the other four categories). It is true that the Temple in the Old Testament could be viewed as a *power place* and that the three great feasts (Passover, Pentecost and the Feast of Tabernacles) could be understood as *power times*. However, this doesn't necessarily mean we can "borrow" times or places from Islamic cultures and view them as valid power places or times. *Power places* and *power objects* borrowed from Israel's neighbors – such as altars, high places, sacred pillars, and Asherim (2 Chronicles 14:3) – were a great stumbling block to God's people. These borrowed "forms" of worship resulted in syncretism and gross idolatry. Similarly today, I believe that putting special emphasis on *power times* or *power places* runs a high risk of syncretism.[31]

The major difference between miracle and magic is not primarily at the level of form or methodology. As we note above, there can be many external or superficial similarities between the two. Yet at least five major differences distinguish magic and miracle in the New Testament.

The crucial difference is the source of the power. Magic can be evaluated phenomenologically. That is, the forms and phenomena of magic can be studied by, for example, an atheistic anthropologist. However, we must evaluate these forms and phenomena *ontologically*, that is, we must understand the "beings" behind the forms. While both miracle and magic are supernatural, miracles come from God, magic from Satan. This may be easy for us to understand, but it isn't necessarily so for people from power-oriented societies.

All demonstrations of power are not from God. Thus, the Bible encourages us to evaluate manifestations of power ontologically: "Beloved, do not believe every spirit but test the spirits to see whether they are from God; ... By this you know the Spirit of God: every spirit that confesses that Jesus Christ has come in the flesh is from God, and every spirit that does not confess Jesus is not from God" (1 Jn 4:1-2; cf. 1 Co 12:3). Manifestations of power not having a Christ-centered focus are demonic.

Miracles are based on relationship with God. Whereas magic approaches the spirit realm through manipulation, Christians approach the living God through supplication. We cannot cajole or control God. We depend on him for power. Intimacy with him is the foundation for every dimension of our walk. Relationship, not ritual, is our basis for power. Faith, not formulas, is the key to biblical miracle.[32] Consequently, questions regarding the power person's relationship with God must be asked. Is this person's walk with God genuine? Do they model a close friendship with God?

Miracles in the New Testament demonstrate the kingdom of God. That is, they must be understood eschatologically–as manifestations of the future kingdom of God breaking into the present. They are not just demonstrations of power, they are signs (or manifestations) of the kingdom of God. As Jesus said, "But if I drive out demons by the Spirit of God, then the kingdom of God has come upon you" (Mt 12:28). Jesus, and then the early church, extended the kingdom through word and deed. Power encounter (the deed of the kingdom) is linked to truth encounter (the word of the kingdom). Manifestations of the kingdom are understood against the backdrop of the message of the kingdom.

Hence, we need to ask questions regarding the nature of this manifestation of power. Does it extend the kingdom in any way? Does it exalt the King?

Miracles have an ethical impact. Because miracles are signs of the kingdom, they reflect the ethics of the kingdom. Kingdom power demonstrates God's love and concern for people. It strengthens us, too, to love them, whereas magic is self-serving and self-centered.

Satan counterfeits or replicates God's signs and wonders. He, too, can heal or cast out demons through a magician. However, he cannot imitate the fruit of the Spirit. Jesus speaks of people who use his name to do mighty works of power. They are described as lawless, with no ethical mooring, and ultimately they will not enter the kingdom (Mt 7:21-23; see also Ac 19:13-16).

By their fruit you will know God's miracle workers. Thus, we must ask, "Does this power person exhibit the fruit of the Spirit in his or her life?" Or "Does this act of power somehow demonstrates God's character?"

True miracles reflect a God-centered, gracious motivation. Biblical demonstrations of power are gracious acts done for God's glory. Hence, a magical view of power is incompatible with biblical miracle at the level of motivation. Magical power exalts the magician rather than the Messiah. Simon claimed to be "someone great" (Ac 8:9). In addition, magical power often has monetary motivations, whereas the message of the kingdom and the miracles of the kingdom are expressions of grace, freely given. "Magical manipulation is a manifestation of the common human quest for a 'salvation by works,' our hunger to control our own destinies, to break free from our need for, and dependence on, divine grace" (Johnson 1997:184).

Consequently, we should ask the question of motivation. "Why does this power person do this?" "What is his or her motivation?" "Who receives the glory?"

Thus miracle differs from magic *ontologically* (its source is God, not Satan), *relationally* (miracle flows from relationship, not ritual), *eschatologically* (miracles are manifestations of the kingdom of God), *ethically* (the power of the kingdom reflects the ethics of the kingdom) and *motivationally* (miracles are gracious acts of power done to glorify God). The table that follows summarizes these themes.

Differences	Magic	Miracle
Ontological	Source is Satan	Source is God
Relational	Focus is on ritual	Focus is on relationship
Eschatological	Manifestation of the kingdom of Satan	Manifestation of the kingdom of God
Ethical	No ethical orientation	Ethical orientation
Motivational	Self-serving and works-oriented	God-centered and grace-oriented

Table 12: Discerning the Differences Between Magic and Miracle

Artemis: A Territorial Spirit?

Was Paul confronting a territorial spirit at Ephesus when he encountered Artemis? While there may be some controversy over how one engages territorial spirits, scholars generally agree that territorial spirits exist. Passages like Daniel 10:12-21 and Ephesians 6:12, supported and illumined by the theology of the kingdom of God, point to the existence of territorial spirits.[33] The Baahithiin certainly believe in territorial spirits![34]

Biblical and extra-biblical evidence indicates that Artemis was in fact a territorial spirit. She had no peers among the gods at Ephesus. Although numerous gods and goddesses were worshipped at Ephesus, Artemis was the supreme spiritual power. Luke vividly portrays the pervasive hold Artemis had on the people of Ephesus, describing her as "the great goddess, worshipped by all of Asia and the world" (v 27). Extra-biblical evidence confirms this extravagant claim. According to the Greek historian, Pausanias,

> All cities worship Artemis of Ephesus, and individuals hold her in honor above all the gods. ... Three other points as well have contributed to her renown, the size of the temple, surpassing all buildings among men, the eminence of the city of the Ephesians and the renown of the goddess who dwells there (1889).

Many engravings on ancients coins and monuments extol Artemis' magnificence. Richard Oster summarizes what his research revealed on this subject: "To those who called upon Artemis she was Savior, ... Lord, ... and Queen of the Cosmos. ... She was a heavenly goddess ... whose being and character could only be described in superlatives" (1976:40). Since Paul elsewhere teaches that sacrifices to idols are really sacrifices to demons (1 Cor 10:19-20), we can conclude that the power behind Artemis was a demon or principality known today as a territorial spirit.[35]

Clearly Paul knew more about the spirit realm than we do. Through both revelation and experience, the apostle understood the kingdom of darkness. Thus, the way he actually deals with Artemis is illuminating. Rather than engaging in what is today called "strategic-level warfare" (a direct confrontation with the territorial spirit through prayer), Paul the apostle focuses on "ground-level" and "occult-level warfare."[36] Paul preached the gospel, cast out demons, and healed the sick (ground-level warfare). This led ultimately to occult-level warfare, in which those who practiced magic repented and burned their magical paraphernalia.

Paul may have done other things to defeat the powers of darkness in Ephesus that Luke did not record. No doubt he did, for he understood his calling in light of spiritual warfare. The resurrected Jesus commissioned him to turn the Gentiles from "darkness to light, and from the power of Satan to the power of God" (Ac 26:18).

If we are commanded to "resist the devil" (Jm 4:7), we can resist territorial spirits. However, the text before us puts the emphasis elsewhere: on the immediate needs of the people whom we are sent to reach. Our emphasis should be there as well.

Summary

Power encounter is a burning issue for church planters among folk Muslims. The four power encounters in Acts highlight ten principles for confronting magic:

- The kingdom of darkness stands behind magicians.
- The fullness of the Spirit is foundational for power encounter.
- Evangelism should emphasize both truth encounter and power encounter.
- Some confrontations with magicians may involve a curse.
- Our authority is in Christ.
- The prayer of command is an important power ritual.
- We may contextualize our approach to magic or realize that God may.
- We should focus on the immediate needs of the people we are reaching and not directly confront territorial spirits.
- Deliverance from magic involves repentance and renunciation.
- Miracle differs from magic ontologically, relationally, eschatologically, ethically and motivationally.

Questions for Reflection and Discussion

1. Review the four confrontations between missionaries and magicians in Acts. Which of these "showdowns" speaks to your context most helpfully? Why?

2. Does Simon (the magician Luke describes in Acts 8) remind you of any shaman in your Muslim community? What form of truth encounter might your "Simon" need?

3. Paul's curse or judgment upon the magician Bar-Jesus (Acts 13) gives us a precedent but not a normative approach. Can you identify any principles that can suggest when such a Spirit-led pronouncement is especially needed or appropriate?

4. Paul did not ask God to cast out the python spirit in Acts 16; Paul commanded the demon to leave. Do you have experience in such exorcism or the "prayer of command"? If so, what have you learned? If not, are you hesitant to exercise such authority?

5. Are you uncomfortable with the idea that Paul adopted contagious magic or power objects in Ephesus (Acts 19)? How did he steer clear of syncretism while using such methods?

6. I believe that power places and power times are forms that should probably be rejected. Do you agree? Why or why not?

7. Do you believe that territorial spirits afflict your community? If so, describe their nature. Do you agree with me that the apostle Paul's example vis-á-vis Artemis in Ephesus indicates that we should not directly confront territorial spirits but should instead focus on ground-level and occult-level warfare? Why or why not?

It will help you to better digest what you're reading if you take the time to reflect on and discuss such questions after each chapter. Also, I would value a glimpse of what you're thinking! I invite you (either now or later) to share with me (r_d_love@hotmail.com) some of your answers to these questions. You may have some good things to teach me.

Notes

[1] While this missionary has yet to raise the dead, he and his team have had a successful contextualized ministry of signs and wonders among their people group.

[2] Taken from a personal prayer letter, dated March 1995.

[3] The names in this story have been changed for security purposes.

[4] See Green 1981:118-122 for a summary of these three types.

[5] According to Kurz, "The narrator [of Acts] engages in a major polemic against all forms of magic" (1993:152). See also Dunn (1996:175), Witherington (1998:98, 222, 397, 578) and Talbert (1997:176-177) for similar conclusions.

[6] Regarding the New Testament era, Hans Dieter Betz notes, "magical beliefs and practices can hardly be overestimated in their importance for the daily life of the people" (1992:41). According to David E. Aune, in the first century AD, "magic was a phenomenon which pervaded the various Greco-Roman cults, Judaism and Christianity" (1980:1519). Edwin M. Yamauchi says that Christians "lived in a world which was steeped with occult beliefs and practices" (1983:199).

[7] According to Howard Clark Kee, "The antithesis between miracles done in Jesus' name and magic ... was already taking shape in the narrative of Acts" (1983: 217). This is especially apparent in Acts 19, which "serves to contrast Christianity with the various magical practices, and so underlines the supernatural power of Christianity" (Newman and Nida 1972:361).

[8] I. Howard Marshall's comments on Acts 8:12 are notable: "This is an interesting combination of themes [the kingdom of God and the name of Jesus], showing how the early church saw the message of Jesus being continued in its own message but at the same time increasingly spoke about the means by which God's kingly power was being manifested in their own time, namely, through the mighty name of Jesus (1983:156).

[9] In the second century, Simon became known as the first gnostic and the arch heretic. But it is difficult to prove that the Simon of early church traditions is the same Simon in this account. Furthermore, what is important for us is how Luke actually portrays Simon in his encounter with Philip, not how the early fathers understood Simon. See Garrett 1989:61-62 and Marshall 1983:153-155.

[10] This is the same Greek word translated as "astonished" in vs 9, 11. It is translated as "amazed" in the NASB.

[11] Why the Holy Spirit did not fall on the Samaritans prior to the coming of Peter and John remains one of those classic puzzles of New Testament

interpretation. See Marshall 1983:157-158; Longenecker 1981:359-360 and Larkin 1995:127-129 for good summaries of the issues.

[12] "The Christian practice of laying on of hands or exorcism may look very much the same, and indeed have a similar effect (cf. 8:9-11 with 8:6, 8, 13), but one of Luke's primary concerns in relating the episodes of 8:17-24 and 19:13-16 is to make clear the difference" (Dunn 1996:109).

[13] Garrett 1989:72, 77. Witherington writes: "God's gift is in God's control" (1998:288).

[14] I have heard missionaries use the lame excuse that we shouldn't confront power-oriented societies at the power level. According to them, truth encounter is all that matters. Besides being unbiblical, this perspective will not bring full deliverance in power-oriented societies.

[15] The Holy Spirit is also called the Spirit of Truth (Jn 15:26; 16:13).

[16] "Pliny, *Natural History* 30.11, says that Cyprus had in his time supplanted previous famed centers of magic" (Talbert 1997:127).

[17] The fullness and power of the Spirit are central themes in Acts (1:8; 2:4; 4:8, 31, 33; 6:8; 9:17; 10:38; 13:52). The Holy Spirit was given that we might be witnesses. Witnessing in Acts, however, includes both bold proclamation and supernatural demonstration. The two go hand-in-hand (2:43; 4:30, 33; 5:12; 6:8; 8:6; 14:1-7; 15:12). Through preaching accompanied by power encounter, the church bears bold, radiant witness to its Lord.

[18] Curses are found in Paul's letters, but they are not pronounced in the context of power encounter or directed against magicians (Gal 1:8, 9; 1 Cor 5:3-5, 16:22; 1 Tim. 1:20). See Aune 1980:1553-1555.

[19] Simon's initial attraction to the gospel was due to seeing signs and wonders and hearing the message of the kingdom. It is true that Peter threatened him with what amounts to a curse (Ac 8:20-24). Nevertheless, there are four important differences between the account of Simon and the account of Bar-Jesus. Although Simon lacked spiritual discernment, he did demonstrate receptivity to the gospel. Ultimately, Peter did not curse Simon. Simon may have listened and repented. Cursing was not part of Philip's initial approach to Simon.

[20] Larkin 1995:237; Stott 1990:264. "The implication of the language used by Luke is that the girl spoke as in a trance: she was inspired, like the priestess at Delphi, by Apollo, who was symbolized by a snake" (Dunn 1996:221).

[21] W.L. Lane describes Jesus' method of using saliva as bordering on magic (1974: 192). Aune is bolder: "The ideas expressed in the story of the women's healing do not border on magic, they are of the essence of Greco-Roman magical notions" (1980: 1536). Graham H. Twelftree's doctoral studies on this subject support Aune's viewpoint. "There is ample evidence showing the use of spittle was part of the healing technique of the ancient world. It is used, for example, in the Babylonian texts, in the magical papyri and in Pliny. And, importantly, the rabbis prohibit its use" (1993:158).

[22] Oster, however, makes an important distinction between magicians' and Paul's use of *power objects*: "While it is true that the idea of power reflected in Acts 19:11ff. is similar to that which supported the idea of relics in the popular

lore of pagans, Jews, and Christians, there seems to be one point which keeps the two from being identical. Lk. gives no examples of the *dunamis* of God permanently residing in certain objects" (1974:37).

[23] A missionary friend told me a modern example of this. He met a Muslim *marabout* who wanted to learn the power verses in the gospel (*Injil*) to enhance his occultic powers.

[24] In fact, the Jews were famous in antiquity for their magic (Alexander 1896:342-379). The book of Acts itself describes two encounters with Jewish magicians (Acts 13:6-12; 19:13-20). There is further historical confirmation in the magical papyri (PGM XXIIb. 1-26) and in the Testament of Solomon (Charlesworth 1983:935-987). Josephus speaks of this phenomena when he describes Solomon's magical prowess: "God granted him [Solomon] knowledge of the art used against demons for the benefit of healing men. He also composed incantations by which illnesses are relieved, and left behind forms of exorcisms with which those possessed by demons drive them out, never to return. And this kind of cure is of very great power among us to this day" (8:45).

[25] That demons communicate through human vessels is documented throughout the New Testament (Mk 1:24; 5:7-12; Ac 16:16-18).

[26] Other New Testament accounts describe the physical impact of demons on people. During an exorcism there are often violent physical manifestations. Jesus commanded demons to come out of a young boy. The response: "After crying out and throwing him into terrible convulsions, it came out; and the boy became so much like a corpse that most of them said, 'He is dead!'" (Mk 9:25-26). Philip's power ministry also encountered disorderly conduct: "In the case of many who had unclean spirits, they were coming out of them shouting with a loud voice" (Ac 8:7). In addition, demons can empower their victims with supernatural strength. The Gerasene Demoniac "had often been bound with shackles and chains, and the chains had been torn apart by him, and the shackles broken in pieces, and no one was strong enough to subdue him" (Mk 5:4).

[27] According to Talbert, "This is a power encounter. It is necessary because believers continue to seek spiritual power from sources other than Jesus. ... They practice a bifurcated religion characterized by dual allegiance and a syncretistic understanding of truth" (1997:177).

[28] Marshall rightly notes regarding the Ephesian believers, "Christians are not fully converted or perfected in an instant, and pagan ways of thinking can persist alongside genuine Christian experience" (1980:312). My personal experience and the experience of missionaries all over the world working in folk Islamic or animistic contexts can testify to the struggle new believers have in these areas. Dual allegiance is an all-too-common problem.

[29] Luke's four summaries highlight Paul's success and indicate that a movement was birthed: "All who lived in Asia heard the word of the Lord" (Ac 19:10). "Fear fell upon them all and the name of the Lord Jesus was being magnified" (Ac 19:17). "So the word of the Lord was growing mightily and prevailing" (Ac 19:20). "Not only in Ephesus, but in almost all of Asia, this Paul has persuaded and turned away a considerable number of people" (Ac 19:26).

[30] The sacraments can be understood in power terms, although the power does not reside in the rituals per se. It is also possible to construe the sacraments as *power times*, since both of these sacraments provide unique contexts for vital demonstrations of kingdom power. For example, the baptism ceremony in one Baahithiin church includes a formal renunciation of magic and a prayer for deliverance. The Lord's Supper also seems to include a power element, for Paul talks about God's judgment being manifest through sickness and death because the Corinthians were taking the Lord's Supper in an unworthy manner (1 Cor 11:27-32).

[31] Even so, there can be unique times and places where God pours out his Spirit and people experience unprecedented power. This often happens during revival or renewal. What I mean is that there is nothing *inherently* special about any time or place when it comes to God's power.

[32] There is a sense in which magicians do have some sort of strange relationship with the spirits they manipulate – at least among the Baahithiin. But the primary orientation of their arts is on ritual and formula, not relationship.

[33] Vern Poythress of Westminster Theological Seminary, a bastion of theological orthodoxy noted for its cessationist view of spiritual gifts, argues convincingly for the reality of territorial spirits (1995:37-49). See also Arnold 1997 for an excellent study of territorial spirits.

[34] According to my experience, when the Baahithiin pray to the ancestor spirits, it is more than just a matter of praying to them as mediators. For it is also true that there is a hierarchy of ancestor spirits. If, for example, the spiritual leader of our community needs to call an ancestor spirit from another city, he must ask permission from the chief ruling spirit in our district of our city. According to tradition, this spirit formerly ruled our district and was a man of great supernatural power. Although frequently described as ancestor spirits, these ruling spirits are also called "the one who rules." According to an informant, "If a Baahithiin enters a new place or territory, he will ask permission of "the one who rules" if it is okay for him to pass by. " But whether they are described as ancestor spirits or "the one who rules," it is clear that the Baahithiin believe in what is now increasingly referred to as territorial spirits.

[35] Wagner's argument that Artemis is a territorial spirit is compelling (1995, 3:171-173; 1996:210-216). This does not mean that Artemis was the only territorial spirit, however.

[36] See Wagner 1995, 3:163-173 for a summary of these three levels of spiritual warfare.

Chapter 9

Power Encounter: Defensive Resistance

Power encounter is a crisis point of encounter in the on-going spiritual warfare between the two supernatural kingdoms, the goal of which is the glory of God.

—**Ed Murphy**

Spiritual Warfare as Resistance

"Rick, I've got a solid background in theology. But my demonology is weak. Since coming to the field, though, I realized I need to rethink things. I read about Paul being thwarted by Satan in 1 Thessalonians 2:18. If Paul could be thwarted by Satan, how much more could I?"

This comment from one of my teammates is typical of many missionaries. Workers frequently cry, "I wasn't ready for this!" They have studied theology, Islamics and missiology, but they weren't prepared for the kind of spiritual warfare they faced when they reached the field. One of the biggest challenges we face is preparing people for spiritual warfare.

True power encounter encompasses more than just the dramatic type of episodes described in previous chapters. Power encounter includes any type of conflict between a believer and the powers of darkness. Thus, any discussion of power encounter must also address spiritual warfare.[1]

Numerous excellent books have been written on spiritual warfare.[2] Thus, this chapter will not attempt to provide comprehensive teaching on spiritual warfare. I merely want to highlight those aspects of spiritual warfare most commonly faced by workers in the Muslim world.

This book encourages church planters to take the offensive for the kingdom of God. Yet the defensive dimension of spiritual warfare also warrants our attention. Church planters need to be prepared to resist Satanic attacks that are *mental*, *moral* and *physical*.

Most battles progress through periods of advance and retreat, times of attack and defense for both armies. One of the major emphases of Paul's teaching on spiritual warfare, outlined in Ephesians 6:10-20, is our defense. Three times Paul exhorts us to "stand firm" against the onslaughts of the evil one (vs 11, 13, 14). We are to dress ourselves in the full armor of God that we "may be able to resist in the evil day" (v 13). In other words, Paul defines spiritual warfare in terms of resistance.

In a helpful parallel passage, Paul teaches that this resistance has *mental* dimensions. "We are destroying speculations and every lofty thing raised up against the knowledge of God, and we are taking every thought captive to the obedience of Christ" (2 Cor 10:5).

He notes two aspects of Satanic encounter in the mental realm. First of all, Paul calls us to destroy speculations and every lofty thing raised up against the knowledge of God. Wrong theological ideas must be deleted; faulty theological thinking must be corrected. A proper view of God has weighty implications. We must wage warfare against any view of God which is unworthy of His majesty, sovereignty or goodness. Theology is important. *There is a Godward approach to spiritual warfare which is undervalued and misunderstood in most "spiritual warfare" literature.*

Second, he calls us to take these thoughts "captive to the obedience of Christ." Purging ourselves of bad thoughts is inadequate. We are commanded to be obedience-oriented in our thinking as well. Paul uses militant language to describe how aggressive we must be in our thought lives. He sees a faulty view of God as something that must be attacked. He describes our thoughts as enemy soldiers who must be captured.

Our minds are the target of Satanic attack. "The lie" is the major weapon of the "father of all lies" (Jn 8:44). An intense battle rages, and the battleground is our mind. Accusations, false guilt, doubt, disobedience, rebellion, lust, malice or fear are some of the most frequent fiery darts that the evil one shoots our way.

At issue is more than mind control and positive thinking. At issue is our view of God, our theology. "We are destroying speculations ... raised up against the knowledge of God." We need to bring both mind and will into complete submission to, and therefore harmony with, the mind and will of God.

Culture stress, marital problems, and tensions on our teams cause many missionaries to doubt God's goodness. When that happens, Satan has an inroad. Anger and depression are common among those in ministry to Muslims. Husbands often battle with anger; wives frequently wrestle with depression. Why? Because we are affected by unbiblical views of God and ministry. Spiritual warfare emphasizes the importance of the renewed mind and the priority of biblical thinking. Spiritual warfare is resistance, and it begins in our mind.

Spiritual warfare also has a *moral* dimension. The mental and moral aspects of spiritual warfare often overlap, since Satan's schemes are often moral. As noted above, Satan's greatest scheme is "the lie" (Gen 3). Paul describes this scheme in slightly different words: "For even Satan disguises himself as an angel of light." Thus, Satan wants to seduce us into compromise and deceive us into error (2 Cor 11:14).

In 2 Corinthians 2:5-11 Paul lists "lack of forgiveness" or an "unwillingness to forgive" as a Satanic scheme. If we don't forgive our brother or sister, then Satan can take advantage of us. Anger can be another scheme of the evil one: "Be angry, and yet do not sin; do not let the sun go down on your anger, and do not give the devil an opportunity" (Eph 4:26-27). Both of these sins destroy the unity of Christ's body. Both of these sins are moral transgressions. Both of these sins provide Satan inroads into our lives.

In addition, Paul describes the armor of God in moral terms. We are commanded to put on the belt of truth and the breastplate of righteousness. Some commentators believe that the belt of truth refers to objective, doctrinal truth, while others think this refers to sincerity or integrity. However, this kind of either/or thinking misunderstands the nature of spiritual warfare altogether. Satan hates truth, whether it is objectively acknowledged or subjectively experienced. This is clearly a "both/and" issue. Objective truth must be subjectively appropriated. Mitton's summary of this issue is helpful.

> Half-truths, prevarications, and disloyal compromises may make for personal comfort and enable us to avoid social awkwardness, but they are poor preparation for decisive Christian action. They put us at a disadvantage when our main concern is to defeat evil wherever it is encountered (1976: 225).

Like the belt of truth, the breastplate of righteousness must be understood both doctrinally and practically. We need to appreciate the importance of both our imputed righteousness and our experiential righteousness. God not only makes us righteous in our standing before him, but he also expects that righteous deeds will flow out of our lives:

- But by his doing you are in Christ Jesus, who became to us wisdom from God, and righteousness and sanctification, and redemption (1 Cor 1:30).
- And put on the new self, which in the likeness of God has been created in righteousness and holiness of the truth (Eph 4:24).
- By this the children of God and the children of the devil are obvious: anyone who does not practice righteousness is not of God (1 Jn 3: 10).

Most Evangelicals would give a hearty "Amen!" to my comments on warfare to this point. Yes, warfare has mental and moral aspects. However, spiritual warfare has *physical* dimensions as well. Most popular books on the subject seldom treat this aspect of warfare.

It is important to realize that the warnings in Scripture about the devil are addressed to believers. He does prowl about "like a roaring lion, seeking someone to devour." Furthermore, Satan can empower objects (charms, amulets and talismans), animals, and locations. (See Ex 7:11-12, Mk 5:13, Rev 2:13 for examples.) He also rules territories (Dan 10:12-13, 20-21; Eph 6:12). Most people who live in the non-Western world believe in and have experienced the power of the kingdom of darkness. Unfortunately, most missionaries are not prepared to deal with these issues.

I was one such missionary. When my wife and I moved into our home among the Baahithiin, we noticed that we began to argue much more intensely than we ever had in America. We chalked up our arguments to culture stress, and I'm sure some of it was. However, we also started seeing fleeting shadows around the house, but both of us were embarrassed to talk about it. After a month, we finally admitted our suspicions. We concluded that we were experiencing demonic attack. We needed to pray over our house and to have what some call a "house cleansing." After we prayed and resisted the devil, according to James 4:7, our intense arguments stopped immediately. The demonic forces that once lived in our home were forced to flee.

A friend's experience also illustrates the physical nature of our warfare:

> [My wife] and I were in the historical ... grand bazaar with our infant daughter who was about six months old at the time. The bazaar was extremely crowded and ... village women were crowding around us and the baby stroller that [our daughter] was in. She was sleeping peacefully when all of a sudden she started shrieking. Immediately, a streaked line, scarlet red, appeared on her face, from above one of her eyes down to the top corner of her lip. My initial reaction was one of horrified shock and helplessness, but in that same moment I put my hand on [our daughter's] body and said, "In the name of Jesus I rebuke you evil spirits who are causing this reaction." I repeated this perhaps once or twice. Then we pushed our way as fast as we could out of the bazaar with the purpose of going to find a doctor. As we were on the way out of the bazaar, [our daughter's] terrified shrieking began to lessen. By the time we were out of the bazaar, it had stopped and the scarlet red streak was

gone. Five minutes had not passed in the whole event. As we examined her closely, we found a red thread on [our daughter's] chest. We think it may have been a talisman thrown on her chest by the ... village women who had been crowding around the baby stroller. I was not from a background that reacted to things like this by rebuking evil spirits. However, because of a very thorough article in an English-language [national] newspaper on the occultic activities in the daily lives of [the people we served], we were alerted to things like this happening. We had been prepared for possible demonic attacks. This same article described how thread and other physical objects are used as talismans to put curses on people.

Timothy Warner, one of the few missionaries writing on the subject of spiritual warfare, tells a similar story.

In a village in Sierra Leone, where I served, early missionaries were given "the devil's hill" on which to build the mission house. No one took the danger of this seriously because "demons couldn't do anything to Christians." When I was on the field I had a nonfunctional theology about such things, but I vividly remember watching the family living in that house go through attacks of physical disease which eventually took them off the field. A recent occupant of that house told me that until two years ago people who came to visit would become ill when they arrived but would lose the symptoms as they left the village. Why the change? Two years ago they finally cleansed the hill in a power encounter. Since that time there have been no more physical attacks. God alone knows how many of his servants have been taken out of the battle because they did not recognize this device of the enemy (1991:89-90).

How can we practically resist these mental, moral and physical attacks of the evil one? First of all, we need to *cultivate our relationship with the Lord*. We need to discipline ourselves for the purpose of godliness (1 Tm 4:7). A disciplined devotional life will not ensure a true knowledge of God nor guarantee our ability to take every thought captive. Yet without a disciplined lifestyle of prayer and Scripture reading, a dynamic relationship with God is difficult to attain. A disciplined devotional life allows us to place ourselves before God so that we can be transformed by the renewing of our minds (Rom 12:2).

The importance of intimacy with Christ is also directly linked to spiritual warfare in Ephesians 6. Paul begins his teaching on warfare with the command to be strong in the Lord (Eph 6:10). The little phrase "in the Lord" describes a crucial dimension to spiritual warfare: union with Christ. This phrase (or its equivalent) appears more than thirty times in the book of Ephesians alone. This strong emphasis on union with Christ indicates that intimacy precedes militancy, worship precedes warfare, and fellowship precedes the fight. A vital, dynamic relationship with Christ, cultivated through prayer and Scripture reading, provides the necessary foundation for spiritual warfare.

The imperative "be strong" is in the present tense, which means that the empowering is to be a moment-by-moment, ongoing experience. This empowering takes place through intimate, ongoing, cleansing communion with the heavenly Father. In my ministry with folk Muslims, I prayed for strength frequently, recalling this command from Ephesians 6:10.

The second thing we need to do is to *resist the devil*. Scripture instructs us repeatedly to pray for deliverance from the devil and the demonic. The Lord's prayer says, "deliver us from the evil one" (Mt 6:13), and Jesus prays that God would keep the church "from the evil one" (Jn 17:15; see also 2 Thes 3:2-3). Paul also speaks about resisting the devil "in the evil day," i.e., when we experience personal and direct attacks from the evil one.

We are commanded to resist the devil (Jm 4:7, 1 Pet 5:9). Jesus resisted the devil directly by quoting Scripture (Lk 4:1-13); Paul cast out demons (the most dramatic aspect of resisting the devil) in the name of Jesus (Ac 16:18; see also Mk 16:17).

Thus there are two aspects to resisting the devil. We should pray for deliverance during those periods when we are not directly under attack by the evil one. We should also firmly resist the devil with the word of God when we are under direct demonic attack (whether mental, moral or physical). "It is written" is our battle cry of victory. We must use the word of God—the sword of the spirit—to defend ourselves and defeat the devil. The name of Jesus is our other major weapon against the evil one.

Dreams and Visions

Folk Muslims not only pursue protection from the devil, they also seek guidance for the future. Dreams and visions play an important role in this pursuit of guidance. While they fit only loosely under the power encounter label, dreams and visions must be understood if we are to truly contextualize the gospel among folk Muslims.[3]

The Bible teaches that dreams and visions are an important medium of divine revelation (Num 12:6; 1 Sam 3:1, 28:6, 15; Hos 12:10). In fact, they are explicitly mentioned or alluded to almost 200 times in the Bible. Furthermore, in the New Testament, dreams and visions are described as characteristic of the age of the Spirit: "young men will see visions ... old men will dream dreams" (Ac 2:17).

While they are not a normal part of the Western Evangelical experience, dreams and visions are biblical, and they play an important role in the life of folk Muslims. God speaks through dreams and visions to convert sinners (e.g., Paul and Cornelius) as well as to encourage and guide his people (e.g., Ananias, Peter, Paul). He does the same today.

The missionary God's method of communication is incarnational. He enters into our world to communicate his message. His revelation is contextual, meeting people where they are. Because many folk Muslims are beyond the reach of the gospel and because many of them are illiterate, dreams and visions are particularly relevant.

Even more conservative expressions of Christianity report the conversion of Muslims through dreams and visions.[4] Just as God used a vision to convert Paul, in like manner he reveals himself to Muslims. Just as God prepared Cornelius to hear the gospel through a vision, so God is preparing a multitude of Muslims to respond to his good news.

God has used dreams and visions in a number of people's lives in our own ministry. Once my teammate and I prayed specifically that God would send a dream to a Muslim with whom we were sharing the gospel. God heard our prayer. Soon afterward our Muslim friend had a dream about Jesus and was converted! A worker's experience in

South Asia is another wonderful example of how God speaks through dreams and visions:

> One afternoon, out of the blue a Muslim rang our gate bell. The doctor who was house-sitting for us answered the gate. The Muslim man told the doctor the following: "Last night I had a dream and in the dream an angel told me that I was to walk down this paved road, turn down this particular dirt road and press these buttons ringing the gate bell for this home. This person that answered the gate would be able to tell me truth. Can you help me?" The doctor said in amazement, "Please come in." After three hours of talking and hearing the truth of Jesus Christ and the claims of Scripture, this Muslim man gave his life over to Christ. The doctor gave him a New Testament in his mother tongue and encouraged him to read as much as he could before their next meeting. The newborn Christian then left.
>
> About three days later, he returned, having read the entire New Testament. He was very excited about his newfound faith and about the things he'd read in the New Testament. He did notice one step of obedience that he hadn't taken and which he wanted to take care of as soon as possible: he asked the doctor if he could be baptized. The doctor was encouraged by his enthusiasm and desire for obedience but very wisely said, "Before I baptize you, I would like for you to publicly confess your newfound faith in Christ. May I suggest that you do this with your wife." The new convert was pretty distraught. Any type of public confession meant that he would be ostracized from his family and could mean that he would pay the ultimate price for his faith.
>
> He went home a little discouraged, not knowing what to do. That night his wife had a dream. In her dream she saw a beautiful garden surrounded by a fence. There was a gate and at the gate stood a gatekeeper. She could see her husband sitting in the garden but she was outside the garden. She started to proceed through the gate into the garden, but the gatekeeper stopped her and said, "Excuse me, you can't come in here." She said, "No, you don't understand. I want to be with my husband." The gatekeeper said, "You can't come in here because this place is reserved for Christians." The woman replied, "I want to be with my husband." The gatekeeper said, "Your husband is a Christian and can be here, but you are not, so you cannot join him in the garden." She awoke, rolled over, shook her husband, looked him in the eyes and said, "Why didn't you tell me you had become a Christian? I want to become a Christian too."
>
> Very early the next morning, the two of them went to the doctor's house and explained the dream. After a few hours the

woman invited Jesus into her heart and she too became a Christian. A few weeks later the husband and wife were baptized together in a river not too far from that particular house.

However, not all dreams come from heaven. Dreams can be psychologically or Satanically inspired as well. Thus, we must teach our new converts discernment. They must learn to examine their dreams and visions in light of Scripture. They also need to submit their dreams and visions to the leaders of their churches to help them discern whether God is speaking.

Practical Issues

Power encounter is a necessary and important aspect of kingdom ministry. For those ministering to folk Muslims, it is particularly important. However, power ministry is not *the* answer to reaching Muslims. It is only one aspect of the task.

It would seem that signs of the kingdom ought to lead people to exalt the king. But usually, folk Muslims just want healing and do not care about its source. In other words, people seeking power do not necessarily seek the Savior. God used my wife and me in a ministry of signs and wonders among Muslims. Though we believe they were more receptive to Christ, few of those healed became believers in Christ!

Many of my friends ministering throughout the Muslim world report the same reaction. One reason for this is folk Muslims' worldview. Because they live in a world of magic and the supernatural, they are not necessarily awestruck by demonstrations of God's power. On the other hand, if we cannot demonstrate God's power, they are even less impressed!

When I first began missionary service, I was looking for that dramatic power encounter that would lead to a major breakthrough among the Baahithiin. I had the encounter but without the breakthrough! It happened during martial arts training.

My instructor was giving me a personal lesson. He started teaching me breathing exercises that were linked to a shoving-type motion. In between exercises, he was telling me stories about the power to knock people over (from a distance without touching them, known as "inner power") as well as the power to heal. He said he himself had often experienced these things. So I asked him if he would give an example, since I had heard many stories about this, but had never experienced it. He told me to get into a certain stance, and then he started to give me the "shove" (from a distance). As he did this, I was praying against the powers of darkness in the name of Jesus. When nothing happened, he asked me to get in another stance. Again, the same shove, the same prayers and the same results. After trying this for a number of times, he asked me if I wanted to try. Since I had never done this before, I copied the "shove" that I had seen. He stood about five feet in front of me. I gave him the shove, simultaneously praying in the name of Jesus. To my shock, he went flying backwards as if a heavyweight boxer had hit him. I hadn't touched him at all, yet a power surged from me that knocked him backwards. This happened a few more times. Finally he stopped, shook his head, prayed, and with a pale, flustered look on his face, he said meekly, "That's enough practice."

This encounter did not lead my instructor to Christ. Why? Because conversion involves truth encounter. He wasn't willing to submit to the true God. Because of my experience, I take great comfort in 2 Corinthians 12:12: "The signs of a true apostle were performed among you *with all perseverance*, by signs and wonders and miracles." The great pioneer church planter describes his ministry in terms of power encounter. His ministry was characterized by the supernatural. It was also characterized by "all perseverance."

Many reject our message from the start. Even those who are healed often reject Christ. Yet with power and "all perseverance," we will see churches established among folk Muslims.

Coworkers in our region have had similar experiences. This couple often prayed for the sick. Some were healed, some weren't. But even when there were manifestations of power, people didn't repent.

Nevertheless, this couple persevered. Within the last few years they have seen breakthroughs because of signs and wonders. In one case, a national couple serving with them cast numerous demons out of a Muslim, who then repented along with his family. The man delivered from demons has become the bridge into the community! Here is the story in their own words.

> Samson [a local shaman], unable to sleep due to the occult forces in his life ... made the rounds from shaman to shaman seeking to be delivered of his powers. However, none were able to free him. ... One evening some time later, Samson went on a rampage, tearing his house apart and shouting wildly. Priscilla and Aquila [the national couple working with our colleagues] ran to his home (200 yards away) and began to cast out demons in the name of "the Lord Isa al-Masih." Not experienced in this, they were amazed to observe many different entities leave him, each with its own name and voice. That night all of his amulets and weapons were burned and buried. Beginning the next day, this shaman, who was once feared by all the neighbors and who had in the past committed hideous sins, was now asking forgiveness of neighbors and witnessing to his family. Several months later, Samson and his wife, his daughter and son-in-law, and one of Aquila's nieces ... were baptized. [They] ... have become the nucleus of a small ... fellowship.

Power encounters, or signs and wonders, are not just necessary for evangelistic breakthroughs. The supernatural breaking in of God's kingdom is also a crucial part of the building up of the church. Two things frequently happen in a folk Islamic context that make power encounter a central part of the pastoral process.

I believe "deliverance" should be an important part of discipling new believers. Folk Muslims who come to Christ have been immersed in the world of spirit powers, charms and amulets. We cannot simply ask them to repent in a general way and believe that this is sufficient. Here's how one team in North Africa integrates deliverance into their discipleship:[5]

> The first thing I do when they come to the Lord is go over the Ten Commandments with them. I especially focus on the first commandment: "You shall have no other gods before Me." Then I

ask them if they have any talismans – since most people groups live in fear of spirits and use talismans. If they have talismans, I ask them to bring it to me the next time we meet. At that meeting we destroy the talisman.[6] They ask for forgiveness, and then we lay hands on them and say, "In Jesus' name, every power that these charms or talisman had are now broken. This man or woman now belongs to the Lord."

Here's what happened with a woman we call Lydia. She couldn't sleep very well because of terrible dreams. The dreams caused her much grief and affected her walk with the Lord. In her dreams, she saw awful things that actually happened afterwards. When we discovered this, we spoke with her and showed her from Scripture that this is not God's will. We took her through the process outlined above. Sure enough, she had a talisman. While we ministered deliverance to her, one of our team members spent the day praying and fasting for Lydia. There was no screaming or dramatic physical manifestations during our prayer for deliverance, but Lydia was set free. She stopped having bad dreams. In fact, after this deliverance God started speaking to her through positive dreams.

Another way to integrate deliverance into discipleship is to link it with baptism. I like this because baptism should be a major turning point in the life of the believer. It is more than just an interesting historical fact that exorcism was a part of baptismal preparation in the early church.[7]

In April 1995 I had the privilege of participating in a baptism that included deliverance. Prior to the actual baptism, the folk Muslim converts being baptized were asked to make a public renunciation of any type of magic. They publicly declared, "I renounce every act of seeking power for myself through magic, charms or amulets of any kind."

The pastor then asked the baptismal candidates whether they had been involved in magic of any kind. Only one man admitted that he had. (In this particular baptism, many of the candidates were teenagers who had not been involved in magic.) Next, the leaders of the church took the man into a different room and ministered deliverance to him. The pastor challenged him to say "Jesus is Lord of my life." The baptismal candidate strained to confess Christ as his Lord. But his words were strangely muffled by an unholy spirit. He looked agitated.

His body had become a battlefield. Internal turmoil and inability to express Christ's Lordship persisted. So we rebuked the evil spirits in the name of Jesus, and commanded them to leave. At the same time we continued to encourage the man to submit himself fully to the Lord. The pastor had him verbally renounce evil spirits and every type of occultic practice. After renouncing the forces of darkness, he convulsed. The spirits left and he was set free. He blurted out with great relief, "Jesus is Lord, Jesus is my Lord!"

This leads to a second point about power ministry among converts from folk Islam.

Converts from folk Islam often revert and seek help from a shaman in times of crisis. Another man in this same congregation had gone to a shaman just prior to the baptismal service described above. When the man who had gone to a shaman heard the prayer of renunciation and heard the testimony of the first man's deliverance, he confessed his sin in this area and the church also prayed for him.

A close friend of mine who has served for more than eight years among folk Muslims has seen much fruit. He has also experienced his share of suffering and setbacks. His training and heritage did not prepare him for addressing the demonic realities he has encountered. He said that the powers of darkness are the hardest thing he has had to face in his ministry. He believes that most of the young converts he works with still suffer from various levels of demonization. Because of this, he now sets aside time at the end of almost every public meeting for prayers of deliverance.

Repentance in a folk Islamic context must involve both renunciation of occultic practices and deliverance from the power of these forces. The texts that have been most helpful to me in this regard are Deuteronomy 18:9-15 and Acts 19:18-20. In Deuteronomy, spiritism of any kind is described as detestable and forcefully denounced. Instead of going to a shaman, Moses calls the people of God to listen to the coming prophet–the prophet Jesus (compare Acts 3:19-24).

As noted previously, Acts 19 deals with these issues in a complementary fashion by illustrating the nature of repentance for folk Muslims. New believers need to publicly confess their occult practices and destroy every charm and amulet regardless of their monetary value.

Power encounter plays an important role in reaching folk Muslims. Power encounter is not *the* key to the kingdom, as some people from a signs and wonders background may assume. However, it is an essential key to reaching folk Muslims, as those from a more traditional Evangelical background often fail to realize.

Questions for Reflection and Discussion

1. Anger and depression are common among those in ministry to Muslims. Is this reflected in your team or among your co-workers? To what extent do you believe this anger or depression is rooted in unbiblical views of God or ministry?

2. What Satanic schemes have you recognized in your ministry? Where have you inadvertently given Satan inroads into your team's life? Have you received the help you need to thwart Satan's schemes and curtail his inroads?

3. How can you and your colleagues (both expatriate and national) gain greater discernment in examining dreams and visions in the light of Scripture?

4. As you review your context and ministry, how might you effectively integrate deliverance with discipleship?

It will help you to better digest what you're reading if you take the time to reflect on and discuss such questions after each chapter. Also, I would value a glimpse of what you're thinking! I invite you (either now or later) to share with me (r_d_love@hotmail.com) some of your answers to these questions. You may have some good things to teach me.

Notes

[1] The more I have studied how Paul addressed power issues in the Ephesian literature (Ac 19-20; Ephesians 1 & 2 Timothy), the more I have realized that his approach was more comprehensive than just power encounter. Thus, instead of writing solely about power encounters, I have coined a quasi-technical term, "confronting the powers," which includes power, truth and moral encounter.

[2] See Anderson 1990; Arnold 1992b, 1997; Subeck 1975, 1984; Green 1981; Harper 1984; Murphy 1992; Kraft 1992; Moreau 1997; Wagner 1990; Warner 1991 and Wimber 1987.

[3] Steyne and Burnett emphasize the importance of dreams in the broader animistic world as well. "Dreams serve as one of the chief sources of revelation from the spirit world to man. ... Dreams are, therefore, accepted as a normative way to receive guidance" (Steyne 1989:133; see also Burnett 1988:61).

[4] A field director for the Southern Baptists described their denomination's experience with dreams and visions: "The tendency seems to be that God uses dreams and visions in the early stages of breakthrough. But once the church is established there seem to be less dreams and visions. Muslims become attracted to the gospel through the new community."

[5] This is a summary of an interview I had with a couple leading a team in North Africa.

[6] I enjoyed listening to the stories of how they destroy the talisman. Many of the talismans are packets of leather with verses from the Quran in them. The men wear them in their turbans, while the women wear them in their hair. Because the leather is old and dry, it is difficult to burn. So one way they get rid of the talisman is to bury it. But it is more common to put it down the toilet!

[7] See Arnold 1997:107-112 and Harper 1984:26.

Chapter 10

Moral Encounter

There is no more Godlike work to be done in this world than peacemaking.
— **John Broadus**

Magic and Moral Encounter

I once asked some of my Baahithiin friends if there was any type of magic that enabled people to better love and serve others – in other words, a positive or productive type of magic. After a moment of reflection, a few of my friends mentioned one type of white magic. One friend said because this type of white magic is used to build harmonious relationships, he thought it could be described as a type of productive magic. However, another friend further explained, "If person A is angry at person B and threatens him, person A can use [this magic] against B so that B will have mercy on him and love him." Hence, the ultimate goal of this form of magic is not love and service, but protection and control. Similarly, the national encyclopedia of one country describes another kind of protective magic: "With this [magical power] a person can make his enemies fall in love with him, and without realizing it, they will want to follow the desires of the person who has this [magic]. An employee can also use it so that his employers love him."

A magical view of power is self-serving. By contrast, there is a moral dimension to God's power. *God's power is distinct in two ways: it either demonstrates God's love or strengthens believers to love.*

First, power encounter demonstrates God's love because it is a manifestation of God's kingdom (Mt 12:28; Jm 2:8). "God's purpose in ministering in power is always to show love. ... If ministry is not done in love, it is not done in God's way" (Kraft 1989:138). Second, the purpose of power in our lives is love (Eph. 3:16-19). "Whereas the supernatural power tapped through magical practice has the individual in view, the instructions surrounding God's power imparted to believers has others in view. The power of God strengthens the believer *to love*" (Arnold 1992a:170, emphasis added). Demonstrating God's love, reflecting the ethics of the kingdom: this is moral encounter.

My wife and I have had the privilege of studying under some of the best missiologists in America. We learned many invaluable lessons about strategy, culture and contextualization. Yet virtually every one of our teachers has neglected one important emphasis.

After serving eight years among the Baahithiin and several more years in mission leadership, I am convinced that there needs to be a whole new emphasis on character for church planters. I heard little about character before I began missionary service, but it was one of the most important aspects of church planting that I had to learn – the hard way.

Character, I believe, is one of the neglected keys to church planting. Most people would agree that character is an important theme in Scripture. As good Evangelicals, we acknowledge the importance of *character*, but in practice we exalt the need of *competence*. Gifting is usually more highly valued than godliness.

In fact, we do need gifted, competent people to start and maintain church-planting movements in the Muslim world. To see breakthroughs among Muslims, we need to be competent in our ministries. However, the road leading to competence is through the valley of character. There is a vital link between character and God's kind of competence. This link is crucial to our task.

When I began working among the Baahithiin in 1984, "character development" was not one of the top priorities on my list. While I acknowledged theoretically that Paul emphasized the priority of character for church leaders (1 Tm 3:1-8, Tit 1:5-9), I had little sense of its practical relevance for my church-planting effort.

However, years of ministry have changed my focus. The first leader of our fellowship fell into adultery. After that, we had a church split over character problems. Through it all, we had to put up with constant bickering in our fellowship.

The character development of our leaders finally became a top priority. Character development is not only crucial, it is also painfully slow. It is hard enough to make Mark Muslim into Bill Believer, but it takes blood, sweat and tears to turn Bill Believer into Earl Elder! I don't know how many times I lost heart because those I was training to be leaders continually made decisions based upon their emotions and cultural values instead of the Word of God.

Perhaps the greatest character flaws among the Baahithiin are what might be called "hurt feelings" and "a grudge or revenge." A gentle, highly emotional people, the Baahithiin are easily offended and rarely forgive. They quickly experience "hurt feelings" and then tenaciously hold on to their "grudge."

Therefore, our ministry focused on the issue of forgiveness. We spent the majority of our time counseling about forgiveness, teaching about forgiveness and mediating forgiveness. For me, training young disciples to love and forgive each other is one of the hardest aspects of church planting. It is a tearful, tiring process.

Another major character problem among the Baahithiin is divorce. Divorce is rampant, and true marital intimacy is generally unknown. Since couples easily experience "hurt feelings" and "grudges," the marriage bonds are fragile.

One couple, members of our house church, came to our house to tell us that they were going to get a divorce. After three intense hours of counseling and prayer, they finally rejected the notion and began to work at their marriage. They later became leaders in the church.

Marriage became a central aspect of church life for us. We put on marriage seminars, did pre-marital counseling, and spent hundreds of hours focusing on the family. However, this was not what we had planned or expected. We wanted to do the great work of pioneer church planting. Yet we found that the greatest pioneer church planter of all time says that elders must "manage their households well" (1 Tm 3:4, 5). To plant churches, we must train elders. If we are going to train elders, we must train them how to manage their households well!

Character is not only an important aspect of church planting, it is also a central element of our own *competence* as church planters. Jesus told the Pharisees that their followers would become twice the sons of hell that they were (Mt 23:15). No doubt the Pharisees imparted their character flaws to their followers. Anyone who is actively involved in personal discipling knows the truth of this verse.

As some people say, "God has to do it *to* you before he can do it *through* you!" In other words, we can only plant loving, forgiving churches if we are loving and forgiving people. Our competence may enable us to master the language, adapt to the culture and win the lost. However, churches that will stand in the Muslim world can only be planted by men and women of character. There needs to be moral encounter.

Jesus' teaching about true and false prophets is especially relevant for ministry to folk Muslims in regards to moral encounter. In the Sermon on the Mount, Jesus speaks of people who prophesy, cast out demons and perform many miracles. Like folk Muslims, these people understand and seek power, and like folk Muslims, these false prophets lack character. Morality is not linked with their miracles. Jesus explains how to discern a true prophet from a false prophet and thus discern the source of "power encounters." According to Jesus, "You will know them by their fruits" (Mt 7:16, 20). Character is the essential credential of a true prophet.

Power encounter alone is not enough. Satan has power, and folk Muslims operate in power. Moral encounter is what separates the true from the false. Church planters need to demonstrate the values of the kingdom as godly, moral people.

One missionary in a North African country told me of people who had been scrutinizing his life for years to see whether he was righteous. Ultimately, his godly life gave him credibility with the people and an open door to preach Christ. In South Asia, another missionary couple had a similar experience. After ten years of watching their lives, the people concluded that there was something different about these missionaries. They wanted to know what it was. Moral encounter opened the door to truth encounter.

The two important most vital aspects of kingdom ethics as they relate to church planting are love and peace.

Love

The church is a community of the king, and it must be ruled by the law of the king, which is the law of love. "If, however, you are fulfilling the royal law [or the law of the king] according to the Scripture, 'You shall love your neighbor as yourself,' you are doing well" (Jm 2:8).

At the heart of true community, love reflects one of the most central aspects of kingdom ethics. In fact, the most pervasive theme in New Testament ethics is the command to love (Morris 1981). Both Jesus and Paul emphasize that love summarizes the whole of the Old Testament (Mt 22:34-40; Gal 5:14). Perhaps Paul's threefold emphasis in Romans is most clear:

> Owe nothing to anyone except to love one another; for he who loves his neighbor has *fulfilled the law*. For this, "You shall not commit adultery, You shall not murder, You shall not steal, You shall not covet," and if there is any other commandment, it is *summed up* in this saying, "You shall love your neighbor as yourself." Love does no wrong to a neighbor, love therefore is *the fulfillment of the law* (Rm 13:8-10, *emphasis added*).

Love not only summarizes the Old Testament, it is also the goal of New Testament ethics. We are commanded to love more than 40 times in the New Testament. A short summary of some of these commands highlights the pervasiveness of love.

"Abide in my love" (Jn 15:9).

"Let love be without hypocrisy" (Rm 12:9).

"Pursue love" (1 Cor 14:1).

"Let all that you do, be done in love" (1 Cor 16:14).

"Through love serve one another" (Gal 5:13).

"Walk in love" (Eph 5:2).

"Put on love ... the perfect bond of unity" (Col 3:14).

"Above all, keep fervent in your love" (1 Pet 4:8).

"Let us love one another" (1 Jn 4:7).

"Keep yourselves in the love of God" (Jud 21).

Paul summarizes the pervasive love ethic of the New Testament, saying, "But *the goal of our instruction is love* from a pure heart and a good conscience and a sincere faith" (1 Tm 1:5 *emphasis added*). Jesus calls love the true mark of discipleship. "By this all men will know that you are my disciples, if you have love for one another" (Jn 13:35).

What does love mean in practical terms? How does the law of the king relate to the establishment of committed communities? Notice the original context of the second commandment: "You shall not take vengeance, nor bear any grudge against the sons of your people, but you shall love your neighbor as yourself; I am the Lord" (Lv 19:18). In its original setting, love is the opposite of taking revenge or bearing a grudge. Thus, both exegetically and practically, love overcomes grudges, something central to community life.

Three other New Testament passages explain how love expresses itself in overcoming grudges. 1 Peter 4:8 says, "Above all, keep fervent in your love for one another, because love covers a multitude of sins." Peter begins this exhortation with the phrase "above all." In other words, love has to be our highest priority. He challenges us to be fervent in our love. Love doesn't just happen naturally. We can't be lackadaisical about love. Wholeheartedness and zeal must characterize our pursuit of love. Prayer for a fresh outpouring of God's love in our hearts and meditation on verses about love are practical ways to become fervent in our love for one another.

Peter concludes by explaining why we need to be fervent in our love for one another, saying, "because love covers a multitude of sins." Our flesh has a strong tendency to be critical and to focus on the negative in others. True love does not.

In many situations, the road to reconciliation is simple: we need to overlook minor offenses. As Proverbs 19:11 says, "A man's discretion makes him slow to anger, and it is his glory to overlook a transgression." Since God does not deal harshly with us every time we sin, we should be willing to treat others in a similar fashion. *We should make every effort to overlook inconsequential wrongdoing.*

True love does not, however, cover all sins. If the sin is significant, creating a wall between persons, or if the offense will do serious harm to God's reputation, to others, or to the offender, it must be confronted. 1 Peter 4:8 ("love covers a multitude of sins") must be balanced by Revelation 3:19, in which Jesus says, "Those whom I love, I reprove and discipline." In other words, true love will reprove. In fact, reproof in this particular verse is proof of Christ's love for his church. Love covers and love confronts, depending on the situation.

The famous "love chapter" gives further insight into the practice of love through "overcoming grudges." In 1 Corinthians 13:4-6, love is described as "not taking into account a wrong suffered." In other words, true love is forgiving (Eph 4:32, Col 3:13).

To summarize: The second commandment defines love as overcoming grudges. The New Testament mentions at least three dimensions to this process of overcoming grudges: love covers, love confronts, love forgives. This kind of love plants churches that last.

Peace

Peace is another important aspect of kingdom ethics. The link between the kingdom of God and peace is most explicit in Paul's teaching: "For the kingdom of God is not a matter of eating or drinking, but righteousness, peace and joy in the Holy Spirit" (Rm 14:17).

Peace is a work of God (Jn 14:27; 16:33; Eph 2:14; Rm 5:1). But peace is also the work of his people. It is easy to pontificate about the peace of

Christ theoretically. It is difficult to become a peacemaker practically. Yet peacemaking is central to moral encounter (and church planting).

We define peacemaking as resolving conflict, restoring and building harmony in relationships (Love 1995). It is both reactive (resolving conflicts, restoring relationships) and proactive (building harmony in relationships). As church planters, we must teach our disciples the "how-to's" of right relationships as summarized through peacemaking.

The priority and importance of peacemaking depends on one's definition of the church. If the church is perceived to be an institution or an organization, then peacemaking isn't central to its life or ministry. Thousands of traditional churches in the United States carry on without much peacemaking. On the other hand, if you define the church as a community (the body of Christ), then peacemaking is a crucial, urgent need.

It is especially urgent in the Muslim world, where most churches are house churches. House churches don't last very long without peacemaking. If you don't get along with someone, you can't transfer membership to some other church down the block. There *are* no other churches down the block!

We could summarize the centrality of peacemaking for church planting in a syllogism:

- The church is community.
- There is no community without peacemaking.
- Therefore peacemaking is central to church planting and church life.

Other terms have been used to describe the process of peacemaking. Some people prefer to use the word "reconciliation," while others favor the term "church discipline." But the term "peacemaking" encompasses both aspects.

Historically, one of the marks of the true church was peacemaking or "discipline" as summarized in the Belgic Confession of 1561: "The marks by which the true church is known are these: if the pure doctrine of the gospel is preached therein; if she maintains the pure administration of the sacraments as instituted by Christ; if church discipline is exercised in punishing sin" (Laney 1985:43).

Two things are worthy of note in this confession – one positive, one negative. Positively, it highlights the centrality of church discipline in church life. Church discipline is one of the marks of the true church. You cannot have a church without peacemaking. Negatively, it defines the goal of church discipline as punishing sin. Unlike the New Testament, this confession makes no mention of restoring relationships and winning the straying person.

Ronald Wallace makes some pertinent historical observations regarding this negative orientation in church discipline:

> Discipline in the first and second centuries seems to have had the forgiveness and winning back of the erring, rather than their punishment, as its aim. ... From the fourth century, discipline began to show undesirable features. More concern came to be shown for the sanctity of the congregation as a whole than for the expelled individual ... the pursuit of discipline became in some quarters more important than the pastoral care of the individual (1974:302).

Because of this, modern advocates of church discipline go to great pains to define the more positive dimensions of this peacemaking process. J. Carl Laney says, "Church discipline is God's loving plan for restoring sinning saints" (1985:14). John White and Ken Blue write about church discipline that heals (1985). According to Jay Adams, the purpose of church discipline is "to win the brother, to bring about peace – peaceful relations, peaceful communication, peaceful friendship between two. Brothers ought to be at peace with one another" (1981:72).

The explicit purpose of peacemaking or discipline according to the New Testament is threefold, to promote:

- the glory of God,
- the welfare of the church, and
- the restoration of the sinner.

Peacemaking is done first of all to glorify God. He is glorified when unbelievers see our good deeds, and he is blasphemed when they see sin in the church (Mt 5:16, 1 Pt 2:12, Rm 2:24). Thus, we promote his glory and honor his name when we keep his commandments and deal with sin biblically. Second, the goal of peacemaking is the welfare of the church. We are commanded to guard the purity and unity of the body (1 Cor 5:1-13; Rm 15:5-7, 16:17-18; Eph 4:3; Tit 3:10-11). Finally, the purpose of peacemaking is restoration, the winning back of an erring brother (Mt 18:15-17).

While much of the New Testament focuses on the more typical aspects of peacemaking (rebuking, forgiving, restoring), there are cases of excommunication. At Corinth, a man was excommunicated for moral reasons; he was living in an incestuous relationship (see 1 Cor 5). In 1 Timothy 1:18-20, Paul describes excommunication for doctrinal reasons. Hymenaeus and Alexander were expelled from the church for their false teaching.

Because we live in a fallen world, we are forced to focus on the reactive or restorative dimensions to peacemaking. "How can we be reconciled once we are alienated?" is the key question in most cases.

We are commanded to be peacemakers because of the importance of unity in the body of Christ (Jn 17:21-23, Eph 4:1-3).

- "So then let us pursue the things which make for peace" (Rm 14:19).
- "Pursue peace with all men" (Hb 12:14).
- "Seek peace and pursue it" (1 Pt 3:11).

The word translated "pursue" in the three verses above is the Greek word, *dioko*, which means "to strive for, aspire to or follow zealously." We must be diligent and wholehearted in our pursuit of peace. Peacemaking demands active, persistent effort. And the peace we are pursuing is not just the absence of strife, but rather the development of harmony and intimacy in our relationships.

The whole church is commanded to operate as peacemakers – but it is the special task of the spiritually mature:

> Brethren, even if a man is caught in any trespass, you who are spiritual, restore such a one in a spirit of gentleness, looking to yourself, lest you too be tempted (Gal 6:1).

Although the New Testament describes spirituality in many ways (abiding in the vine, fighting the good fight, taking up the cross, the fruit of the Spirit, holiness, etc.), Galatians 6:1 clearly underscores the fact that truly spiritual people are peacemakers. They seek to restore those who have fallen into sin or reconcile those who are enemies. In other words, "The way you and I respond to someone who sins indicates whether or not we are spiritual" (Laney 1985: 83).

Galatians 6:1 contains three important aspects of spirituality: the who, the what and the how. First of all, the *who*: the context links spirituality with the fruit of the Spirit (Gal 5:22-23). Second, the *what*: the characteristics of spirituality listed in the fruit of the Spirit must find expression in the often difficult work of peacemaking. Or conversely, the one who manifests the fruit of the Spirit will be a peacemaker! Third, the *how*: the ministry of peacemaking must be carried out in a spirit of gentleness, humility and vigilance. We must gently restore the erring brother, all the while being on guard, because we ourselves can be tempted.

Why is peacemaking so important? Peacemaking is commanded of believers. Peacemaking defines spirituality. Moreover, God promises a blessing to those who are peacemakers: Blessed are the peacemakers, for they shall be called the sons of God (Mt 5:9).

The emphasis of the pronouncement of blessing here is on divine approval more than on our personal happiness. In other words, peacemakers have the approval of God on their lives! They are called sons of God because they are acting like their Father, the God of Peace (Phl 4:9, 1 Ths 5:23) who sent the Prince of Peace (Is 9:6) to bring about a world of peace (Lk 2:14). "There is no more Godlike work to be done in this world than peacemaking."[1]

Summary

If we are to establish communities of the King, then truth encounter and power encounter must be accompanied by moral encounter. The law of the kingdom is love (Jm 2:8). The fruit of the kingdom is peace (Rm 14:17). Blessed are the church planters who are also peacemakers!

Questions for Reflection and Discussion

1. What is your "game plan" for character development in your team and among new leaders of fledgling churches?

2. What are the predominant character flaws among your people of service? What does this suggest for teaching and other forms of discipleship?

3. In your context do you recognize false prophets whose miracles are not matched by morality? What should be your response to such false prophets?

4. To what extent has your training prepared you for effective peacemaking and church discipline? How will you fill the gaps in your preparations?

It will help you to better digest what you're reading if you take the time to reflect on and discuss such questions after each chapter. Also, I would value a glimpse of what you're thinking! I invite you (either now or later) to share with me (r_d_love@hotmail.com) some of your answers to these questions. You may have some good things to teach me.

Notes

[1] Broadus quoted in Carson 1984:135.

Chapter 11

Cultural Encounter

The development of strategies for world evangelization calls for imaginative pioneering methods. Under God, the result will be the rise of churches deeply rooted in Christ and closely related to their culture.

— The Lausanne Covenant #10

The Role of Ritual

By nature, I recoil from rituals. I come from a church background that is anti-ritual, and I was raised in California in a time and place when non-conformity was highly valued. Furthermore, I know enough about church history to realize that rituals often deteriorate into lifeless forms.

However, the Bible is more positive about rituals than I am. In fact, central to Christian worship are the sacraments of baptism and the Lord's Supper. Both of these rituals are concrete illustrations of the gospel — visual aids, if you will. Baptism exemplifies our union with Christ in his death and resurrection (Rm 6:3-5), and the Lord's Supper proclaims the death of Christ (1 Cor 11:23-26). God makes good use of ritual!

Even if God weren't committed to ritual, folk Muslims are. Like most people in the world, folk Muslims' lives progress through formal traditions and well-defined rituals. Ceremonies and rituals are not optional. They are a pervasive fact of life for folk Muslims. Therefore, church planters must work with the emerging church to develop appropriate rituals. I call this process cultural encounter. The gospel of the kingdom must find expression in culture.

The word "ritual" can be defined broadly to describe anything from the etiquette of daily greetings to the solemnity of sacred ceremonies. In this wide sense, ritual is almost synonymous with the learned behavioral patterns of a people, a central element of every culture.

Ritual retains its broad ramifications even in the narrower focus of religion. Religious ritual serves numerous social functions. Rituals preserve culture and give individuals a sense of group identity. Religious rituals also reinforce the social order, producing a feeling of solidarity between its members.

Effective church planters must understand these broad social functions of religious ritual. However, their primary concern should be to understand ritual as it relates to folk Muslims' perspective of the spirit realm. In this sense, ritual is "the heart of religious behavior ... 'the meat which goes on the bones of ... beliefs' " (Lehman and Myers 1985: 50). To understand a people's religious ritual is to comprehend what they really believe.

According to Steyne, "Ritual articulates the formula for eliciting help from the spirit world ... an effective system of manipulation. ... Through ritual, that is, right ritual, man seeks to tap into a power source" (1989:96), This definition highlights two important elements of ritual: it seeks *power* through the use of *manipulation*.

David Burnett describes three kinds of religious rituals: Life-Cycle, Calendar and Crisis Rituals (1988:93-106). *Life-Cycle Rituals* are rites of passage, transition rituals that mark the important stages of life such as birth, circumcision, marriage and death. *Calendar Rituals*, by contrast, are not related to stages of life, but rather to points on the calendar. In many cultures, calendar rituals are related to the agricultural cycle. However, among folk Muslims they are linked to the Islamic calendar. The commemoration of Muhammad's birth, the breaking of the fast after *Ramadan* (the month of fasting) known as *Id ul-fitr*, and *Id ul-adha*, which commemorates Abraham's sacrifice of a lamb in place of Ishmael[1] are the most significant in the Islamic calendar. After conversion, folk Muslims would most likely want to celebrate the birth of Jesus as well as his death and resurrection. *Crisis Rituals* are usually precipitated by unforeseen events, such as sickness, accidents, curses, droughts, unexpected death. They are carried out in order to ameliorate problems, or restore health and harmony in life. Whereas life-cycle and calendar rituals are predictable and generally celebrated by the society as a whole, crisis rituals deal with the unpredictable and usually benefit only a small group or a single individual.

The following section focuses on the life-cycle rituals of the Baahithiin in order to illustrate how the gospel might be contextualized in indigenous cultural forms.

Life-Cycle Rituals

Every culture responds to the biological stages of human life with some sort of life-cycle rituals. These rites reveal the people's assumptions about the nature and destiny of human beings and their place in the world. They provide a window into the group's understanding of the spirit realm. The figure that follows describes the major life-cycle ceremonies the Baahithiin observe.

Life-cycle ceremonies are at the heart of Baahithiin religion. At the core of each ceremony is the communal feast (*haflat musaalaha**), which is celebrated at every stage of the life-cycle. That the *haflat musaalaha* goes beyond the bounds of orthodox Islam causes no concern to the Baahithiin. A veteran missionary to folk Muslims writes:

> With no twinge of conscience or sense of conflict, a faithful Baahithiin Muslim can confess at the mosque, "There is no God but Allah, and Muhammad is his Prophet," then go home to an animistic spirit feast. This spirit feast is the real heart-felt religion of the people of [our region]. Almost all the people would observe spirit feasts.

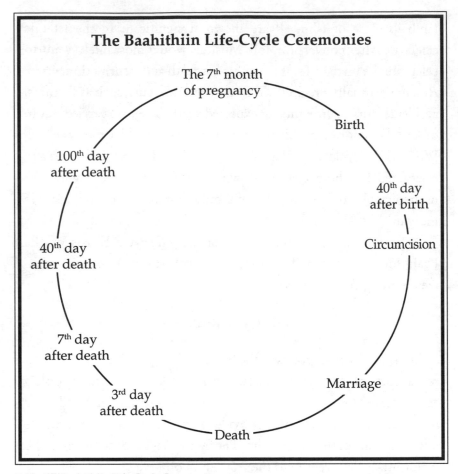

Table 13: Baahithiin Life-Cycle Ceremonies

The meaning and purpose of the *haflat musaalaha* can best be understood linguistically. The words in Baahithiin convey the basic meaning of bringing something into a state of well-being, safety, security or harmony. These communal feasts enable the Baahithiin to maintain and carefully guard the social and spiritual well-being of the community. It helps them keep relationships between people and the supernatural in proper balance.

There are prescribed occasions for the *haflat musaalaha*, linked to the Baahithiin life-cycle (birth, circumcision, marriage and death), and there are spontaneous feasts celebrated during important occasions such as harvest, graduation or moving. These feasts can be simple or elaborate, depending on the situation and financial ability of the host.

While feasts vary (depending on the community, purpose and the people), there are a number of elements found in almost every communal feast. The house is the ritual center. All the furniture is moved from the front room, and straw mats are placed on the ground where the people sit in a circle. Every *haflat musaalaha* formally begins when the host (or his representative) opens the ceremony with an expression of gratitude for the attendance of the guests, a statement of the purpose of the *haflat musaalaha* and an apology for all its possible shortcomings (e.g., the language used may not be polite enough, the food may not taste good, the house may be run down and so forth).

Next, an Islamic leader will pray. This prayer is different from what most Westerners know as prayer. It is actually a recitation from the Quran, asking for blessing and protection. This part of the ritual often includes the burning of incense and food offerings to the ancestor spirits. After the prayer, many feasts include an Islamic chant confessing the oneness of God. "There is no God but Allah" is repeated in chorus by all the participants, as many as 100 times or sometimes even for an hour. Then everyone eats a rice meal together. These meals usually consist of a bowl of rice with side dishes of vegetables, potatoes and chicken. A slice of cake and bananas are eaten after the meal to "clean one's mouth" and the participants all drink tea. The guests often bring food, described as "blessing", home from the *haflat musaalaha*. At some feasts, the food they bring home may be a full meal, while at others it may consist only of a piece of cake.

These feasts have significant social and spiritual functions. Socially, these communal feasts provide a community get-together, a time to draw near to one another and strengthen relationships. However, more than just social "chit-chat" takes place. It is also a time for the elders to discuss community issues. According to one of my informants, the *haflat musaalaha* has two functions: to address the ancestor spirits and to address Allah. "We have to ask for help from the ancestor spirits. Since they are dead, they are closer to God than we are. So, we ask for help and we also ask for permission to put on a *haflat musaalaha* because many people will come and might disturb them. We give thanks to God and ask for his blessing too."

Cultural Encounter for the Kingdom

What follows are some concrete examples of cultural encounter (or contextualization) from the Baahithiin life-cycle rituals that developed through a long and complex process. Various aspects of the rituals have been adopted, confronted or substituted.[2]

Many aspects of the Baahithiin life-cycle rituals, especially as they are expressed in the *haflat musaalaha*, can be adopted without change. For example, the home should remain the ritual center. This is especially significant for Baahithiin outreach. A large social barrier already stands between Christians and the Baahithiin. If these communal meals are celebrated in a church building instead of the home, significant evangelistic opportunities are lost.

We did not continue the practice of burning incense and giving offerings. The use of incense in ritual prayer has its roots in animism/Hinduism, whereas the giving of offerings is linked to ancestor worship. Because of these strong idolatrous connotations, we felt they must be confronted. I hasten to add, however, that since both of these practices have Old Testament precedent, it may be possible to transform these rituals.[3]

The prayer, reading of the Quran, and chanting can easily be transformed through the process of substitution. Prayer in the *haflat musaalaha* usually has two directions, which reflect the Godward and the Satanward dimensions of spirituality. There is a request for blessing (Godward) and a request for deliverance (Satanward). Both aspects are thoroughly biblical. The concept of "blessing" is central to Scripture and reflects an important element of biblical prayer (Nm 6:24-26, Ps 67).

Blessing is not only an important concept of Scripture but also may be a valuable bridge to reaching Muslims. In his book, *Blessing in*

Mosque and Mission, Larry Lenning argues that blessing is a holistic, power-laden concept that is central to both Islam and Scripture. He concludes:

> First, Christians and Muslims alike look to God as the source of all blessings. This fact, plus additional factors such as the strong emphasis on the blessing of Abraham, indicate the potential of blessing as a theological bridge to Islam. Second, the influence of blessing through effective media, personal evangelism, and dialogue reveals the fact that this has become a missiological bridge to Islam. Finally, and for the author most significantly, the dynamic impact of ritual indicates that blessing has great potential as a liturgical bridge to Islam (1980:115).

Prayers for deliverance should also be an important element in our prayers. In the Lord's Prayer, Jesus taught us to pray "deliver us from evil" (literally "the evil one," Mt 6:13). In his high priestly prayer, Jesus himself prayed, "Keep them from the evil one" (Jn 17:15). In addition, two times in the New Testament we are called to "resist the devil" (Jas 4:7, 1 Pet 5:9).

We can easily substitute the reading of Scripture for the reading of the Quran. In place of the Islamic chant ("There is no God but Allah"), we can develop a culturally relevant confession of faith. At one contextualized *haflat musaalaha* I attended, the Islamic chant was replaced with John 17:3, "And this is eternal life, that they may know you, the only true God, and Jesus Christ whom you have sent."

The following description of a contextualized *haflat musaalaha* is taken from my field notes in May 1991:

> Mr. and Mrs. Umar*, members of a Baahithiin church called Miyaah Hayyah* (which means 'Living Water'), recently moved to a new neighborhood. So they wanted to put on a *haflat musaalaha* to pray for protection from the forces of darkness and ask for blessing from God. Over 35 people (25 of these Baahithiin Muslims) squeezed into the Umars' little home. Twenty of these gathered in the front room where the ceremony was held (all men), ten women gathered in the back room and a handful of latecomers sat outside. Mr. Umar opened the ceremony in traditional Baahithiin fashion with an Arabic greeting. Next, he thanked the guests for coming to his *haflat musaalaha* and especially honored the leaders of the community. He then asked for forgiveness. "I ask for your pardon

because my house is too small, the food isn't that good and I can't speak Baahithiin very well." After that he quoted the state philosophy of religious diversity. First of all he mentioned the fact that all national citizens believe in the oneness of God. Second, he pointed out that state philosophy gives citizens freedom of religion. He then closed his short speech by asking those people who confess a different religion than he does to merely witness the ceremony.

Next, the leader of Miyaah Hayyah, Mr. Fuad*, clad in the traditional holy man attire, gave a similar Arabic greeting. After making a joke about his accent, he proceeded to quote the Quran and Baahithiin proverbs as examples of his theme: We can receive protection and blessing from Allah because he is a loving God. Miyaah Hayyah next sang two songs, both of which emphasized love. The first song was from Ps 103, the second song was taken from the love chapter, 1 Cor 13. These songs were in Baahithiin, using their musical scale as well as a distinctive Baahithiin musical instrument.

Mr. Fuad then read a confession taken from numerous verses in the Bible:

I confess that there is one God. There is no God but Allah. And you shall love the Lord your God with all your heart, with all your soul and with all your mind. Also, you shall love your neighbor as yourself. However, this is love, not that we loved God but that he loved us and sent Isa al-Masih [Jesus the Messiah] to die for our sins. So, this is eternal life, that we might know the only true God and Isa al-Masih [Jesus the Messiah] whom he has sent.

Next, Mr. Fuad used the Lord's Prayer as a basis to pray for protection and God's blessing. However, instead of beginning with the word "Father" (which is very offensive to Muslims), he prayed to God, "who loves us like a father loves his children." Because Mr. Fuad was sensitive in his choice of words, the whole gathering repeatedly echoed "Amen" at the end of each petition. The gap between Christian and Muslim was bridged, at least for the moment, and without compromising theologically. The traditional rice cone was placed in the middle of the gathering, and Mr. Umar cut off the top and gave it to the oldest man present. After that the rest of the food was brought out and everyone feasted.

Besides a lot of joking around, many people commented on the songs. The Scripture songs, put to a blend of traditional and pop Baahithiin music, touched the hearts of the people. People talked into the evening, and Mr. Fuad had ample opportunity to draw near to this new network of people as well as to share some from Scripture. (He explained, for example, that the words that touched their hearts about love, "Love is patient, love is kind," etc., are from the Bible.)

It's been over a week since the *haflat musaalaha*, but neighbors are still commenting on it. Some of the neighbors have also been visiting regularly since the ceremony. Mrs. Umar's family (all Baahithiin Muslims) asked who the holy man was. They also commented repeatedly, "This ceremony was totally Baahithiin. We didn't know Christians did this. And we didn't know that you prayed to the Lord God, we thought you only prayed to Jesus!" Mrs. Umar's parents have also told her that they wouldn't mind if her younger brothers and sisters joined her in her religion.

Developing contextual rituals for life-cycle ceremonies and other important rites is not enough. The church must be contextualized at every level. Thus among the Baahithiin we adopted and adapted many forms from the communal meal and various art forms for our Christmas and Easter celebrations. Our churches have also integrated many of these same forms into their meetings and liturgies.

Culturally relevant church rituals are being developed throughout the Muslim world. A women's fellowship in the Middle East provides another illustration of this kind of cultural encounter.

Let me take you to a meeting in a home in [the capital]. Present are two missionary women and half a dozen poor [national] women. These women had, over the course of the past nine months, each confessed their faith in *Isa al-Masih* (Arabic for Jesus the Messiah). Several of them had known each other previous to their contact with our team. Several of them worked for us as house helpers.

The first of them who had come to faith had met weekly with a mixed-gender group at an evening fellowship. But because it was inappropriate for them to travel across the city alone at night, they requested a separate meeting – for women only – during the daytime. In need of a neutral word with which we could refer to the evening fellowship meeting, we chose "the Tree." This new women's group, we called "the Flower."

Outside the room on a tray are cookie crumbs and half-empty glasses of tea. We've just finished a half-hour of conversation before the beginning of the meeting. As the [national] *sheikha* (leader) ushers us into the prayer room, our shoes pile up outside the door. We adjust the scarves over our heads to prepare for prayer. The women stand shoulder to shoulder, lifting their hands as the *sheikha* calls out in Arabic: *Allahu akbar* ... "God is great. I testify that there is no God but God, and *Isa* is the word of God."

The women begin to tell God how much they appreciate what he has done in their lives. They pray for one another's children to be healed of various sicknesses. They ask God to bring their husbands to faith in *Isa*. They ask him for jobs for this friend or that relative.

A few minutes later, these spontaneous prayers end as the *sheikha* leads the group in a responsive chorus that begins *Abana illethi fi samawaat* ... "Our Father, who art in heaven ..." After the prayers, everyone settles on the wide Persian carpet that stretches across the floor.

We continue the meeting by singing a number of worship choruses, mostly to Middle Eastern tunes, that we had learned from a few local Christians. (We replaced the Arabic "Christian" term for Jesus, *yesua*, with *Isa*, the term for Jesus that Muslims recognize.) Unaccustomed to this kind of sing-along, the women are – frankly – pretty lousy singers. But they are joyfully making the noise of praise to *Isa*.

Since most of the group are illiterate, we chant responsively a few verses from the Gospels that we have been working to memorize. "Jesus said, 'I am the way, the truth, and the life. No one comes to the Father but through me.'" And, "Jesus said, 'Come to me, all you who are weary and burdened, and I will give you rest.'" Or, "The thief comes only to steal and kill and destroy; I have come that they may have life, and have it to the full." This chanting form of memorization was familiar to them, since that is the way Muslims commit the Quran to memory.

The lesson for the day focuses on Jesus' teaching about the kingdom of God in Matthew 20. As the text is read, the women are encouraged to listen for the commands as well as the promises of Jesus. (As an occasional teacher to this group, I found that their closeness to the culture of Jesus meant that they often helped me understand the content of the gospel in a fresh new light.)

One of the women has been attending the group for several weeks. A quiet, reserved young woman, she wears the clothes that mark her as a strict Muslim. We call her "Composed."

Despite the fact that she knew very little Arabic, my teammate Kim has been living out the gospel with "Composed" for nearly a year. Kim has shown her the "Jesus" film and tried to answer her many, many questions about who Jesus is. Kim also set to rest a number of her misconceptions (promulgated by Islamic teachers) about what it means to follow Christ. She has come today wanting to be baptized.

Before she is baptized, we formally ask "Composed" five questions. These questions focus on beliefs that are typical stumbling blocks for Muslims.

- Do you believe that *Isa* is the word of God in human flesh?
- Do you believe that he died on the cross?
- Do you believe that his death on the cross paid for your sins?
- Do you believe that God raised him from the dead?
- Are you willing to obey him and follow him as your lord and master?

She answers all in the affirmative. Lacking a baptismal pool, we "immerse by sprinkling," pouring water over her head and pronouncing her baptized "in the name of the Father, and of the Son, and of the Holy Spirit."

Then, with one of these precious, illiterate women leading the recitation of the ceremonial words of 1 Corinthians 11 from memory, we together break bread and share the cup of the Lord's Supper.

A friend working among Muslims, John Travis*, has developed an extremely helpful tool for contextualization. He calls it the C1-C6 Spectrum, describing six possible ways the church could contextualize in a Muslim setting (see following table). This model is useful in a variety of contexts.

The C1 model reflects a wholesale rejection of contextualization. This approach uses traditional Western church forms and the language of trade rather than the language of the people group. The C2 model is basically the same, except that the C2 approach does use the language of the people group. For example, a Kazak church would be C1 if it used traditional Western forms and spoke Russian. It would be C2 if it used traditional forms but spoke Kazak.

Ideally a C3 church tries to contextualize by avoiding both Western and Islamic forms. Thus, the C3 approach looks for models of church life outside the mosque. Traditional rituals, ceremonies, arts and aspects of culture that are not part of Islamic belief or practice provide contextual possibilities for the C3 church planter. This approach may be more difficult to apply in the Arab world, since Arab culture and Islam are intimately related. In non-Arab countries, where Arabic and Islamic forms are more of a veneer over deeply held cultural beliefs and practices, it may be easier to develop C3 churches. In fact, C3 contextualization should probably be our goal in various Muslim countries.

C1-C6 Spectrum

A range of church/fellowship structures presently or potentially available to Muslim-backgound believers based on commonly-used linguistic, cultural and religious forms.*

C1   **Traditional** church structure; using **national or trade language**. Reflects Western churches in practices and styles.

C2   **Traditional** church structure; using **local or heart language**. Very similar to C1.

C3   **Contextualized** church structure; **ethnic/local arts** and **culture** reflected.

C4   **Contextualized** church structure; **ethnic/local arts** and **culture** reflected and some **biblically acceptable/usable Islamic forms** and **traditions**.

C5   **Congregations of Messianic Muslims.** Like "Jews for Jesus" movement. This has emerged in some Muslim countries, generally through people movements.**

C6   **Clusters of "secret believers" within Islam.** Such believers have little if any contact with other Christians. Many have found Christ through dreams, miracles or the Quran. Limited fellowship with other C6-type believers.

Table 14: C1-C6 Spectrum

*N.B. This chart is only an attempt to graphically portray some of the individual and congregational socio-religious dynamics and processes that take place when Muslims become followers of Jesus. The C1-C6 range is not exhaustive, nor does it place value judgments on any one form. It has been created primarily as a point of reference for ongoing discussion and development of strategies. There is no traditional theological bias: any believer (C1-C6) could hold a variety of Biblical theological positions, e.g. Arminian/Calvinist, Pentecostal/non-Pentecostal, etc.

** C5 represents the generally perceived boundary between Christianity and Islam as institutions (religious organizations). This means that to some in the community, a C5 follower of Christ would be seen as being an unique kind of Christian; to others he would appear to be an unorthodox Muslim. As the case of Messianic Jews, the question of their true identity is raised: "Are they really Christians, or Muslims?" To a large extent, the answer is a matter of a person's perspective. In the final analysis only God knows, because He looks beyond the form to the heart.

A C4 church not only adapts to culture but also adopts biblically acceptable Islamic forms and traditions. This level of contextualization forces us to ask deeper theological questions. It is one thing to adapt to a culture and quite another thing to relate to a religion. How do we relate to non-Christian religions in general and to Islam in particular?

Paul's letter to Romans is a good starting point. In Romans 1:18-32 we have Paul's description of what theologians call "general revelation." Paul makes two central affirmations about God's dealing with humanity. First of all, Paul speaks of *revelation*. Paul emphasizes the clarity of God's revelation. He says it is "evident" (v 19), "clearly seen" (v 20), and "understood" (v 20). Of all humanity, he says, "they are without excuse" (v 20); "they know God" (vs 21, 28); and "they know the ordinances of God" (v 32). Next, he describes the content of revelation, affirming that all can perceive God's invisible attributes, external power, and divine nature and that all acknowledge his right to judge (vs 20, 32).

Second, Paul speaks of *suppression and substitution*. Although God has clearly and emphatically revealed himself to all people, through suppression of truth (by unrighteousness, v 18) and substitution of truth (they exchanged the glory of God, vs 23, 25) they have perverted God's revelation.

Paul teaches the principles of divine revelation and human rejection. Thus, there is a divine/demonic tension that is characteristic of all men and all religions. According to Bavinck:

> All the great religions in history are man's answer embodying this mysterious process of repression .... In the 'night of power' of which the ninety-seventh sura of the Koran speaks, the night when the 'angels descended' and the Koran descended from Allah's throne, God dealt with Mohammed and touched him. God wrestled with him in that night and God's hand is still noticeable in the answer of the prophet, but is also the result of human repression. The great moments in the history of religion are the moments when God wrestled with man in a very particular way. ... It includes the divine approach and human rejection. This rejection is hidden because man apparently is seeking God and serving him, but the God he seeks is different from the true God because of the uncanny process of repression and exchange that enters in. It seems to me that we can

thus formulate the testimony of the Bible concerning human religions (1981:125).

Although non-Christian religions are fundamentally in error, undisputed truths about God, man and sin can be found in varying degrees in them. Also, the great religions of the world frequently display a sensitivity to the spiritual dimension of life, finding expression through their adherents' persistence in devotion and readiness to sacrifice. Personal virtues like gentleness, patience, and serenity of temper along with social virtues such as concern for the poor and nonviolence are also prized in many religions of the world.

The religion of Islam has a greater degree of truth than most religions. Islam has built-in theological bridges or starting points for communication, which can be employed for the kingdom. Why is Islam the religion closest to Christianity except for Judaism? Vos' humorous illustration says it well.

> There is a story of a woman who sent a manuscript of poetry to a publisher, hoping that it would be published in book form. The publisher rejected it, sending a note saying, 'Dear Madam: Your poetry is both good and original. But unfortunately the part that is good is not original, and the part that is original is not good.' It might be truly observed that in Islam that which is good is not original, but borrowed from other faiths, while that which is original is not good (1965:62).

We need to exploit these built-in theological bridges by using a C4 approach to church planting. A C4 approach is not only concerned about crossing bridges to communicate the gospel with Muslims. A C4 approach also wants to break down unnecessary barriers to the gospel. A C4 approach challenges Christians to reexamine their own cherished traditions and beliefs. Just as we do not want to acritically accept Islamic forms and beliefs, neither do we want to baptize our own practices and perspectives as if they were all from God.

For example, do we need to have a building to plant a church? Do pastors have to graduate from Bible school or seminary to pastor a church? What are the Christian forms of prayer? Does the Bible say anything about closed eyes and folded hands? It does say a lot about bowing down to the ground and lifting hands to the Lord–forms usually equated with Islam! (See Ex 4:31, 12:27; Ps 63:4, 95:6; 1 Tm 2:8). At a deeper level, do we have to call Jesus the "Son of God," or are there other titles just as biblical but more relevant to Islam (Messiah? Savior? Word of God, Mediator)?[4]

"Though a corruption of Christian teaching, Islam can be used to help correct Christian practice–particularly through its uncompromising emphasis on the transcendent character of God" (Inch 1982:73). In fact, as noted earlier, according to J. Dudley Woodberry, "what have come to be known as the 'pillars' of Islam are all adaptations of previous Jewish and Christian forms!" (Gilliland 1989:282).

Therefore, a fully biblical position regarding Islam affirms its elements of both truth and error. However, Islam is fundamentally in error. Because of this, the emphases of the three aspects of contextualization (adoption, transformation and confrontation) will be on transformation and confrontation.

A C5 approach to contextualization is often described in terms of "messianic Muslims" or "Jesus mosques.[5] However, a C5 approach is no different from a C4 approach at a theoretical or theological level. Both seek a contextualization that is relevant and prophetic, an approach that adapts to culture yet submits to Scripture.

The difference between a C4 and C5 approach is threefold. First of all, the context should determine one's contextual practices. If there is a Christian presence, as is the case in most cities, it may be difficult to use a C5 approach. It could confuse the Muslim populace and possibly cause resentment among Christians, since in most cases they would not understand. A C4 approach is hard enough on traditional Christians!

Second, the degree of Islamicization would determine which approach is best. It would be unwise and even uncontextual to imitate Islamic forms of prayer in a country where the Muslim majority rarely pray. The goal of a C5 approach is not to impose a form, but to use those forms that are most meaningful to the new converts.

Third, there is a difference in terminology. While a C4 approach prefers to use non-Christian religious terminology, those using a C5 approach are very strict in this regard. Traditional Christian terminology is not used. A C5 approach has no orientation to the traditional church in any way.

The concepts of Messianic Muslims and Jesus Mosques mean different things to different people. Practically, a whole continuum of possibilities exist—some syncretistic, others biblical. For example, to model the church after Friday's prayers in the mosque (even with Christian content) and use that as the sole example of church life is clearly sub-biblical. The *umma* (community) of Islam must be transformed into the Body of Christ. We cannot merely follow Islamic liturgy. We must gather in small groups to obey the "one another" verses of the Bible.

In recent years a C5 movement has taken place in South Asia. Reported estimates of the number of converts range from 10,000 to 100,000. (An independent study identified 4,500 followers of Christ in a sample of the villages surveyed.) Many observers are exuberant about this work, while others remain skeptical, claiming syncretism. Several factors have contributed to this movement. One of the most important is a contextual translation of the Bible that uses Islamic terminology. Some expatriate pioneers have also been influential.

I believe that two different C5 churches could be basically identical in their forms, yet one could be contextual while the other would be syncretistic. The difference is at the level of meaning. As I noted earlier in my discussion on contextualization, this emphasis on meaning is at once the most profound and difficult aspect of contextualization. In fact, the battle for Biblical contextualization against heretical syncretism is fought here. Change at the meaning level comes through the Spirit-led study of the Scriptures in community. It involves a sustained effort at reinterpreting old Islamic forms and giving them new biblical meaning (cf. Parshall 1988).

A C6 development in Muslim ministry has happened and will continue to happen. However, it should never be an intentional strategy. New Testament Christianity is characterized by boldness, not secret believers. The very last verse in the book of Acts summarizes the church's goal. We need to be "preaching the kingdom of God and teaching concerning the Lord Jesus Christ with all openness, unhindered" (Acts 28:31).

The following table may help determine what level of contextualization is appropriate for what context. The four quadrants describe four different ways a people perceive themselves. The table is easy to understand and makes analysis simple. The ethnographic research necessary to arrive at valid conclusions, however, is difficult. Contextualization is not only concerned about cognitive categories and ritualistic behavior. It must also be deeply concerned about the "feelings" of the people. A people's self-perception has strong emotional overtones.

Charting Islamic Identity and Practice Among Folk Muslims

Low Identity High Practice	High Identity High Practice
Low Identity Low Practice	High Identity Low Practice

Table 15: Charting Islamic Identity and Practice Among Folk Muslims

Quadrant 1 (low identity and high practice) means that this Islamic people group does not emotionally identify with Islam, but faithfully practice their religion. Quadrant 1 is more a theoretical possibility than a practical reality. I've never met nor heard of Muslims like this.

Muslims in quadrant 2 (high identity and high practice) strongly identify with and faithfully practice their religion. In general, quadrant 2

Muslims reflect orthodox Islam, though one could still be a folk Muslim in quadrant 2. I suggest that quadrant 2 Muslims may require a C5 level of contextualization. Some Muslims in the Arabian Gulf may fit this category.

Quadrant 3 Muslims (low identity and low practice) neither strongly identify with nor faithfully practice their religion. They are good candidates for a C3 approach to contextualization. Muslims in the former Soviet Republics, such as the Kazaks or Tajiks, may fit this category.

Quadrant 4 (high identity and low practice) Muslims strongly identify with Islam emotionally but do not reflect it in their practice. A C4 or a C5 approach would be most relevant to Muslims in this quadrant. There are numerous Muslims in Southeast Asia who fit this category.

Summary

Life for most folk Muslims centers around formal traditions and well-defined rituals. These are a pervasive fact of life for folk Muslims. Therefore, we must work with the emerging church to develop appropriate biblical rituals, through a process I call cultural encounter. The gospel of the kingdom must find expression in culture, especially in life-cycle rituals, calendar rituals and crisis rituals. The C1-C6 contextualization spectrum, which illustrates the potential levels of contextualization, and the Islamic identity chart, which shows types of Islam, can give church planters among folk Muslims a greater sensitivity to their context.

Questions for Reflection and Discussion

1. Which ceremonies and rituals are especially relevant to evangelism, discipleship, and church planting among your people? What is the spectrum of opinions among your co-workers in how to address these ceremonies and rituals?

2. Summarize the life-cycle ceremonies among your community. Which of these ceremonies do you find most redemptive or "neutral," and which do you find most problematic? Where do you suggest adoption, confrontation, and transformation?

3. As you review the C1-C6 spectrum, which church structures seem most appropriate for your setting, and why? To what extent does table 15 help you decide? What possibilities and problems can you envision for the simultaneous outworking of two or more models in the same setting?

It will help you to better digest what you're reading if you take the time to reflect on and discuss such questions after each chapter. Also, I would value a glimpse of what you're thinking! I invite you (either now or later) to share with me (r_d_love@hotmail.com) some of your answers to these questions. You may have some good things to teach me.

Notes

[1] The Islamic version of this sacrifice differs from that in Genesis 22. Muslims believe that Ishmael, not Isaac, was the son offered up to God.

[2] For a discussion of these terms, refer to Chapter 4.

[3] The key issue regarding the use of these forms centers around their perceived meaning. If someone chooses to use these forms, there should be a sustained effort at reinterpreting them, so that the old forms take on new meanings.

[4] A cursory reading of the various titles of Jesus in John 1 is an excellent starting point for Christological contextualization.

[5] For an illustration of this, see Winter and Hawthorne 1992:D-141-144.

*a pseudonym

Chapter 12

Thy Kingdom Come

Our look at popular Islam pushes the issue of kingdom power very much to the forefront. ... People are sick and in need of healing; by magic or by Christ? People require help in a world of hostile, occult "beings," by alliance with evil spirits, or with the Holy Spirit? ... For too long, it would seem, in Christian witness among Muslims, there have been no power encounters because there have been no power bearers.

        – Bill Musk

Three-fourths of the Muslim world, approximately 800 million people, are folk Muslims–confessing the greatness of Allah, yet fearing spirits. They have heard little or nothing of the Messiah who came to destroy the works of the devil. They have not heard the good news of the one who came to deliver them from the domain of darkness and transfer them into the kingdom of light.

I believe that an effective church-planting ministry among folk Muslims will include truth encounter, power encounter, moral encounter and cultural encounter. The church-planting team and then the emerging church need to preach the good news that Jesus came to destroy the works of the devil (truth encounter), confront the powers of darkness through exorcism and healing (power encounter), model the values of the kingdom (moral encounter), and express the reality of the kingdom through culturally relevant rituals (cultural encounter).

Kingdom ministry has a relevance far beyond folk Muslims. This approach can be effective among animists, Hindus and Buddhists as well. A kingdom orientation is bearing fruit in many diverse ministries in the West, too.

But my burden is for Muslims–the largest bloc of unreached peoples in the world. This is the major evangelistic challenge facing the church today. Muslims comprise the final frontier of the Great Commission. Many have assumed that Muslims are so resistant they cannot be won. The truth is that Muslims are not so much resistant to the gospel as they are neglected by Christians. For hundreds of years, the church has virtually ignored the Muslim world.

In our day, God is doing a new thing! He is putting Muslims on the agenda of the church. There is an unprecedented openness to the gospel among Muslims. Hundreds of missionaries to Muslims have been sent out through many different mission agencies within the last decade. Missions like Youth With A Mission and Operation Mobilization are now involved in long-term church-planting efforts among Muslims. The Assemblies of God, Southern Baptists, WEC International, International Missions (now Christar), SIM International, Pioneers and Navigators are just a few of the mission agencies making a significant impact on the Muslim world. Frontiers has more than 600 missionaries seeking to share the love of Christ with Muslims; these missionaries, on approximately 100 teams, have seen thousands of Muslims come to Christ and have established more than 70 fellowships of Muslim-background believers.

The kingdom of God is advancing in the Muslim world. *In fact, more Muslims have come to Christ in the past 25 years than in the previous 1,400 years of missions history combined!* This is a positive step in light of church history. However, in light of more than one billion Muslims, it is barely a ripple. The laborers are few. Muslims remain the least-reached peoples on earth.

Hundreds of millions of Muslims wake up every morning with no church, with no Bible, with no one to tell them about the way, the truth and the life. Five times a day they hear "God is great" ringing from the mosque. Who will be the first person to tell them that God is love?

It is time for the church to move out in kingdom power to see the King exalted in this final frontier.

Lord of the harvest, hallowed be your name. May your people so honor, revere and love your name that they will do whatever it takes to see your name glorified in the Muslim world. May your kingdom come upon the church. May the power of your kingdom shake your church so that thousands of new workers are sent out to plant churches throughout the Muslim world! Amiin.

Questions for Reflection and Discussion

1. What examples can you give from your own ministry regarding the convergence of truth encounter, power encounter, moral encounter, and cultural encounter?

2. Which parts of this book have you found most helpful or relevant to your ministry? Which parts have you found most difficult or unclear? With which parts do you most disagree, and why?

3. As you near the end of this book, what questions about ministry to folk Muslims are uppermost in your mind? Which questions or issues do you think I have neglected or have inadequately addressed? Can you point me to tools or resources I might find helpful?

It will help you to better digest what you're reading if you take the time to reflect on and discuss such questions after each chapter. Also, I would value a glimpse of what you're thinking! I invite you (either now or later) to share with me (r_d_love@hotmail.com) some of your answers to these questions. You may have some good things to teach me.

Appendix 1

The Master Builder's Blueprint:
A Model of Pioneer Church Planting

The Master Builder's Blueprint

Paul described the church-planting task in terms of a building and himself as a "wise master builder" (1 Cor 3:9,10). The word "master builder" (in Greek, *architekton*) "refers not simply to a 'carpenter', *tekton*, but to the one who serves as both architect and chief engineer" (Fee 1987:138). Thus, as the leader of a church-planting team, Paul saw himself as the supervisor. His task was to oversee the work performed by his fellow laborers who were building a spiritual temple in Corinth.

"The Master Builder's Blueprint" helps us visualize what is involved in the task of pioneer church planting.[1] This blueprint emerged as I developed as a team leader. As a young team leader, I encouraged everyone to "go out and love the Baahithiin." After numerous complaints from my teammates, I realized that loving people into churches is not something most people do intuitively. The blueprint helped the team visualize the steps involved in church planting.

The Foundation
Of course, the most important part of the building is its foundation. The foundation determines the size of the building. In church planting among Muslims, strong foundations are crucial.

Without them missionaries won't persevere and churches won't be planted.

The Master Builder's Blueprint

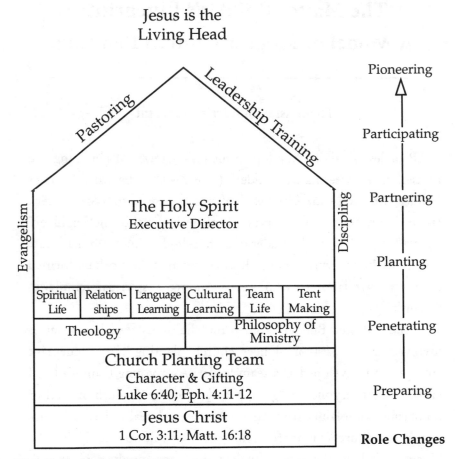

Table 16: The Master Builder's Blueprint

The First Layer: Jesus Christ

The Bible teaches that Jesus Christ is the foundation of the church (1 Cor 3:11). Jesus is the "precious corner stone" (1 Pet. 2:5), and the church planter must understand this both as a doctrinal truth and as a spiritual reality.

Jesus also describes himself as the church builder: "I will build my church and the gates of Hades will not prevail against it" (Mt 16:18). Church planting, first and last, is his idea and his work. More than pious platitudes, these words must be vital convictions. Countless times during my church-planting experience I had to return to these basic promises to regain perspective and hope. When the going gets tough—and it will—these truths function as the sword of the Spirit against the discouraging lies of the evil one. The church of Jesus Christ *will* be established among people from every tongue, tribe and nation (Rv 5:9, 7:9).

The Second Layer: The Character and Gifting of the Team

The character of the individuals on the church-planting team will greatly affect its success or lack thereof. Spiritual transformation lies at the heart of church planting, for we can only reproduce in others what the Spirit of God has produced in us. To plant spiritually transformed churches requires spiritually transformed people. Church planting is more than the implementation of a well thought-out strategy. We must not only dispense information; we must impart life (2 Cor 3:5,6).

Paul centered on this strategy. Colossians 1:28 describes Paul's priority in church planting: "We proclaim him, admonishing every man and teaching every man with all wisdom, that we may present every man complete [perfect] in Christ." Paul's goal was godliness. His aim was no less than to present every person perfect in Christ.

But he did not simply teach and exhort people about godly character. Paul modeled his message. He repeatedly called his converts to imitate him as he imitated Christ (1 Cor 4:16, 11:1). He encouraged new believers to follow his example (Phil 3:17): "The things you have learned and received and heard and seen in me, practice these things" (Phil 4:9).

The apostle Paul puts equally strong emphasis on character when describing the qualities of church leadership. Paul does mention that teaching and sound theology are important (1 Tm 3:2; Ti 1:9). Still, even a cursory reading of 1 Timothy 3 and Titus 1 shows that he puts a much greater emphasis on character.

Team members' spiritual gifts also play a crucial role in church planting. A team full of administrators and "mercy show-ers" will not be the most effective in a pioneering situation. The best teams will have a balance between apostle-evangelist types and pastors and teachers. Those with the gift of miracles or faith also prove valuable to the task.

Of course, God is sovereign. He uses a multitude of approaches and a wide variety of people to plant churches. We rejoice that he accomplishes his task through "earthen vessels" (2 Cor 4:7). Nevertheless, the gift-mix will either enhance or hinder the team's church-planting progress.

The Third Layer: Theology and Philosophy of Ministry

What we believe (our theology), and how we prioritize and live out our beliefs (our philosophy of ministry), greatly affect the type of churches we plant. Moreover, folk Muslims confront us with a whole array of unique questions.

What is necessary for worship, and what is negotiable? When should baptism take place? Is the church primarily a place or a people a building or a body? Does making disciples best take place in a classroom or should it be informal and incarnational?

Teams must hammer out a doctrine of the Holy Spirit. Is the fullness of the Holy Spirit a doctrine to believe or a dynamic reality to be experienced? Does the Holy Spirit empower us as a church-planting team for signs and wonders? Or does the Holy Spirit only convict us and Muslims about our sin?

Our doctrine of revelation will affect our views regarding contextualization. Are the beliefs and practices of our target people all demonic, or can many of them be transformed? Do we want to plant churches that are firmly rooted in Christ and closely related to their culture (contextualization) or do we want to reproduce the forms and traditions that we have learned in our sending churches (replication)?

Teams should ask and answer questions like these before they begin to plant churches. Much of this book describes how the theology of the kingdom affects church planting.

Our philosophy of ministry shapes our church-planting strategy as well. Our theology describes what we believe. Our philosophy of ministry focuses more on how we live out our beliefs. It describes our greatest values and highest priorities. A philosophy of ministry functions as a framework for discerning and deciding. It helps screen ideas and experiences and enables decisions based on explicit biblical principles.

If our theology and philosophy of ministry are well-defined, then the church-planting task is much easier. Our theology and philosophy of ministry help us to envision what kind of churches we want to plant as well as the steps involved in planting those kind of churches.

The Fourth Layer: Spiritual Life, Relationships, Language Learning, Culture Learning, Team Life, and Tentmaking

When I originally developed the Master Builder's Blueprint, this fourth layer was the entire foundation. I focused on these six tasks of a new missionary in order to help the team with the all-important management question: "How are we supposed to use our time?"

Since we were in a pioneer setting, we didn't have a nice clear-cut job description. Pioneering work involves much ambiguity. But these six building blocks greatly reduced our team's stress level and helped us stay on track with our goals.

Spiritual Life. All that we are and do as believers, team leaders, and church planters is founded on our spiritual life. A disciplined devotional life, crucial in any ministry, is especially important in a pioneer setting where supportive fellowship is usually lacking and spiritual warfare is particularly intense. In the words of Paul, we must discipline ourselves for the purpose of godliness (1 Tm 4:7).

Relationships. Close relationships with our target people is key to church planting. We will be most effective in language and culture learning, and ultimately in church planting, if we have numerous and close relationships with the people we serve.

In our Master Builder's Blueprint we separate relationships, language learning, and culture learning. Ideally, these three foundation stones will be integrated. However, people have different learning styles. Some people are highly relational and are weak at the more analytical or reflective dimensions of language and culture learning. On the other hand, some people are more bookish and prefer learning language with a helper, a tape recorder and a book. They minimize going "face to face" and downplay the relational dimensions to the task. Either extreme will produce sub-par church planters. Consequently, the Master Builder's Blueprint breaks down the one task of relational language and culture learning into three components so that none of these components will be overlooked or minimized.

To become accepted by our target group and effectively communicate Christ, we must become culture learners. We must come to understand our people group intimately by establishing deep relationships while we learn the language.

Team Life. The dynamics of team life, which are crucial to understand, include four stages: forming, storming, norming and performing.[2] In the forming stage, expectations are unclear and interactions are superficial. This is the honeymoon stage. The second stage (storming) is characterized by conflict and resistance to the group's task and structure. This is where personality differences, work styles and fleshly behavioral patterns emerge. The team must learn to deal with differences. The third stage (norming) is when the group develops a sense of cohesion. Members accept the team and establish norms for resolving conflicts, making decisions and completing assignments. The fourth stage (performing) is the payoff stage, when the group has a structure, a purpose, and a role. It is ready to tackle its task. At this stage, the team begins to bear fruit for the kingdom.

Tentmaking. Four important issues relate to tentmaking. First of all, we need to find credible tentmaking roles among our target people. Whether in business, education, or whatever we do, our role must make sense to those we are seeking to reach. Tentmaking is not a "covering" for reaching the lost; it is a platform for ministry. Because of this, we must do it heartily as unto the Lord, with excellence.

Second, we need to be wise in describing why we live among the target people we serve. I am concerned about the ethics of truth-telling. I have seen my fellow workers make what could have been serious security breaches (by spilling too much of their story) because they felt trapped by someone's questions. Others have just lied. (They repented quickly, however!) Finding an appropriate and truthful way to respond to our friends' question is important issue for the success of our mission and the integrity of our lives.

When asked various questions about his identity, Jesus did not always give full disclosure, yet he always told the truth. At the same time, he did not always answer others' questions about his ministry.[3] Neither must we. When people asked me why I came to my country of service, I gave various answers. Sometimes I told them I came to teach. Other times, I mentioned the beauty and adventure of living in that country. I also said I came to do research. In the right setting, I would say that God had sent me to the country. All of these answers were true. The wise person doesn't need to give the same answer to everyone.

Establishing an identity while maintaining security in restricted-access countries can create a stressful living situation. To live in a country as a tentmaker with the goal of planting churches among Muslims is not easy. However, one of the reasons for stress resides in our inability to live bi-vocationally. Sometimes missionaries think we are alone in our calling to live this way. Yet God has called the vast majority of Christians in the world to be bi-vocational. We all need to make a living while working to extend the kingdom. Missionaries simply have the challenge of doing so cross-culturally.

Third, we need to manage our time wisely. We can busy ourselves with "tentmaking" activities and forget the main reason we have been sent. We must do everything we can to integrate our lifestyles around church planting. Even though we are bi-vocational, our secular vocation must be chosen and lived out in such a way as to maximize impact for the kingdom.

Some tentmakers' vocation is merely *workable*, that is, their visa allows them to stay in the country, but their role doesn't make sense. For example, saying you are a businessmen, working 10 hours a week and living among the poor doesn't fit the typical American businessman's image. Other people stress the importance of being *viable*, that is, their work must make sense to their target people. Teaching English at least 20-30 hours a week fits with the role of a teacher. Yet it is possible to have a viable role and not be strategic. In my country I had a viable role as a teacher, but most of my students were not from the people group of my major focus. Ideally, we want to have a vocation that goes beyond being workable and even viable. We want it to be *strategic*, that is, it not only makes sense to the people we serve, but also gives the church planter much face-to-face time to share the gospel in a natural setting.

Fourth, we need to develop security guidelines to help us communicate freely with our supporters, fellow missionaries and our mission agency without jeopardizing our status in the country. Secure e-mail, pseudonyms, and code terms are three of the most practical tactics most teams employ.

The Building

Evangelism

Before beginning missionary service in 1984, I had been involved in practically every type of evangelism: concert evangelism, door-to-door evangelism, street preaching, visitation evangelism, power evangelism and literature evangelism. One assumption characterized all of these approaches: a "harvest methodology." A harvest methodology assumes that people are receptive to the gospel and need only to hear it clearly presented. This method knows nothing of working with ignorant or unreceptive people.

I soon learned that this harvest methodology wouldn't work among Muslims. (I won't comment on its effectiveness or lack thereof in America!) Every time someone asked me about my religion, I would preach Christ crucified. Rather than finding a receptive ear, I lost my audience and the cause of Christ was not advanced. Repeated failures led me to re-examine Scripture, and then I experienced a paradigm shift.

Clearly the most helpful model of evangelism in a pioneer context is a "sowing methodology." The parable of the sower and many other passages describe evangelism in agricultural terms (Mk 4; Mt 13; see also Jn 4:34-38; Gal 6:7-9). We need to use a sowing methodology, while maintaining a harvest mentality. Pioneer evangelism progresses much like farming. It is not just a one-time event, but an on-going process of plowing, sowing, cultivating and reaping.

The Engel Scale adapted to a Muslim context (table 17) describes the process of people coming to Christ and is directly related to a sowing methodology.[4] Studying this scale will help us discern where people are in their movement toward Christ and how to share the aspect of truth most relevant to their needs.

An understanding of social webs or networks is also crucial for the evangelistic step in church planting. If we evangelize with networks in mind, perceiving people in terms of their networks of influence or relationships and not just as individuals, the gathering stage of church planting is simplified. By working within the natural social webs, evangelism leads more naturally to churches.[5]

The natural extension of our evangelism should be the friends and relatives of our contacts or converts. Donald McGavrin describes these networks as the "bridges of God".[6] Jesus used these relational bridges for outreach. After calling Matthew to follow him, Jesus went to Matthew's house where he met his network (described as tax-collectors and sinners by the Pharisees, Mt 9:9-13). Paul used the same approach when he led Lydia's household and the Philippian jailor's house to Christ (Ac 16:15, 31-34).

Evangelism from a kingdom perspective includes what is called "power evangelism." Exorcism and healing are part of the evangelistic package of the New Testament, addressed earlier in this book.

The Engel Scale	
-8	Awareness of Allah but no effective knowledge of gospel
-7	Establish positive rapport with missionary
-6	Restudy of Quranic verses on Jesus and clarification of misconceptions
-5	Initial awareness of gospel through the Scriptures
-4	Awareness of fundamentals of gospel through Scriptures
-3	Grasp of the implications of the gospel
-2	Recognition of personal need
-1	Challenge and decision to follow Christ
	Conversion
+1	Evaluation of the decision
+2	Incorporation into a fellowship of believers
+3	Active propagators of the gospel

Table 17: The Engel Scale adapted to a Muslim context

Discipling

We need to help new believers develop basic spiritual foundations and practices in their lives through "the show and tell method" of training. This type of training is what I mean by discipling. First, we show our disciples how to live and minister. Then we tell them how it's done until they can do it on their own, producing a five-step discipleship loop like this:

1) I do it.
2) I do it and you watch.
3) You do it and I watch.

4)   You do it and report back.

5)   You do it (and begin the process again).

This process can be summed up in the maxim: "Give a man a fish and he'll eat for a day; teach a man how to fish and he'll eat for a lifetime."

While discipling involves some personal, one-on-one occasions, it is carried out primarily in small groups. Although Jesus ministered to multitudes, he focused primarily on discipling twelve men. While Paul criss-crossed the Roman world planting churches, he was always discipling leaders, such as Timothy, Titus, Epaphroditus, Prisca and Aquila, Luke, and Silas (1 Cor 4:16, 11:1; 2 Tm 2:2; 1 Thes 2:4-12; Eph 4:11-12).

Pastoring

While the church planter should give indirect leadership as much as possible, it is usually necessary to pastor the young church for at least a short time. In this context, we help young leaders emerge. They are trained best in the context of Body life.

We found that nationals cannot automatically lead better than the missionary. Just because nationals thoroughly understand their language and culture does not necessarily mean they can give spiritual leadership to the church. Like leaders in any culture, they need training. Nationals can't lead best, but trained nationals can!

Three elements comprise "pastoring" for the church planter. First, help the church obey the "one another" verses of Scripture (Jn 13:34-35, Eph 5:18-19, Col 3:16, Jas 5:14-16, 1 Cor 14:26, Acts 2:41-47, Acts 4:32-35, Heb 10:24-25). More than 40 times the New Testament commands the church to minister to one another. The recent emphasis in the Western church on study groups, recovery groups, and cell groups is not a new trend. It recovers the original biblical emphasis. Ministry to one another is a major function of the church. Ministry should not flow just from the missionary to the converts. New converts must encourage, serve and pray for one another immediately.

Second, teach them how to maintain good relationships and restore broken ones. This is what I call peacemaking (Mt 5:9, 23-24; Mt

18:15-17; Rom 12:18, 14:19; Heb 12:14; Gal 6:1). Peacemaking is the key to true community and the only way the church can endure in a hostile environment.[7]

Third, help new believers discover and develop their spiritual gifts (Rom 12:3-8, 1 Cor 12-14). The more people are using their gifts, the healthier the church will be. Qualitative and quantitative church growth depends on the use of our spiritual gifts (Eph 4:11-16, 1 Pt 4:10-11).

These three elements of pastoring – ministering to one another, peacemaking, and using spiritual gifts – relate directly to team life as well.

Leadership Training

Leadership training is a higher level of discipling, preparing stable Christians to become leaders in the body. Five aspects of leadership training are worth noting.

First of all, the best leadership training takes place in the context of small groups (Body ministry) because it gives us opportunities to see who is serving, who is sensitive, and who is gifted. Leaders are those who demonstrate leadership in the church and who facilitate Body life (Eph 4:11-12, 1 Pt 5:3, 3 Jn 9). Second, leadership training includes the development of godly character, the major qualification of New Testament leadership (1 Tm 3:1-7, Ti 1:5-9). Third, leadership training involves teaching the skills of evangelism, Bible study, counseling, teaching/preaching, visitation, organizing events and leading meetings. Fourth, we teach our emerging leaders theology and the process of theologizing. According to Paul, they must be able to teach sound doctrine and refute false teaching (Ti 1:9).

Fifth, leadership training should be integrated into an overall equipping ministry in the church. In other words, the church planter develops a training track in the church with numerous stages, including the discipling of new believers, the equipping of small group leaders, and the training of elders. Only certain people on your team can train others at this level. In fact, the ability to train leaders is what distinguishes the Master Builder from ordinary Christian leaders.[8]

The Living Head of the Church

Jesus is the head of the church. He promised, "I will build my church." He founded the church, builds the church and longs to rule the church in our day-by-day life together. Paul often describes Jesus as the head of the church (Eph 1:22, 4:15, 5:23; Col 1:18, 2:19), a metaphor of his leadership or ruling. Moreover, Jesus is the present head of the church. He is with us when we gather in his name and when we are serving him in the world (Matt 18:20, 28:20). The literal presence of Christ within the church is foundational to a vital church life. It is not just a doctrinal proposition but a dynamic reality!

Because Jesus is the present head of the church, we need to hear his voice and obey it. We must train our young believers to continually submit to him, call upon him for guidance and seek to hear his voice (Jn 10:14,27). Otherwise, the believers will depend upon us instead of on Jesus. We need to help them seek the voice of the living head of the church—primarily through the word of God, prayer and the people of God and secondarily through dreams and visions. (Of course, they must be taught discernment when using these modes of guidance; that is, they need to learn to examine all things in light of Scripture.)

The Executive Director of the Church

At the center of the Master Builder's Blueprint is the Holy Spirit. While Jesus is the foundation of the church and its living head, the Holy Spirit is the executive director! The Holy Spirit empowers, gifts, guides and purifies his people (Acts 1:8, 4:31, 8:29, 13:1-4, 15:28, 16:6-7; Rom 12:3-8; 1 Cor 12:28; Eph 4:11-12; Gal 3:5; Eph 5:18-20; Gal 5:16-23). If folk Muslims are to experience deliverance from the unholy spirits of their past, they must encounter and enjoy the Holy Spirit in their lives.

Role Changes in the Church Planting Process

Tom Steffen wisely notes that "church planters pass through a number of role changes. These transitions call for relinquishing one's power so that others are empowered to mature in character and ministry skills. Such role changes facilitate the church planting cycle" (1993:37).

As with any quality management or leadership, the church planter must begin with the end in mind: a reproducing church with its own indigenous leadership. The next step is to work backwards from that goal to understand the process necessary to reach that end.[9] This process requires the church planter to take different roles during the different stages of the church-planting process.

Role changes are not always easy. Stress and conflict normally accompany the process. Thus, the more clearly we understand and communicate these stages to others, the easier the transitions will be.

The church-planting team can expect seven role changes in the church planting process:

1. Preparing. Before arriving on the field, the church planting team prepares spiritually, theologically and ministerially. Developing the vision and hammering out an initial philosophy of ministry are part of this period. This also the time to recruit and build the team. The church planter's primary role is that of a learner.

2. Penetrating. In many parts of the Muslim world, the work of language and culture learning, or penetrating, can take a very long time. Church planters develop an incarnational lifestyle modeled after Jesus and the apostle Paul (Jn 1:1,14,18; 1 Cor 9:19-23). While maintaining the role of learner, the team members begins to bond to the people they serve.

3. Planting. Like a farmer, the church-planting team begins to sow the seed of the gospel, looking for receptive people or fertile soil. Their main role is as evangelists.

4. Parenting. The church planters lead others to Christ and begin to work on reaching the new believers' networks. After a small fellowship comes into being, the team begins parenting them spiritually. They move into the role of teacher.

5. Partnering. The church has begun to mature, and the church planters focus more on training new leaders. As leaders mature, they take on more and more responsibility. The team begins this stage as trainers and end as advisors, following the five-fold discipleship loop mentioned earlier. They submit to the counsel of the new leaders, partnering with them.

6. Participating. The church-planting team leaves the church and become absentee advisors. Through correspondence and visits, they continues to encourage and strengthen the church.

7. Pioneering. The mobile missionary team moves on to new territory to do new pioneer church planting, and the church itself begins to pioneer by planting new churches. In this way, reproduction is built into our role changes.

These role changes apply most specifically to cross-cultural workers in pioneer settings. When local churches plant sister churches, it may not be necessary to go through all of these stages. In addition, not every member of the church-planting team will go through these seven stages. Some on the team may be gifted primarily as evangelists and will not be much involved in leadership development, for example. Nevertheless, the team as a whole will experience these role changes.

The Master Builder's Blueprint outlines the theoretical foundations and practical steps to church planting. The blueprint helps people visualize the building of the church and understand the process involved.

As noted above, the theoretical foundations to church planting prepare us for fruitfulness. Jesus is the foundation of the church. Our character and gifting, theology, and philosophy of ministry provide further biblical building blocks for the foundation. Next comes the missiological layer of the foundation. Our spiritual life, relationships, language and culture learning, team dynamics and tentmaking opportunities enable us to penetrate the culture of the people we serve.

The four practical steps to church planting are pictured as the actual "building." The walls and roof of the Master Builder's Blueprint involve four activities: evangelism, discipling, pastoring and leadership training. These four activities take place concurrently with our role changes. We move progressively from planting, to parenting, to partnering, to participating and finally on to pioneering elsewhere. At the center of these church planting activities hovers the Holy Spirit—guiding and empowering the team. Over all these activities, the Lord Jesus reigns as living head, reminding us that church planting begins and ends with Jesus.

Notes

[1] See the Frontiers Church Planting Phase and Activity List (Appendix 2) for an excellent complementary guide to church planting.

[2] I first heard of these four stages from a leader in Youth With A Mission, then saw the stages again a decade later in Parker 1990. This summary of the four stages comes from my own experience of team dynamics.

[3] 1 Samuel 16:1-13 illustrates truth-telling for the tentmaker in a politically sensitive situation. Notice the parallels between the church-planting tentmaker and Samuel. God gives Samuel two things to do. His highest priority is to anoint David as king (church planting). However, because it is a politically dangerous situation, God also gives Samuel the task of offering a sacrifice (tentmaking).

[4] Adapted from Dayton, Edward R. *That Everyone May Hear*. Monrovia: MARC, 1979:40 and McCurry, Don *The Gospel and Islam*, 1978:178).

[5] The Greek term for relational networks is *oikos*. See Neighbor 1990 for a summary of *oikos* evangelism.

[6] See Winter and Hawthorne 1992, B-1 37-156.

[7] For a fuller explanation of peacemaking, see chapter 10, Moral Encounter.

[8] See Morris 1993 for a very helpful approach to leadership training in the church.

[9] See Appendix 2, Frontiers' Church Planting Phase and Activity List, for an excellent summary of these issues.

The Frontiers Church-Planting Phase and Activity List

The first version of this tool was developed in 1994 by Dick Scoggins, Dan Brown, and Tim Lewis for utilization with Frontiers church-planting teams. Since then the "Phase and Activity" list has been refined and applied not only to Frontiers teams but also to other teams in other contexts.

Dan Brown, the Field Director of Frontiers, comments, "In effect, this list is actually two-tools-in-one:

"1. *A Yardstick*. Seven clear phases, with definitions that endeavor to make as clear as possible what phase a team is at, and precisely when the team will pass into the next phase. This is particularly clarified in the 'Definition' and 'When Begun' sections found at the beginning of each phase.

"2. *A Guidebook*. While it's not a 'cookbook', nor a list of mandatory steps that all teams must do, it does identify most of the concerns you should be focused on in each phase, and it gets you thinking ahead into the next phase. This gives invaluable insights into what the team's priorities ought to be.

"A tool such as this does not diminish a church-planting team's need for creativity and ingenuity from the Spirit to find the keys that will unlock the doors in your particular context. But when it's clear to the whole team where the work is at and where it needs to go, then it's also easier for people to see how they fit in and to gain a vision for how they can make their particular contribution."

* * * * *

Church Planting Phases
Phase & Activity List (Edition 2.0, February 1998)
by Dick Scoggins, Dan Brown & Tim Lewis

PHASE 1: Launching the Team

Definition: Preparing the team. Initial church-planting (CP) plans and strategies. When begun: When the Aspiring Team Coordinator (ATC) has officially been "knighted" by the General Director (GD) to become a Designated Team Coordinator (DTC).

1. **Research** best information available on language, history and culture of country and target group
2. Prepare a **vision statement**
3. Develop **Memorandum of Understanding (MOU)**
4. Get church **approval**, support (each team member/TM)
5. Plan a **strategy** paper
6. (Each TM) secures adequate prayer, financial **support**
7. **Recruit** a team
8. Get the team to **own** the vision and strategy for CP
9. Complete **TC checklist**

PHASE 2: Preparing to Sow

Definition: Learning the language, adjusting to the culture, becoming "belongers" in society. When begun: Most of the team is on-site (and, usually, engaged in aggressive language-learning).

1. **TMs "land,"** secure suitable housing, arrange for their (initial) entry strategy
2. Resolve **conflicts** arising in the **home**
3. Address **conflicts** arising in the **team**

4. Develop a **team life** which spiritually sustains members

5. **Goal-setting** and planning for the team

Language and Culture Adjustment:

6. TMs work hard at learning the **target language**

7. Language-learning **program & accountability** in place

8. Learn how to **survive** in area chosen, get comfortable, and enjoy life in the country

9. Enable a **family** to do the same

10. Start **residency** procedure on basis of strategy

11. Develop **multiple relationships** of varying depth with target persons

12. Enable **family** members (wives and children) to develop **relationships** with target persons

13. Bring **redemptive** elements into your relationships

14. Enhance **character** through the stress of adapting personally, as a family, and as a team to culture

15. Discover and collect any evangelistic **tools** available in your target language

PHASE 3: Sowing

Definition: The noble work of evangelism. **When begun:** *Most of the team are spending most of their ministry time on evangelism, as opposed to language learning.*

1. **Memorize** parts of the Word (e.g., parables or miracles, etc) in the target language

2. Learn to **share Biblical truths** in the language

3. Develop a **sympathy for the gospel** in friends

4. Develop a **strategy for reaching** receptive people and their closest relationships (family or friends) as a group

5. Begin **evangelistic Bible studies** (e.g. using "Discovery Course" material)

6. Encourage contacts to **bring** some committed relations

7. Prayerfully **evaluate** your friends for a prospective man of peace: can he bring others with him?

8. Prayerfully **identify** one or more potential men or women of peace among your relationships (you may more readily identify women, especially where men are not responding but women are)

9. **Lead** someone to commit to follow Jesus

PHASE 4: Discipling Begins!

Definition: Discipling one or more Muslim-Background Believers (MBB) from the target group. Both parties should recognize this as an on-going process working toward the maturing of the MBB in character and service for Christ. **When begun:** *Begin regular discipleship with a MBB of the target group (regardless of how he/she came to Christ).*

1. **Challenge** one or more believers (man or woman of peace, if possible) to be discipled by you (or other TM), that they might grow "unto the full measure of Christ"
2. **Model** Christ's lifestyle before this man and his network
3. Have believer include some of his family or friends in the **discipling** process (see below)

Disciple the believer(s) to:

4. Fully understand his new identity as a child of God by **faith, not works** (are there tendencies to return to "works" mindset of Islam?)
5. Understand the purpose of **baptism** as an outward sign of the death of self and rebirth in Christ
6. Relate Bible **stories** which will impact life practices
7. Develop a regular habit of turning to Scripture to deal with specific **life problems** as they arise
8. **Recognize sin** in personal life and respond by repentance, confession and developing new life patterns
9. **Live out** Christ's life in extended family (e.g., Matt. 5-7)
10. Develop godly patterns of **loving spouse**, e.g., resolving conflict, forgiveness, reconciliation
11. Develop godly patterns of **child rearing**
12. Implement godly patterns of **conflict resolution** with others
13. Understand the place and function of **suffering** in believer's life, and be able to apply it to own life
14. Practice **godly response** to those hostile to his faith (eg., government, family, employer, friends)
15. Understand the Biblical perspective on local **occult practices** and godly alternatives and responses
16. Be ready to give a **reason for their faith** in a non-fearful, non-combative but prepared way
17. **Share** the good news with family/friends
18. Begin to identify his **gifts and calling**

19. Become familiar with **God's plan** for the extension of the Kingdom in Acts

20. Team women begin **discipling women** in Titus 2:3-5 skills and in submission to husbands

PHASE 5: Beginning the Church

Definition: The ministry of gathering MBBs together and leading that fellowship toward maturity. During this phase the church planter (CPer) exerts significant influence in the community.

Criteria for when begun:

GROUP COMMITMENT: To meet together regularly for the purposes of fellowship in Christ, teaching, prayer, etc.

SIZE: Three or more MBBs (with at least two being of the target group).

BREADTH: not specified

LEADERSHIP: not specified; presumably the CPer is doing all or mostly all the leading and teaching at first

STRENGTH: not specified; usually pretty fragile at first

Goal: Numerical growth and maturing of the group, with the MBB's committed to one another as expression of the Body of Christ (Phase 5 goal = Phase 6 criteria for when begun).

1. Family/friends begin to **explore good news** together

2. Three or more believers agree to **follow Christ** in a committed community

3. CPer **shares God's plan** for forming Kingdom communities among family/friends

4. Believers **embrace God's plan** for Kingdom communities and, together with CPer, decide on a culturally meaningful pattern for regular gatherings

5. Believers learn to recognize and maximize **spiritual gifts** in the emerging community of believers

6. The older believers understand the **"one another"** verses of Bible and how this defines community

7. Older believers have settled on appropriate way to determine fellowship in community (eg, **covenant**)

8. Community has become **identifiable** (eg, via covenant)

9. The community is celebrating the **Lord's table**

10. The community is **meeting together** regularly for meaningful worship, instruction, and prayer

11. The believers are doing the work of **evangelism**

12. Community gatherings are **culturally attractive**

Church Planters begin to phase out:

13. **Responsibilities** between CPer and leaders **defined**

14. Withdrawal of most of the CPers **from meetings**

15. Withdrawn CPers focus on **starting new communities** of believers (PHASE 4)

16. Remaining CPer(s) take **lower profile** in meetings

PHASE 6: Leadership Development

Definition: Preparing the fellowship for being on their own as a church. Developing a plurality of men who can soon assume eldership. Main focus of CPer(s) is developing multiple leaders (2 Tim. 2:2), rather than ministering to the fellowship.

Criteria for when begun:

GROUP COMMITMENT: The MBB's have covenanted (or otherwise expressed their commitment) to one another, and see their assembling together as an expression of being a local church.

SIZE: 10 or more MBB's regularly involved (including believing children). This does not necessarily mean that meetings average 10 or more, just that there is some sort of regular involvement (of MBB's, not just seekers).

BREADTH: 3 or more married men MBB's regularly involved.

LEADERSHIP: At least 1 key MBB man who clearly seems to be an "elder in the making," who is assuming more and more leadership and teaching responsibilities, and whom the others see as a leader.

STRENGTH: Not all hidden believers with hidden faith. Some MBB's are baptized and have already faced into persecution or serious threats and come out well, maintaining their faith and their "confession of Christ before men" (Mt.10:32).

Goal: Appointing 2 or more elders (preferably 3 or more). See Phase 7 "when begun."

Leaders Emerge:

1. Older believers have **baptized** new believers

2. Older believers are **discipling** new believers (see above)

3. Older women **teach** newer **women** Titus 2 skills

4. Older, more mature men trained to take **leadership** of community gatherings
5. Believers take responsibility for Biblical **instruction**
6. Older believers are **presiding** at the Lord's table
7. Initial leaders emerging, functioning as **shepherds**
8. **Growth in godliness** in their homes sets pace for others
9. Gifts encouraged and developed for **edification**

Peacemaking Skills Exercised by the Community:

10. Forbearing and **forgiving**
11. Confronting, exhorting, reproving **erring members**
12. Shunning, "disfellowshipping" **those persisting in sin**

Train and recognize leaders:

13. **Character developed** in context of marriage
14. (Team) **leadership concepts** taught, implemented
15. Discerning the **will of the Lord** by leaders and community taught and practiced
16. Leaders' place in conflict and peacemaking in the community taught, practiced (**Peacemaking**, PHASE 6)
17. Emerging elders recognized (provisional **leadership**)
18. **Mature women** recognized in ministry
19. **Conflicts** about leadership appointment dealt with
20. Leaders begin shepherding and church discipline
21. Leaders looking for **new men** to develop as leaders
22. Leaders begin **discipling new leaders** (See discipling, PHASE 4 and above, this PHASE)
23. CPer often absent from community meetings, **leaders lead**
24. CPer often **absent** from leadership meetings
25. Elders formally **ordained**

PHASE 7: Reproducing & Exiting

Definition: Developing church-reproduction, other new CP efforts, or assisting the new church for a temporary period. The CPer(s) are not making a career out of working with the one church they have planted, but are working with national believers to plant more churches.

Criteria for when begun:

GROUP COMMITMENT: Same as Phase 6.

SIZE & BREADTH: Same as Phase 6, and of sufficient "critical mass".

LEADERSHIP: Plurality [i.e. minimum of 2] of biblically-qualified MBB elders recognized and installed in the first church. Local authority and responsibility for shepherding that church rests solely in the hands of indigenous leaders.

STRENGTH: same as Phase 6.

Reproduction Begins:

1. Intense **teaching** on reproducing communities
2. Community **embraces goal** of reproducing
3. Members begin to look for **new men of peace** around whom to start another community
4. **New gathering** (Bible Study) started or owned by church (if started by other CPers)
5. Leaders begin to **network** with emerging leaders of new gathering, taking some responsibility for their training
6. Leaders formally **recognize** newer emerging leaders (provisional elders)
7. Leaders of two communities start **meeting** regularly
8. Elders take more **responsibility** to develop leaders in the new community
9. New community **meeting** started
10. Communities care for each other – **resources shared**
11. **Peacemaking** skills among leaders (of different communities) practiced
12. Elders (possibly with CPer) **lay hands** on new elders in the newer community
13. **Relationship** between communities and leaders worked out, **formalized** (eg, covenant)
14. Peacemaking **skills** between communities and leaders of different communities **exercised**
15. CPer **commends** the old community to God and leaves community meetings. May sometimes visit.
16. CPer redefines relationship to leaders as **coach**. No longer attends leadership meetings unless invited
17. New **churches started** without a CPer

Great Commission Vision:

18. **Vision developed** to plant churches beyond local area
19. Vision includes recognizing, training and sending **national CPers** to other cities/countries
20. **Vision given** by leaders to congregation

21. **Means** of sending teams of nationals devised
22. **CPers sent out** either with F team or other teams
23. **New clusters** of communities started
24. **National teams** of CPs sent out

For further explanation of this tool and its utilization in Frontiers, review the article by Dan Brown in the April 1997 issue of the **Evangelical Missions Quarterly**. *To obtain reprints of that article, contact* emis@wheaton.edu *or Evangelical Missions Information Service, PO Box 794, Wheaton, IL 60189, USA.*

For further information on Frontiers, point your Web browser to www.frontiers.org, or contact one of the following addresses: (1) for USA inquirers, contact Frontiers, PO Box 31177, Mesa, AZ 85275-1177; (2) for inquirers from other countries, contact Frontiers IHQ, PO Box 4, High Wycombe, Bucks HP14 3YX, UNITED KINGDOM.

Bibliography

Alexander, P. S.
  1986   "Incantations and Books of Magic." In *The History of the Jewish People in the Age of Jesus Christ.* Vol. 3. Emil Schurer, ed. Pp. 342-379. Edinburgh, Scotland: T. and T. Clark.

Arnold, Clinton E.
  1992a   *Ephesians: Power and Magic. The Concept of Power in Ephesians in Light of Its Historical Setting.* Grand Rapids, MI: Baker.

  1992b   *Powers of Darkness: Principalities and Power in Paul's Letters.* Downers Grove, IL: InterVarsity.

  1993   "Magic." In *Dictionary of Paul and His Letters.* Gerald F. Hawthorne, Ralph P. Martin, and Daniel G. Reid, eds. Pp. 580-583. Downers Grove, IL: InterVarsity.

  1996   *The Colossian Syncretism: The Interface Between Christianity and Folk Belief at Colossae.* Grand Rapids, MI: Baker.

  1997   *3 Crucial Questions about Spiritual Warfare.* Grand Rapids, MI: Baker.

Aulen, Gustaf
  1986   *Christus Victor.* New York: MacMillan.

Aune, David E.
  1980   "Magic in Early Christianity." In *Aufstieg und Niedergang der Romishen Welt* 2.23.2:1507-1557. Berlin, Germany: Walter DeGruyter.

Babit, Frank Cole
  1928   *Plutarch's Moralia.* Vol. 2. The Loeb Classical Library. London: William Heinemann.

Banks, Robert
  1988   *Paul's Idea of Community: The Early House Churches in Their Historical Setting.* Grand Rapids, MI: Eerdmans.

1993   "Church Order and Government." In *Dictionary of Paul and His Letters.*
            Gerald F. Hawthorne, Ralph P. Martin, and Daniel G. Reid, eds. Pp.
            131-137. Downers Grove, IL: InterVarsity.

Barker, G. W.
1977   "Ephesians, Letter of Paul to the." In *The Zondervan Pictorial
            Encyclopedia of the Bible.* Vol. 2. Merrill C. Tenney, ed. Pp. 316-324.
            Grand Rapids, MI: Zondervan.

Barr, James
1961   *Semantics of Biblical Language.* Oxford, England: Oxford University.

Barrett, Charles Kingsley
1963   *The Pastoral Epistles.* Oxford, England: Clarendon.

1977   "Paul's Address to the Ephesian Elders." In *God's Christ and His
            People: Studies in Honour of Nils Alstrup Dahl.* J. Jervell and W. A.
            Meeks, eds. Pp. 107-121. Oslo: Universitetsforlaget.

Barth, Markus
1974   *Ephesians.* 2 vols. New York: Doubleday.

Bavinck, Johan Herman
1960   *An Introduction to the Science of Missions.* Philadelphia, PA:
            Presbyterian and Reformed.

Becker, Jurgen
1993   *Paul: Apostle to the Gentiles.* Louisville, KY: Westminster/John Knox.

Beker, J. Christiaan
1984   *Paul the Apostle: The Triumph of God in Life and Thought.*
            Philadelphia, PA: Fortress

Best, Ernest
1993   *Ephesians.* New Testament Guides. Sheffield, England: JSOT.

Betz, Hans Dieter, ed.
1992   *The Greek Magical Papyri in Translation Including the Demotic Spells.*
            Chicago, IL: University of Chicago.

Bietenhard, Hans
1977   "Onoma." In *Theological Dictionary of the New Testament.* Vol. 5.
            Gerhard Kittel, ed. Pp. 242-283. Grand Rapids, MI: Eerdmans.

Birkey, Del
1991   "The House Church: A Missiological Model." *Missiology* 19(1):69-79.

Blue, Bradley
1993   "Acts and the House Church." In *The Book of Acts in Its Graeco-Roman
            Setting.* Pp. 119-189. Grand Rapids, MI: Eerdmans.

Bratcher, Robert G., and Eugene A. Nida
1982   *Translator's Handbook on Paul's Letter to the Ephesians*. London:
            United Bible Societies.

Bruce, Fredrick F.
1942   *The Speeches in the Acts of the Apostles*. London: Tyndale.

1961   *The Epistle to the Ephesians*. Grand Rapids, MI: Revell.

1974   "The Speeches in Acts—Thirty Years Later." In *Reconciliation and
            Hope: New Testament Essays on Atonement and Eschatology Presented
            to L.L. Morris on His 60th Birthday*. R. Banks, ed. Pp. 53-68. Grand
            Rapids, MI: Eerdmans.

1977   *Paul: Apostle of the Heart Set Free*. Grand Rapids, MI: Eerdmans.

1982   *The Epistle to the Galatians: A Commentary on the Greek Text*. Grand
            Rapids, MI: Eerdmans.

1984   *The Epistles to the Colossians, to Philemon and to the Ephesians*. Grand
            Rapids, MI: Eerdmans.

1988   *The Book of the Acts*. New International Commentary on the New
            Testament. Revised edition. Grand Rapids, MI: Eerdmans. (1st edition,
            Eerdmans, 1954.)

1990   "The Significance of the Speeches for Interpreting Acts." *Southwestern
            Journal of Theology* 60(3):20-28.

Bubeck, Mark
1984   *Overcoming the Adversary*. Chicago, IL: Moody.

Burnett, David
1988   *Unearthly Powers: A Christian Perspective on Primal and Folk
            Religions*. Eastbourne, England: MARC.

Carson, Donald A., ed.
1993   *Biblical Interpretation and the Church*. Grand Rapids, MI:
            Baker.

1993   *Biblical Interpretation and the Church: Text and Context*.
            Grand Rapids, MI: Baker and Carlisle: The Paternoster Press.

1996   *The Gagging of God: Christianity Confronts Pluralism*. Grand Rapids,
            MI: Zondervan.

Charlesworth, James H.
1983   *The Old Testament Pseudipigrapha*. Vol. 1. New York: Doubleday.

1985a   *The Old Testament Pseudipigrapha*. Vol. 2. New York: Doubleday.

1985b   *The Old Testament Pseudipigrapha and the New Testament*. Cambridge,
            England: Cambridge University Press.

Chastain, Warren
    1993   "Contextualization: Some Questions, Criticisms, and Suggestions."
            Frontlines. No. 8 (Summer):1, 3.

Childs, Brevard S.
    1970   *Biblical Theology in Crisis*. Philadelphia, PA: Westminster.

    1993   *Biblical Theology of the Old and New Testaments: Theological
            Reflection on the Christian Bible. Minneapolis*, MN: Fortress.

Cohoon, J. W., and H. Lamar Crosby
    1951   *Dio Chrysostom*. Vol. 3. The Loeb Classical Library. Cambridge:
            Harvard University Press.

Conn, Harvie M.
    1984   *Eternal Word and Changing Worlds*. Grand Rapids, MI:
            Zondervan.

    1985   "Urban Church Research: Methods and Models." Syllabus, Westminster
            Theological Seminary.

    1988   *Inerrancy and Hermeneutics. A Tradition, A Challenge, A Debate*.
            Grand Rapids, MI: Baker.

Conzelmann, Hans
    1987   *Acts*. Philadelphia, PA: Fortress Press.

Coote, Robert T. and John Stott, eds.
    1980   *Down to Earth: Studies in Christianity and Culture*. Grand Rapids,
            MI: Eerdmans.

Cranfield, Charles E. B.
    1979   *The Epistle to the Romans*. Vol. 2. The International Critical
            Commentary. Edinburgh: T. and T. Clark .

    1985   "Diakonia in the New Testament." In *The Bible and Christian Life*. Pp.
            69-87. Edinburgh: T. and T. Clark.

Cullmann, Oscar
    1949   *The Earliest Christian Confessions*. London: Lutterworth Press.

    1951   *Christ and Time*. London: SCM.

    1956   *The Early Church*. London: SCM.

    1967   *Salvation in History*. New York: Harper and Row.

Davis, John Jefferson
    1980   "Contextualization and the Nature of Theology." In *The Necessity of
            Systematic Theology*. 2nd edition. John Jefferson Davis, ed. Pp. 169-
            190. Grand Rapids, MI: Baker.

Deissmann, Adolf
1901   *Bible Studies*. Edinburgh, Scotland: T. and T. Clark .

1927   *Light from the Ancient East*. London: Hodder and Stoughton.

Dibelius, Martin
1956   "The Acts of the Apostles as an Historical Source." In *Studies in the Acts of the Apostles*. H. Greeven, ed. Pp. 102-108. New York: Charles Scribner's Sons.

Dickason, Fred C.
1975   *Angels, Elect and Evil*. Chicago: Moody.

Dodd, Charles H.
1929   "Ephesians." In *The Abingdon Bible Commentary*. F. C. Eiselen, E. Lewis, and D. G. Downey, eds. Pp. 1222-1225. New York: Abingdon.

1936   *The Apostolic Preaching and Its Developments*. London: Hodder and Stoughton.

Dunn, James. D. G.
1973   *Baptism in the Holy Spirit*. London: SCM.

1975   *Jesus and the Spirit: A Study of the Religious and Charismatic Experience of Jesus and the First Christians as Reflected in the New Testament*. London. SCM/Philadelphia: Westminster.

1977   *Unity and Diversity in the New Testament*. London: SCM.

1988   *Romans 9-16*. Word Biblical Commentary. Vol. 38b. Dallas, TX: Word.

1998   *The Theology of Paul the Apostle*. Grand Rapids, MI: Eerdmans.

Dyrness, William.
1983   *Let the Earth Rejoice! A Biblical Theology of Holistic Mission*. Westchester, IL: Crossway Books.

1990   *Learning about Theology from the Third World*. Grand Rapids, MI: Zondervan.

Edelstein, Emma J. and Ludwig Edelstein
1945   *Asclepius: A Collection and Interpretation of the Testimonies*. Vols. 1-2. Baltimore: Johns Hopkins.

Elliston, Eddie
1993   "Paul's Final Encounter with the Ephesian Elders." In *Handbook 1. Leaders, Leadership and The Bible: An Overview*. J. Robert Clinton, ed. Pp. 223-227. Pasadena, CA: Barnabas.

Erickson, Millard
1988   *Christian Theology*. Grand Rapids, MI: Baker.

1993   *Evangelical Interpretation: Perspectives on Hermeneutical Issues*. Grand Rapids, MI: Baker.

234 MUSLIMS, MAGIC AND THE KINGDOM OF GOD

Erdemgil, Selahattin
1997   *Ephesus: Ruins and Museum*. Istanbul: Net Turistik Yayinlar.

Eustathius
n.d.   *Commentarii ad Homeri Odysseam*. Thesaurus Linguae Graecae.

Fee, Gordon D.
1993   *New Testament Exegesis*. Gracewing: Fowler Wright Books and
            Louisville, KY: John Knox.

1994   *God's Empowering Presence*. Peabody, MA: Hendrickson.

1994   *Gospel and Spirit: Issues in New Testament Hermeneutics*. Peabody,
            MA: Hendrickson.

Ferguson, Everett
1996   *The Church of Christ*. Grand Rapids, MI: Eerdmans.

Fernea, Elizabeth Warnock
1980   *Street in Marrakesh: A Personal Encounter with the Lives of Moroccan
            Women*. Garden City, NY: Anchor.

Filson, Floyd V.
1939   "The Significance of the Early House Churches." *Journal of Biblical
            Literature* 58:105-112.

Frazer, James George
1963   *The Golden Bough*. Abridged edition. Vol. 1. New York: Macmillan
            Publishing Company.

Fung, Ronald Y.K.
1980   "Charismatic Versus Organized Ministry? An Examination of an
            Alleged Antithesis." *The Evangelical Quarterly* 52:195-214.

1982   "The Nature of the Ministry According to Paul." *The Evangelical
            Quarterly* 54:129-146.

1984   "Function or Office? A Survey of the New Testament Evidence."
            Evangelical Review of Theology 8 (1):16-39.

Gaffin, Richard B.
1979   *Perspectives on Pentecost*. Philadelphia, PA: Presbyterian and
            Reformed.

Garrett, Susan
1989   *The Demise of the Devil: Magic and the Demonic in Luke's Writings*.
            Minneapolis, MN: Fortress.

Gartner, B.
1955   *The Areopagus Speech and Natural Revelation*. Lund: C. W. K.
            Gleerup.

Gasque, W. W.
1974   "The Speeches of Acts: Dibelius Reconsidered." In *New Dimensions in New Testament Study.* R. N. Longenecker and M.C. Tenney, eds. Pp. 232-251. Grand Rapids, MI: Zondervan.

1989   *A History of the Interpretation of the Acts of the Apostles.* 2nd edition. Peabody, MA: Hendrickson. (1st edition, Eerdmans, 1975.)

Geertz, Clifford.
1971   *Islam Observed.* New Haven: Yale University Press.

Getz, Gene A.
1984   *Sharpening the Focus of the Church.* Wheaton, IL: Victor Books.

Gilliland, Dean S.
1989   *The Word Among Us: Contextualizing Theology for Mission Today.* Dallas, TX: Word.

Goerner, H. Cornell
1979   *All Nations in God's Purpose.* Nashville, TN: Broadman Press.

Goppelt, L.
1982   *Theology of the New Testament.* Vol. 2. Grand Rapids, MI: Eerdmans.

Green, Michael
1975   *I Believe in the Holy Spirit.* London: Hodder and Stoughton.

1981   *I Believe in Satan's Downfall.* Grand Rapids, MI: Eerdmans.

Gritz, Sharon Hodgin
1991   *Paul, Women Teachers, and the Mother Goddess at Ephesus.* Lanham, MD. University Press of America.

Grudem, Wayne
1988   *The Gift of Prophecy in the New Testament Today.* Wheaton, IL: Crossway Books.

1994   *Systematic Theology.* Grand Rapids, MI: Zondervan.

Gundry, Stanley
1979   "Evangelical Theology: Where *Should* We Be Going?" *Journal of the Evangelical Theological Society* (22)1:3-13.

Guthrie, D.
1979   *New Testament Introduction.* Downers Grove, IL: InterVarsity.

1981   *New Testament Theology.* Downers Grove, IL: InterVarsity.

Haenchen, Ernst
1971   *The Acts of the Apostles: A Commentary.* Oxford, England: Blackball/Philadelphia, PA: Westminster.

Harmon, A. M.
1947   *Lucian.* Vol. 3. The Loeb Classical Library. Cambridge: Harvard University.

Harrison, Everett F.
1986   *Interpreting Acts: The Expanding Church.* Grand Rapids, MI:
              Zondervan.

Hawthorne, Gerald F., Ralph Martin, and Daniel G. Reid, eds.
1993   *Dictionary of Paul and His Letters.* Downers Grove, IL: InterVarsity.

Hay, David M.
1973   *Glory at the Right Hand.* Nashville, TN: Abingdon Press.

Hemer, C. J.
1989a   "The Speeches of Acts:1. The Ephesian Elders at Miletus." *Tyndale
              Bulletin* 40(5):77-85.

1989b   *The Book of Acts in the Setting of Hellenistic History. WUNT* 49. C.H.
              Gempf, ed. Tubingen, Germany: Mohr.

Hesselgrave, David J.
1978   *Communicating Christ Cross-Culturally.* Grand Rapids, MI: Zondervan.

1984   *Counseling Cross-Culturally.* Grand Rapids, MI: Baker.

Hiebert, Paul G.
1982   "The Flaw of the Excluded Middle." *Missiology: An
              International Review.* Vol. 10 (January): 35-47.

1985a   *Anthropological Insights for Missionaries.* Grand Rapids, MI: Baker.

1985b   "Epistemological Foundations for Science and Theology." *Theological
              Students Fellowship Bulletin* 8(4):5-10.

1985c   "The Missiological Implication of an Epistemological Shift."
              Theological Students Fellowship Bulletin 8(5):12-18.

1989   "Power Encounter and Folk Islam." In *Muslims and Christians on the
              Emmaus Road.* Pp. 45-62. Monrovia, CA: MARC.

Hull, John M.
1974   *Hellenistic Magic and the Synoptic Tradition.* SBT Vol. 28. Naperville,
              IL: Allenson.

Illinois Greek Club, The, trans.
1948   *Aeneas Tacticus, Aslepiodotus, Onasander.* The Loeb Classical Library.
              Cambridge, MA: Harvard University Press.

Jeffery, Arthur
1938   *The Foreign Vocabulary of the Quran.* Baroda, Pakistan: Al-Biruni
              Oriental Institute.

Johnson, Dennis E.
1997   *The Message of Acts in the History of Redemption.* Phillipsburg, PA:
              Presbyterian and Reformed.

Johnstone, Patrick
 1986   *Operation World*. Bromley, Kent: STL Books.

Jones, Horace Leonard
 1949   *The Geography of Strabo*. Vol. 2. The Loeb Classical Library.
             Cambridge: Harvard University.

 1950   *The Geography of Strabo*. Vol. 6. The Loeb Classical Library.
             Cambridge: Harvard University.

Kaiser, Walter C. Jr.
 1981   *Toward an Exegetical Theology*. Grand Rapids, MI: Baker.

Kallas, James
 1961   *The Significance of the Synoptic Miracles*. Great Britain: Talbot.

 1966   *The Satanward View: A Study in Pauline Theology*. Philadelphia, PA:
             Westminster Press.

 1968   *Jesus and the Power of Satan*. Philadelphia, PA: Westminster.

Kee, H. C.
 1983   *Miracle in the Early Christian World*. New Haven, CT: Yale University.

 1986   *Medicine, Miracle and Magic in New Testament Times*. Cambridge,
             England: Cambridge University.

Kelly, J. N. D.
 1976   *Early Christian Doctrines*. 5th edition. San Francisco, CA: Harper and
             Row.

 1986   *A Commentary on the Pastoral Epistles*. Grand Rapids, MI: Baker.

Kittel, Gerhard, ed.
 1968   "Theos" in the *Theological Dictionary of the New Testament*. pp. 65-
             119, vol. III. Grand Rapids, MI: Eerdmans.
Koentjaraningrat
 1990   *Javanese Culture*. Singapore: Oxford.

Koester, Helmut
 1995   *Ephesos: Metropolis of Asia*. Harvard Theological Studies. Valley
             Forge: Trinity.

Kraft, Charles H.
 1979   *Christianity in Culture: A Study in Dynamic Biblical Theologizing in
             Cross-Cultural Perspective*. Maryknoll, NY: Orbis.

 1980   "The Church in Culture—A Dynamic Equivalence Model." In *Down to
             Earth*. John R. W. Stott and Robert Coote, eds. Pp. 211-230. Grand
             Rapids, MI: Eerdmans.

 1989   *Christianity With Power*. Ann Arbor, MI: Vine.

 1992   *Defeating Dark Angels: Breaking Demonic Oppression in the Believer's
             Life*. Ann Arbor, MI: Servant Publications.

Kurz, William S.
1990   *Farewell Addresses in the New Testament*. Collegeville, MN: Liturgical
            Press.

1993   *Reading Luke-Acts: Dynamics of Biblical Narrative*. Louisville, KY:
            Westminster/John Knox.

Ladd, George Eldon
1968   *The Pattern of New Testament Truth*. Grand Rapids, MI: Eerdmans.

1974   *A Theology of the New Testament*. Grand Rapids, MI: Eerdmans.

1976   *The New Testament and Criticism*. Grand Rapids, MI:
            Eerdmans.

Lambrecht, J.
1979   "Paul's Farewell Address on Miletus (Acts 20, 17-38)." In *Les Actes des
            Apotres: Traditions, Redaction, Theologie. BETL* 48. J. Kremer, ed. Pp.
            307-337. Leuven: Leuven University.

Lane, William, L.
1974   *The Gospel According to Mark*. Grand Rapids, MI: Eerdmans.

Langton, E.
1949   *Essentials of Demonology*. London: Epworth.

Larkin, William J.
1988   *Culture and Biblical Hermeneutics*. Grand Rapids, MI: Baker.

1995   *Acts*. Downers Grove, IL: InterVarsity.

LaSor, William Sanford
1979   "Artemis." In *The International Standard Bible Encyclopedia*. Geoffrey
            W. Bromiley, ed. Vol. 1, Pp. 306-308. Grand Rapids, MI: Eerdmans.

Lehman, Arthur C., and James E. Myers
1985   *Magic, Witchcraft, and Religion*. Palo Alto, CA: Mayfield.

Leith, John, ed.
1973   *Creeds of the Churches*. Richmond, VA: John Knox.

Lessa, William, and Evon Z. Vogt
1972   *Reader in Comparative Religion*. New York: Harper and Row.

LiDonnici, Lynn R.
1992   "The Images of Artemis Ephesia and Greco-Roman Worship: A
            Reconsideration." *Harvard Theological Review* 85(4):389-415.

Liefeld, Walter L.
1995   *Interpreting the Book of Acts*. Grand Rapids, MI: Baker.

1997   *Ephesians*. Downers Grove, IL: InterVarsity.

Lightfoot, J.B.
  1879   *St. Paul's Epistles to the Colossians and to Philemon*. London:
              MacMillan.

  1884   "The Name and Office of Apostle." In *The Epistles of St. Paul to the
              Galatians*. Pp. 92-101. London: MacMillan.

  1893   "The Destination of the Epistle to the Ephesians." In *Biblical Essays*.
              Pp. 377-396. London: MacMillan.

  1893   "The Date of the Pastoral Epistles." In *Biblical Essays*. Pp. 399-418.
              London: MacMillan.

  1893   "St. Paul's History After the Close of the Acts." In *Biblical Essays*. Pp.
              421-437. London: MacMillan.

  1894   *Saint Paul's Epistle to the Philippians*. London: MacMillan.

Lincoln, Andrew T.
  1990   *Ephesians*. Waco, TX: Word.

Lincoln, Andrew T., and A. J. M. Wedderburn
  1993   *The Theology of the Later Pauline Letters*. Cambridge, England:
              Cambridge.

Lingenfelter, Sherwood
  1992   *Transforming Culture*. Grand Rapids, MI: Baker.

Longenecker, Richard N.
  1981   "Acts." In *The Expositor's Bible Commentary*. Vol. 9. Grand Rapids,
              MI: Regency Reference Library Zondervan.

  1984   *New Testament Social Ethics for Today*. Grand Rapids, MI: Eerdmans.

  1990   *Galatians*. Word Biblical Commentary. Vol. 41. Dallas, TX: Word.

Love, Richard Deane, II
  1995   "A Plea for Missiological Theologians and Theological Missiologists."
              Paper presented at the Evangelical Missiological Society West Regional
              Meeting, United States Center for World Mission, April 7, 1995.
              Pasadena, CA.

MacDonald, Margaret Y.
  1991   *The Pauline Churches*. Cambridge, England: Cambridge University.

Mackay, John A.
  1953   *God's Order: The Ephesian Letter and This Present Time*. New York:
              MacMillan.

Malherbe, Abraham J.
  1987   *Paul and the Thessalonians*. Philadelphia, PA: Fortress.

  1989a   *Paul and the Popular Philosophers*. Minneapolis, MN: Fortress.

1989b   *Moral Exhortation, A Greco-Roman Sourcebook*. Philadelphia, PA: Westminster.

Marchant, E. C., trans.
1946   *Xenophon, Scripta Minora*. The Loeb Classical Library. Cambridge, MA: Harvard.

1953   *Xenophon, Memorabilia and Oeconomicus*. The Loeb Classical Library. Cambridge, MA: Harvard University Press.

Marshall, I. Howard
1983   *The Acts of the Apostles: An Introduction and Commentary*. Tyndale New Testament Commentary. Leicester: InterVarsity/Grand Rapids, MI: Eerdmans.

1989   *Luke: Historian and Theologian*. 2nd edition. Grand Rapids, MI: Zondervan.

1992   *The Acts of the Apostles*. New Testament Guides. Sheffield, England: JSOT Press.

Martin, Hubert M. Jr.
1992   "Artemis." In *The Anchor Bible Dictionary*. David Noel Freedman, ed. Vol. I. Pp. 464-465. New York: Doubleday.

Martin, Ralph P.
1967-68   "An Epistle in Search of a Life Setting." *Expository Times* 79:296-302.

1976   *Worship in the Early Church*. Grand Rapids, MI: Eerdmans.

1981   *Reconciliation: A Study of Paul's Theology*. Atlanta, GA: John Knox Press.

1993   "Creed." In *Dictionary of Paul and His Letters*. Gerald F. Hawthorne, Ralph P. Martin, and Daniel G. Reid, eds. Downers Grove, IL: InterVarsity.

McCown, Chester C.
1923   "The Ephesia Grammata in Popular Belief." *Transactions and Proceedings of the American Philological Association* 54:128-140.

McCurry, Don M., ed.
1979   *The Gospel and Islam*. Monrovia, CA: MARC.

1980   "An Introduction to Islam and The Gospel and Islam," lecture notes. Pasadena, CA: Samuel Zwemer Institute.

McGavran, Donald
1974   *The Clash Between Christianity and Cultures*. Washington: Canon Press.

McQuilkin, J. Robertson
1977   "The Behavioral Sciences Under the Authority of Scripture."

Journal of the Evangelical Theological Society 20:31-43.

1992   *Understanding and Applying the Bible.* Chicago, IL: Moody.

Meeks, Wayne, A.
1983   *The First Urban Christians: The Social World of the Apostle Paul.* New Haven, CN: Yale.

Metzger, Bruce. M.
1944   "St. Paul and the Magicians." *Princeton Seminary Bulletin* 38(1):27-30.

1975   *A Textual Commentary on the Greek New Testament: A Companion Volume to the United Bible Societies' Greek New Testament*, 3rd Edition. New York: United Bible Societies.

Minar, Edwin L., F.H. Sandbach, and W.C. Helmbold, trans.
1961   *Plutarch's Moralia.* Vol. 9. Table Talk 5. Loeb Classical Library, Cambridge, MA: Harvard University Press.

Mitton, C. L.
1976   *Ephesians.* London: Oliphants.

Montefiore, C. G. and H. Loewe
1974   *A Rabbinic Anthology.* New York: Shocken.

Morosco, Robert E.
1974   "Conceptions of Spiritual Powers in the Pauline Corpus." Th.D. dissertation, Fuller Theological Seminary.

Morris, Leon
1974   *The Apostolic Preaching of the Cross.* Grand Rapids, MI: Eerdmans.

1994   *Expository Reflections on the Letter to the Ephesians.* Grand Rapids, MI: Baker.

Moulton, James Hope
1930   *A Grammar of New Testament Greek.* Edinburgh, Scotland: T. and T. Clark.

Moulton, James Hope and George Milligan
1929   *The Vocabulary of the Greek Testament.* Parts 1-9. Hodder and Stoughton: London.

Muller, Richard A.
1991   *The Study of Theology.* Grand Rapids, MI: Zondervan.

Murphy, Ed.
1992   *The Handbook for Spiritual Warfare.* Nashville, TN: Thomas Nelson.

Musk, Bill
1989   *The Unseen Face of Islam.* London: MARC.

Mussies, G.
1995   "Artemis." In *Dictionary of Deities and Demons in the Bible*. Karel
        Van der Toorn, Bob Becking and Pieter W Van der Horst, eds. Pp.168-
        180. Leiden, Holland: Brill.

Newman, Barclay M. and Eugene A. Nida
1972   *The Acts of the Apostles*. UBS Handbook Series. New York: United
        Bible Societies.

Neufeld, Vernon H.
1963   *The Earliest Christian Confessions*. Grand Rapids, MI: Eerdmans.

Nida, Eugene A.
1975   *Message and Mission*. Pasadena, CA: William Carey Library.

Niebuhr, H. Richard.
1956   *Christ and Culture*. New York: Harper and Row.

O'Brien, P. T.
1982   *Colossians, Philemon*. Word Biblical Commentary. Vol. 44. Waco, TX:
        Word.

1984   "Principalities and Powers: Opponents of the Church." In *Biblical
        Interpretation and the Church: Text and Context*. D. A. Carson, ed. Pp.
        110-150. Exeter, England: Paternoster.

Osborne, Grant R.
1991   *The Hermeneutical Spiral: A Comprehensive Introduction to Biblical
        Interpretation*. Downers Grove, IL: InterVarsity.

Oster, Richard E.
1974   "A Historical Commentary on the Missionary Success Stories in Acts
        19:11-40." Ph.D. dissertation, Princeton Theological Seminary.

1976   "The Ephesians Artemis as an Opponent of Early Christianity." In
        Jahrbuch fur Antike und Christentum 19:24-44. Munster Westfalen.

1990   "Ephesus as a Religious Center under the Principate, I. Paganism Before
        Constantine." In *Aufstieg und Niedergang der Romishen Welt* Part II:
        Principate. 18(3):1662-1728. New York: Walter De Gruyter.

1992   "Christianity in Asia Minor." In *The Anchor Bible Dictionary*. Vol. 1.
        David Noel Freedman, ed. Pp. 938-954. New York: Doubleday.

Page, Sydney H.T.
1996   *Powers of Evil: A Biblical Study of Satan and Demons*. Grand Rapids,
        MI: Baker and Apollos.

Parshall, Phil
1983   *Bridges to Islam*. Grand Rapids, MI: Baker.

Paton, W.R.
1948   *The Greek Anthology*. The Loeb Classical Library. Cambridge, MA: Harvard University Press.

1972   *Polybius: The Histories*. The Loeb Classical Library. Cambridge: Harvard University Press.

Patzia, Arthur G.
1993   *Ephesians, Colossians, Philemon*. New International Biblical Commentary. Peabody, MA: Hendrickson Publishers.

Penner, Erwin
1983   *The Enthronement Motif in Ephesians*. Ph.D. dissertation, Fuller Theological Seminary.

Powlison, David
1995   *Power Encounter: Reclaiming Spiritual Warfare*. Grand Rapids, MI: Baker.

Poythress, Vern Sheridan
1987   *Symphonic Theology: The Validity of Multiple Perspectives in Theology*. Grand Rapids, MI: Zondervan.

1995   "Territorial Spirits: Some Biblical Perspectives." *Urban Mission* 13(2):37-49.

Preisendanz, Karl
1973   *Papyri Graecae Magicae*. Vol. 1. Stvtgardiae in Aedibvs B.G. Tevbneri.

1974   *Papyri Graecae Magicae*. Vol. 2. Stvtgardiae in Aedibvs B.G. Tevbneri.

Ramsay, William M.
1907   *The Cities of St. Paul*. London: Hodder and Stoughton.

1925   *St. Paul the Traveller and the Roman Citizen*. London: Hodder and Stoughton.

1953   *The Bearing of Recent Discovery on the Trustworthiness of the New Testament*. Grand Rapids, MI: Baker.

1996   *Historical Commentary on the Pastoral Epistles*. Mark Wilson, ed. Grand Rapids, MI: Kregel.

Reicke, Bo
1957   "The Constitution of the Primitive Church in the Light of Jewish Documents." In *The Scrolls and the New Testament*. Krister Stendahl, ed. Pp. 143-156. New York: Harper.

Reid, D.
1982   "The Christus Victor Motif in Paul's Theology." Ph.D. dissertation, Fuller Theological Seminary.

1993   "Principalities and Powers" and "Triumph." In *Dictionary of Paul and His Letters*. Gerald F. Hawthorne, Ralph P. Martin, and Daniel G. Reid, eds. Pp. 746-752. Downers Grove, IL: InterVarsity.

Ridderbos, H.
1977   *Paul: An Outline of His Theology*. Grand Rapids, MI: Eerdmans.

Robinson, J. A.
1979   *Commentary on Ephesians*. Grand Rapids, MI: Kregel.

Rolfe, J.C.
1951   *Suetonius*. The Loeb Classical Library. Cambridge, MA: Harvard University.

Rommen, Edward.
1993   "The De-Theologizing of Missiology." *Trinity World Forum* 19(1):1-4.

Sage, Evan T.
1949   *Livy*. The Loeb Classical Library. Cambridge, MA: Harvard University.

Schillebeeckx, Edward
1980   *Christ: The Experience of Jesus as Lord*. New York: Seabury.

Schlier, H.
1961   *Principalities and Powers in the New Testament*. Freiburg, Germany: Herder.

Schnackenburg, Rudolf
1991   *The Epistle to the Ephesians*. Edinburgh, Scotland: T and T Clark.

Segal, Alan F.
1981   "Hellenistic Magic: Some Questions of Definition." *In Studies in Gnosticism and Hellenistic Religions*. R. van den Brock and M. J. Vermaseren, eds. Pp. 349-375. Leiden, Holland: Brill.

Silva, Moises
1987   *Has the Church Misread the Bible?* Grand Rapids, MI: Zondervan.

1990   *God, Language and Scripture*. Grand Rapids, MI: Zondervan.

1994   *Biblical Words and Their Meaning: An Introduction to Lexical Semantics*. Grand Rapids, MI: Zondervan.

Spradley, James P.
1979   *The Ethnographic Interview*. New York: Holt Rinehart and Winston.

1980   *Participant Observation*. New York: Holt Rinehart and Winston.

Spradley, James P., and David W. McCurdy
1980   *Anthropology: the Cultural Perspective*. New York: John Wiley and Sons.

Steffen, Tom A.
1993   *Passing the Baton: Church Planting that Empowers.* La Habra, CA: Center for Organizational and Ministry Development.

Stewart, Z., ed.
1972   *Arthur Darby Nock: Essays on Religion and the Ancient World.* Vol. 1. Oxford, England: Clarendon.

Steyne, Philip M.
1989   *Gods of Power.* Houston, TX: Touch Publications.

Stott, J. R. W.
1973   *Guard the Gospel: The Message of 2 Timothy.* Downers Grove, IL: InterVarsity.

1979   *God's New Society: The Message of Ephesians.* Leicester, England: InterVarsity.

1986   *The Cross of Christ.* Leicester, England: InterVarsity.

1990   *The Message of Acts.* Leicester, England: InterVarsity.

1996   *Guard the Truth: The Message of 1 Timothy and Titus.* Downers Grove, IL: InterVarsity.

Stott, John R.W. and Robert T. Coote, eds.
1980   *Down to Earth.* Wheaton, IL: Lausanne Committee for World Evangelization.

Strauch, Alexander
1988   *Biblical Eldership: An Urgent Call To Restore Biblical Church Leadership.* Littleton, CO: Lewis and Roth.

1992   *The New Testament Deacon.* Littleton, CO: Lewis and Roth.

Strelan, Rick
1996   *Paul, Artemis, and the Jews in Ephesus.* Berlin, Germany: Walter de Gruyter.

Streeter, B. H.
1929   *The Primitive Church.* London: MacMillan.

Swamidoss, Andrew Washington
1979   "The Speeches of Paul in Acts 13, 17, 20." Ph.D. dissertation, Fuller Theological Seminary.

Talbert, Charles H.
1974   *Literary Patterns, Theological Themes and the Genre of Luke-Acts.* Missoula, MT: Society of Biblical Literature.

1997   *Reading Acts: A Literary and Theological Commentary on the Acts of the Apostles.* New York: Crossroad.

Tannehill, Robert C.
1994   *The Narrative Unity of Luke-Acts*. Minneapolis, MN: Fortress.

Thackeray, H. St. J. and Ralph Marcus
1950   *Josephus*. Vol. 5. The Loeb Classical Library. Cambridge, MA:
            Harvard University.

Thiselton, Anthony C.
1980   *The Two Horizons: New Testament Hermeneutics and
            Philosophical Description*. Grand Rapids, MI: Eerdmans.

1992   *New Horizons in Hermeneutics: The Theory and Practice of
            Transforming Biblical Reading*. Grand Rapids, MI: Zondervan.

Tippett, Alan
1987   *Introduction to Missiology*. Pasadena, CA: William Carey
            Library.

Travis, John
1998   "Must all Muslims leave 'Islam' to follow Jesus?" *Evangelical
            Missions Quarterly*, 34:3 (October 1998).

Trebilco, Paul
1994   "Ephesus." In *The Book of Acts in its Graeco-Roman Setting*.
            D. W. J. Gill and C. Gempf, eds. Pp. 302-354. Grand Rapids, MI:
            Eerdmans.

Twelftree, Graham H.
1993   *Jesus the Exorcist: A Contribution to the Study of the Historical
            Jesus*. Peabody, MA: Hendrickson.

Unger, M.
1952   *Biblical Demonology*. Wheaton, IL: Scripture Press.

1971   *Demons in the World Today*. Wheaton, IL: Tyndale.

Van Engen, Charles
1996   *Mission on the Way: Issues in Mission Theology*. Grand Rapids,
            MI: Baker.

Van Roon, A.
1974   *The Authenticity of Ephesians*. Vol 39 of *Supplement of the
            Novum Testamentum*. Leiden, Holland: Brill.

Versnel, H.S.
1996   "Deisidaimonia." In *The Oxford Classical Dictionary*. 3rd edition.
            Simon Hornblower and Antony Spawforth, eds. P. 441. Oxford,
            England: Oxford.

von Campenhausen, Hans
1969   *Ecclesiastical Authority and Spiritual Power*. J. A. Baker, trans.
            Stanford, CA: Stanford University.

Vos, Gerhard
1979   *Biblical Theology*. Grand Rapids, MI: Eerdmans.

Wagner, C. Peter
1988   *How to Have a Healing Ministry without Making Your Church
            Sick!* Ventura,CA: Regal Books.

1991   *Territorial Spirits*. Chichester, England: Sovereign World.

1994   *Spreading the Fire*. Ventura, CA: Regal Books.

1995   *Lighting The World*. Ventura, CA: Regal.

1995   *Blazing the Way*. Ventura, CA: Regal.

1996   *Confronting the Powers*. Ventura, CA: Regal.

Wagner, C. Peter and F. Douglas Pennoyer, eds.
1990   *Wrestling with Dark Angels*. Ventura, CA: Regal.

Warner, Timothy M.
1991   *Spiritual Warfare*. Wheaton, IL: Crossway.

Wax, Murray and Rosalie
1962   "The Magical World View." *Journal for the Scientific Study of
            Religion* 1(2):179-188.

1963   "The Notion of Magic." *Current Anthropology* 4(5):495-503.

Wessing, Robert
1978   *Cosmology and Social Behavior in a West Java Settlement*.
            Athens: OH: Ohio University Center for International Studies.

Whiteley, D. E. H.
1966   *The Theology of Paul*. Philadelphia, PA: Fortress.

Wild, R. A.
1984   "The Warrior and the Prisoner: Some Reflections on Ephesians
            6:10-20." *Catholic Biblical Quarterly* 46:284-298.

Williams, David J.
1993   *Acts*. New International Biblical Commentary. Peabody, MA:
            Hendrickson.

Willowbank Report
1978   "Gospel and Culture." In *Down to Earth: Studies in
            Christianity and Culture*. 1980 Robert T. Coote and John Stott,
            eds. Pp. 308-342. Grand Rapids, MI: Eerdmans.

Wimber, John
1987   *Power Healing*. San Francisco, CA: Harper and Row.

Wink, W.
1984   *Naming the Powers*. Philadelphia, PA: Fortress.

Wilson, J., Christy, Jr.
1980   *Today's Tentmakers*. Wheaton, IL: Tyndale.

Witherington, Ben, III
1998   *The Acts of the Apostles: A Socio-Rhetorical Commentary*. Grand
              Rapids, MI: Eerdmans.

Woodberry, J. Dudley
1989   "Contextualization Among Muslims: Reusing Common Pillars."
              In *The Word Among Us*. Dean Gilliland, ed. Pp. 282-312. Dallas,
              TX: Word.

1990   "The Relevance of Power Ministries for Folk Muslims." In
              Wrestling with Dark Angels. C. Peter Wagner and F. Douglas
              Pennoyer, eds. Pp. 311-337. Ventura, CA: Regal.

1992   "The View from a Refurbished Chair." An inaugural address
              delivered at Fuller Theological Seminary. Pp. 1-9.

1998   Personal interview with author. Pasadena, CA, March 6.

Woodbridge, John D. and Thomas Edward McComiskey, eds.
1991   *Doing Theology in Today's World*. Grand Rapids, MI:
              Zondervan.

Wu, J. L.
1993   "Liturgical Elements." In *Dictionary of Paul and His Letters*.
              Gerald F. Hawthorne, Ralph P. Martin and Daniel G. Reid, eds.
              Pp. 557-560. Downers Grove, IL: InterVarsity.

Yamauchi, E.M.
1983   "Magic in the Biblical World." *Tyndale Bulletin* 34:169-200.

1984   "Pre-Christian Gnosticism, the New Testament and Nag
              Hammadi in Recent Debate." *Themelias* 10(1):22-27.

1993   "Gnosis, Gnosticism." In *Dictionary of Paul and His Letters*.
              Gerald F. Hawthorne, Ralph P. Martin, and Daniel G. Reid, eds.
              Pp. 350-354. Downers Grove, IL: InterVarsity.

Zwemer, Samuel
1920   *The Influence of Animism on Islam*. London: Central Board of
              Missions.

Index